METHUEN LIBRARY REPRINTS

Sebastien le Prestre de Vauban

SEBASTIEN LE PRESTRE DE VAUBAN
Bust by Coysevox

Sebastien le Prestre de Vauban
1633-1707

by

Sir Reginald Blomfield, M.A., R.A., F.S.A.

Hon.D.Litt., Hon. Fellow of Exeter College, Oxford, Hon. Member of the
Royal Academy of Belgium, of the American Academies of Arts and
Letters and the American National Academy of Design, of the Société des
Architectes Diplômés of France, etc.

With a Portrait, 11 Halftone Illustrations
by the Author, 16 Line Plates, and 3
Diagrams

BARNES & NOBLE, Inc.
New York
METHUEN & CO. Ltd
London

First published, 1938

This edition reprinted, 1971
by Barnes & Noble, Inc.
and Methuen & Co. Ltd.

Barnes & Noble ISBN 389 04149 1
Methuen ISBN 416 60740 3

Printed in the United States of America

27 JUN 1971

PREFACE

VAUBAN was perhaps the greatest military engineer that has ever existed, and it is strange that in a country such as England, which in the last hundred years has produced many able engineers, nobody has yet written his life. A few years ago M. Daniel Halévy's life of Vauban was translated by Major Street, but M. Halévy's eloquence and enthusiasm leave one rather breathless, and one must look elsewhere to learn what Vauban actually did and the sort of man that he really was. For this purpose three works are indispensable: (1) the *Abrégé des Services du Maréchal de Vauban*, edited by Augoyat, Lieutenant-Colonel of Engineers, 1839; (2) *Le Prestre de Vauban. Sa famille et ses écrits*, by Rochas d'Aiglun, Lieutenant-Colonel, 1910; and (3) *Vauban*, 1633–1709, by P. Lazard, Colonel of Engineers, 1934. The first is a summary statement of Vauban's military services, prepared by himself; the second by Colonel Rochas d'Aiglun includes a life of Vauban, extracts from his *Oisivetés* and his letters to Louvois and his successors, a work of immense research admirably edited; the third by Colonel Lazard gives an exhaustive life of Vauban, with a masterly analysis of his career as an engineer, soldier, artillerist, and reformer. The only criticism I would make on Colonel Lazard's work is that there is no adequate index to a book of over six hundred pages. I am indebted to these three works for most of the facts of the life of Vauban.

Colonel Lazard gives a complete bibliography of all books, papers and documents relating to Vauban. My authorities for the notes on military fortifications in the sixteenth and seventeenth centuries are given in a short bibliography at the end of this book; not the least

important of them is a delightful book of maps, with geo-
metrical plans of the most famous forts in Europe at
the time, published at Amsterdam in 1702, and entitled
*"Atlas Portatif ou le Théâtre de la Guerre en Europe, conte-
nant les Cartes Géographiques avec le plan des villes et forteresses les plus exposées aux révolutions présentes"*. Having
regard to the date (at the outbreak of the War of the
Spanish Succession) this volume is of first-rate value as
historical evidence in regard to Vauban's fortifications.
I do not find it mentioned in any of the authorities,
and there is no copy in the British Museum. This copy
was picked up by my son in Holywell Street, Oxford, in
1913. A glossary of terms used in fortifications in the
seventeenth century is given at the end of this book.
Quotations, for which no reference is given, are from
Vauban's writings, the *Abrégé*, the *Oisivetés*, or his letters.
If I have allowed myself some little licence in phrases
here and there, the reason is that it is impossible to read
Vauban's letters without to some extent falling into his
delightfully free use of the vernacular. Vauban always
used the word that came to him as the immediate expres-
sion of his thought, without regard to formal elegance,
and it is for this reason that his letters are such excellent
reading.

Much of Vauban's work has disappeared, superseded
by later methods of fortification, or swept away by the
relentless advance of the speculative builder, as has
happened at Dunkerque, Lille, Charleville, and most
prosperous commercial towns. Sometimes, as at Charleroi,
Mons, Bayonne, Valenciennes, Bois-le-Duc, the Town-
planner has levelled the ramparts, and converted them
into pleasant boulevards; sometimes, as at Maubeuge, he
has been guilty of almost incredible vandalism. At La
Rochelle the railway station, completed in 1923, occupies
the site of a famous hornwork. To realize the scope and
purpose of Vauban's fortifications, one must go to quiet

places left behind by the tide of trade, such as Gravelines or Bergues or Le Quesnoy, once strong fortresses, now quiet, uneventful places where nobody finds it worth his while to pull the ramparts down—and in these places Nature is doing her best to hide Vauban's works with trees and briars and brambles. It is for these reasons, and also on account of my sincere admiration for Vauban himself, that I have ventured on this account of his work.

September 1937   REGINALD BLOMFIELD

CONTENTS

ILLUSTRATIONS

IN THE TEXT

[1] From Drawings by Sir Reginald Blomfield
[2] From the *Atlas Portatif*, 1702
[3] From Belidor, *La Science des Ingénieurs*, 1729
[4] From Fournier, *Traité des Fortifications*
[5] From Scamozzi, *L'Idea della Architettura Universale*, 1615
[6] From Perret, *Des Fortifications et artifices*, 1594

Sebastien le Prestre de Vauban

CHAPTER I

*The family of Vauban—Vauban's boyhood—Semur—He enlists under
Condé—The Fronde—A gentleman cadet—Clermont—Sainte Ménehould—
Swims a river under fire—Offered a commission, but declines—Taken
prisoner—Employed by Mazarin at siege of Sainte Ménehould—Given
commissions in the regiments de Bourgogne and la Ferté—Sieges in the
Netherlands—End of War with Spain—The funeral of the maltôtier—
Vauban's marriage.*

"SEBASTIEN LE PRESTRE, Chevalier, Seigneur de Vauban,
Bazoches, Pierre Pertuis, Pouilly, Cervan, la Chaume,
Epiry, le Creusot, et autres lieus, Maréchal de France,
Chevalier des Ordres du Roi, Commissaire Général des
Fortifications, Grand Croix de l'Ordre de Saint Louis, et
Gouverneur de la Citadelle de Lille, naquit le premier
jour de Mai 1633—d'Urbain le Prestre et d'Aimée de
Carmagnol. Sa famille est d'une bonne noblesse du
Nivernois et elle possède la seigneurie de Vauban depuis
deux cent cinquante ans."—Magnificent and nearly all
true—This is how Fontenelle[1] introduces his éloge on
Vauban, given in the year of his death in 1707. In his
enthusiasm for his subject Fontenelle was not quite
accurate. The "bonne noblesse", when investigated,
resolves itself into descent from a notary of Bazoches, a
small town in the Morvan, a few miles south-west of
Avallon, who in 1555 bought part of a small fief near
Bazoches. His son Jacques became an "Écuyer, Seigneur
de Champignolle et de Vauban, Châtelain de Bazoches"
and served with the "Arrière-Ban" in 1595, and two of his
sons were killed when serving with the Arrière-Ban.[2]

[1] Bovier de Fontenelle, a famous man in his time, was perpetual Secretary of
the Academy of Sciences, who lived to be a hundred, and composed admirable
obituary notices of his colleagues of the Academy. He also wrote discourses on
Sir Isaac Newton and the Plurality of Worlds, the latter of which was discussed
in nearly every capital of Europe.

[2] The Arrière-Ban was composed of holders of fiefs who were bound to serve
when summoned by the King. Vauban says it was quite useless. Voltaire (*Le
Siècle de Louis XIV*, chap. xii, 154) says: "Les possesseurs des fiefs étaient dans
l'obligation d'aller à leurs dépens à la guerre, pour le service de leur seigneur
souverain, et de rester armés un certain nombre des jours."

Jacques le Prestre, who lived to the age of 96, and had eight children, seems to have been impecunious, for in 1618 he had to apply to his relations for help, and all that they could do for him was to give him 50 livres douze sous, realized by the sale of some cloth, silk and buttons. Jacques was the father of Urbain le Prestre, born in 1602, who in 1630 married Edmée Carmignolle, and it was their son Sebastien, born on May 15, 1633, who became the famous engineer known as "Vauban". Urbain le Prestre, who was styled "Escuyer, Sieur de Vauban et Champignolle", served in the cavalry, in the Regiment d'Enghien in 1636-7, came out with the Arrière-Ban in 1639-41, and was taken prisoner in a battle at Sedan. After this he appears to have settled down at Saint Léger-des-Foucherest,[1] a little village south-east of Avallon, and spent the remainder of his life in planting trees in the ungrateful soil of the Morvan, and teaching his neighbours how to graft their fruit trees.

Urbain died in 1652, leaving a son and a daughter. The son Sebastien was baptized in the church of Saint Léger, a village church with a central tower and a broach spire like the tower and steeple of Playden Church near Rye. Sebastien's godfather signed his name on the certificate of baptism, but his godmother, Judith de Hain, could not write, so she made her mark. A patent of nobility was given to Sebastien le Prestre, an uncle and two cousins, in 1667 "en considération de ce que la noblesse des éxposans étoit assez notoire connue et establie, que leur père, ayeul et bisayeul avaient toujours vécu noblement sans avoir jamais fait d'acte dérogeant à leur noblesse." It was stated that such titles as they had, had been burnt in the late wars, and this patent was really granted "en considération des services . . . du Sebastien Le Prestre de Vauban depuis l'an 1653". In 1667 Vauban was already becoming famous, but he could not enter the regiment of Guards without producing proofs of noble birth; hence this patent which seems to me to establish nothing but a growing recognition of his ability.

[1] Now called "Saint Léger Vauban".

Vauban did not, in fact, belong by birth to the French nobility, and when Saint Simon described him as "petit gentilhomme de Bourgogne tout au plus" he was much nearer the mark than Fontenelle, who in the manner of the time, hoped to magnify his hero by misrepresenting his origin. I take Urbain le Prestre, Vauban's father, to have been a small country gentleman. His position was nearer that of the English yeoman or Westmorland "statesman", than that of any one connected with the aristocracy of France, and Vauban himself was a true son of that strange wild Morvan with its granite rocks, its ravines, its oaks and beech and chestnut woods, a harsh land, yet a land with passages here and there of exquisite beauty. In an age when every one who hoped to succeed was a courtier, and the road to advancement lay through intrigue, Vauban remained a countryman to the last. The point of Vauban's extraction and the social status of his ancestors is only important in its bearing on Vauban's thought and attitude to life. He did not belong to the French aristocracy; in actual fact he disliked and despised it, holding that the only aristocracy worth considering was the aristocracy of merit, and one of his last efforts was a mémoire showing how such an aristocracy might be established.[1]

Little is really known of Vauban's boyhood. Legends of his early days were, of course, inevitable. He was said to have run wild in the woods with no friends but the shepherd boys on the hills. One story said that the curé of the village of Saint Léger had given him instruction in the rudiments, in return for Vauban's grooming his horse. Another said that one day he had come across the Prior of the college at Semur who had lost his way, and was wandering about the woods of Rouvray, that Vauban disentangled the Prior, and that the latter educated him in gratitude for his rescue. The only known facts are that the Abbé Orillard, who had baptized Vauban in the church of Saint Léger, did his best for him up to the age

[1] *Pensées Diverses:* "Idée d'une excellente noblesse" and "Des moyens à tenir pour faire une excellente noblesse *par les services*."

of ten, when he was transferred to Semur-en-Auxois, entered at the Carmelite College and educated by the Prior of the college, the Abbé de Fontaine. Here he learnt to read and write, acquired some little knowledge of mathematics and history, and some skill in drawing. Semur is a picturesque little town of some 3,500 inhabitants, some thirty kilometres south of Avallon. It is situated on a rocky hill, surrounded on three sides by a branch of the river Armançon, and all walled in, and here, with occasional visits to his home at Saint Léger, Vauban spent the next seven years of his life, learning his lessons and no doubt ruminating on the walls of the ramparts above the river at Semur. His instincts for design and engineering must have begun to develop themselves in his boyhood, for he was only seventeen when he enlisted under Condé. He was very soon noted for his courage and ability. I do not doubt that he spent most of his holidays among the hills and forests of the Morvan with the sons of local peasants, an admirable training for one who for nearly sixty years was probably the hardest worked man in France.

His father, Urbain Le Prestre, died in 1652, leaving him, Fontenelle says, nothing but a musquet and such education as he had received; in other words, nothing at all, and Vauban now had to make his own career. According to his own account, given in the *Abrégé des Services de M. de Vauban*, drawn up by himself in 1703, "Il a commencé de servir dès l'an 1651, âgé de 17 ans. Il a été assez heureux pour avoir pu continuer depuis ce temps-là jusqu'à aujourd'hui sans aucune interruption, et sans avoir été une seule année soit en paix, soit en guerre, qu'il n'ait été employé utilement hiver et été. . . . Au commencement de ladite année 1651, il entra au service, en qualité de cadet dans le régiment de Condé, Compagnie d'Aunay, ayant une assez bonne teinture des mathématiques et des fortifications, et ne dessinant d'ailleurs pas mal." That he should have picked up any knowledge of fortifications in the Carmelite establishment at Semur by the age of seventeen seems remarkable, and I think that Vauban at seventy may have taken rather a sanguine view of what he was as a boy of seventeen; but it must be remembered that in the seventeenth century the art and science of fortification was very closely studied, and, as will appear later, by the middle of that century was regarded as an important part of a liberal education, so that it is quite possible that Vauban may have picked up a smattering in his school at Semur.

In 1649 Mazarin had imprisoned Condé in Vincennes—an intolerable insult to Le grand Condé, the hero of Rocroi, of Fribourg, and of Nordlingen—and de Retz (afterwards Cardinal), the man who was at the back of "the day of the barricades", wrote a "courier burlesque de la guerre de Paris", and thus addressed Condé in prison. Paris, he said, was going on much as usual, but "vous le vainqueur de Nordlingue, de Rocroi, de Fribourg, de Lens, l'effroi de tous les Castellans, êtes dans le bois de Vincennes".

Condé was released in 1651, but that he, the hero of the day, should have been imprisoned by Mazarin, an Italian, the most hated man in France, was an outrage to be avenged by war, even against the throne. Mazarin had the Queen to back him, but the Parliament and Paris loathed him, and the French aristocracy hated him because he was an Italian, much too successful, far too rich, and because he had the Queen Mother under his thumb. They hoped to drive him out of France, and so began the war of the Fronde, fought not in the interests of France, but merely to further intrigues and gratify personal animosities. Condé was determined to avenge the insult of his imprisonment, and was on the look-out for recruits. He paid a visit to his cousin, Louis de Bourbon, at Vesigneux, near Saint Léger-Foucherest, and here Edmé Carmignole, brother-in-law to Urbain le Prestre and Maréchal des Logis in Condé's Regiment, was able to introduce his nephew to the notice of Condé, and young Vauban was accepted as a Cadet in Condé's Regiment. According to one of the usual legends, Condé was so much impressed by the lad's bravery and intelligence that he said to the bystanders: "Remember, this young man will go far."

The position of cadets was curious, as they were neither in the Army nor out of it. Louis XIV, early in his reign, established two companies of Gentlemen Cadets from fourteen to twenty-five years of age, for those who wished to enter the army but had not sufficient means to do so by purchase. Two cadets were attached to each company of a Regiment. The Cadets lived the life of the privates and had no rights or privileges. They were quartered in barracks and were allowed to go into towns but forbidden the theatres. In 1693 the Companies of Cadets had become so disorganized that Vauban advised their suppression as "les plus mauvais sujets de Royaume".[1] If war broke out the cadets were given temporary rank as sublieutenants or cornets. So Vauban at the age of seventeen, began his career as a cadet, but almost at once was enlisted as a regular. In 1652 he was employed on the fortifications of Clermont in Lorraine, Clermont-en-Argonne, as it is now called, some twenty kilometres west of Verdun. From Clermont he was moved on another fifteen kilometres westward to Sainte Ménehould, which was being besieged by Condé. Sainte Ménehould is situated in the valley of the Aisne, and was of considerable military importance as it commanded the passage of the river. Here Vauban distinguished himself by swimming across the river under fire during an attack on the fort, and the colonel commanding the Condé Regiment was so pleased with him that he offered him a commission as ensign. Vauban declined on the ground that "Il n'était pas en état d'en soutenir le caractère." Vauban was modest about his attainments and exploits, but there can be little doubt that the reason for his refusal was that he could not afford the rank of officer on nothing but his patrimony of a good education and a musquet. Vauban contented himself with the rank of "Maître", in other words, trooper; and instead of continuing with the regiment, he served for a year in the cavalry "pendant lequel il s'est trouvé à plusieurs actions, à l'une desquelles il a été blessé."

[1] See Lazard, *Vauban*, pp. 74-5.

In 1653, while still in Condé's army, Vauban was taken prisoner. He was riding with some troopers, when they were surprised by a party of the King's Horse. The troopers fled in all directions. Vauban managed to reach a narrow place, "un chemin creux", in which the King's Horse could only approach him in single file. Here with characteristic courage he turned and faced his enemies, levelled his musquet at the officer in command, and demanded honourable terms of surrender, namely, that he should not be stripped of his uniform or maltreated, and should not be compelled to march as a prisoner on foot. In those days war was still conducted with some regard to chivalry, though I imagine that a good deal of the fighting in the war of the Fronde was little more than play-acting. Anyhow, the officer in command agreed, and Vauban came off with the honours of war. I am reminded of a somewhat similar incident in the war of the Camisards fifty years later. Cavalier,[1] the famous leader of the Camisards, was pursued by three dragoons. He shot one as he came up, the second as he attacked him and the third as he ran away, but Cavalier was a fierce and desperate man fighting in a war of religion in which no mercy was shown by either side, whereas Vauban was a soldier in a war which was not taken very seriously. In the war of the Fronde there were no great principles at issue, and Vauban, the most humane of men, hated killing anybody. This second exploit seems to have reached the ears of Mazarin, who also was on the look-out for likely recruits. "Feu M. Le Cardinal, informé qu'il avait intelligence dans les fortifications, se le fit amener, et après l'avoir converti, l'envoya au siège de Sainte Ménehould, où il servit en second sous le Chevalier de Clerville." One would like to hear more of this interview at which the Cardinal, wiliest of men, "converted" young Vauban to the service of the King, and then made use of his knowledge of Sainte Ménehould to take the place.

The war of the Fronde ended in 1653. It had always been a ridiculous affair, this "guerre civile—nommée

---

[1] See *Byways*, by Reginald Blomfield, p. 118.

Fronde, d'un jeu d'enfants interdit par la police, et ce fut en effet un jeu, mais abominable".[1] Condé contemptuously called it "la guerre des pots de chambre". Mazarin and the young King who had been present at the siege of Sainte Ménehould were so favourably impressed by Vauban, that Mazarin, now returned to power, made him a small grant of money, and gave him a commission as lieutenant in the Régiment de Bourgogne. This had been Condé's own regiment and his personal property, as it were, and when Condé declared war, it followed its owner in his revolt against Mazarin and the King. After the collapse of the Fronde, it was reconstituted as a Royal Regiment, and it was in this regiment under which Vauban had first enlisted that Mazarin with deliberate irony now offered him a commission. The regiment, indeed, was now known as the "Régiment des Repentis", most of its soldiers having been "rebelles involuntaires et mécontents d'une guerre qui n'était plus qu'une querelle en famille".[2] Vauban was given the charge of repairing the fortifications of Saint Ménehould which had been besieged and captured by Condé in 1652, and recaptured by the Royal troops in 1653. As Vauban had served on these occasions both outside and inside Sainte Ménehould, he must have known the place to its last stone.

France was now at war with Spain and began the interminable series of sieges and attacks on the Flemish frontier. Vauban was moved to Arras, and soon afterwards was placed in charge of the siege of Clermont,[3] and in the year following (1653) of the sieges of Landrecies, Condé and Saint Ghislain,[4] fortified places on the northern frontier still held by the Spaniards. It seems that at these sieges he was more or less in sole charge "presque seul", de Clerville being away on sick-leave. In

---

[1] Lavisse, *Hist. de France*, vii, I, p. 42. See also Voltaire, *Le Siècle de Louis XIV*, chaps. iv and v.

[2] Lazard, p. 109.   [3] Clermont-en-Argonne.

[4] Landrecies is north of Saint Quentin and half-way between Cambrai and Avesnes. There are four Condés in the north of France. The Condé referred to appears to be Condé sur L'Escaut, north of Valenciennes. Saint Ghislain is west of Mons and half-way between Mons and Condé.

1654 he was employed in the siege of Stenay, which lasted thirty-three days. On the ninth day of the siege he was wounded, but "Il y retourna avant qu'il fut guéri. Il y fut encore blessé d'un coup de pierre en attachant le mineur."[1] Vauban's ability as an engineer was now to be officially recognized. In 1655 he was given the rank of "Ingénieur ordinaire du Roi, pour mieux reconnoistre son mérite", on the recommendation of the Maréchal de la Ferté, who had been in command at the siege of Landrecies, where Vauban "s'acquitta fort bien". At the siege of Valenciennes in 1656 he was wounded in the leg; he was taken to Condé L'Escaut, and when the Spaniards attacked that place, though wounded he insisted on being carried to all parts of the fortifications that required his presence. The town, however, was starved into surrender.

It is not easy to follow Vauban's movements in the years which precede his correspondence with Louvois, who succeeded his father as Minister for War in 1666. The *Abrégé* is very sparing of information, and the strong places on the frontiers were constantly changing hands; one year one finds them belonging to Spain; and a year or two later to France. Condé, for example, and Ghislain had been captured by the French in 1653, and in 1655 they were being besieged by the Spaniards. The Spaniards took Condé, but after nine days had to raise the siege of Ghislain. In 1657 Vauban was the engineer of the siege of Montmédy "dont il conduisit seul les attaques", the other three engineers having been killed early in the siege. Vauban must have done well at Montmédy, for the Maréchal de la Ferté, a rough and rather brutal soldier, was so pleased with him that in order to retain his services he gave him a company in his own regiment. It seems that an officer could hold a company in more than one regiment, serving in one but drawing pay in two, for La Ferté gave him another company, this time in the Régiment de Nancy "pour lui servir de pension". Commissions with no duties attached were handed about freely

---

[1] *Abrégé.* I take this to mean that he was wounded in firing a mine.

by commanding officers. Here was Vauban an "Ingénieur ordinaire du Roi", given companies in two regiments, and for all one knows he may have still been holding his commission in the "Régiment des Repentis" given
him by Mazarin in 1653.

In 1657 Vauban was present at the siege of Mardyk,
and after the place fell, spent the winter in reconditioning
its fortifications. The sieges of Ypres, Gravelines and
Oudenarde followed in 1658, and Mazarin was so pleased
with Vauban that he thanked him graciously, "et quoique
naturellement peu libéral, il lui donna une honnée gratification, et le flatta de l'espoir d'une lieutenance aux
Gardes". When inspecting work at Oudenarde by order
of Turenne, he was taken prisoner by the enemy, but
released on parole soon afterwards and exchanged. The
war with Spain ended in 1659. Condé was pardoned, by
the Treaty of the Pyrenees (1659) France obtained some
invaluable bases of operations for future campaigns in
the north, such as Arras, Hesdin, Bapaume and Béthune,
and Louis XIV was betrothed to Marie-Thérèse, the
Infanta of Spain.

Mazarin died in 1661, and this closes the first period of
Vauban's military service. He had not been seen at home
for six years; the whole of this time had been spent on
active service; he had been wounded several times and he
was now recognized as a promising young officer of very
great ability. In 1666 de Clerville gave him a certificate,
recounting his merits and certifying that he had well and
faithfully served His Majesty at "Saint Ménehout, Stenay,
Arras, Clermont, Landrecy, Saint Ghislain, Condé" and
"Valencienne", and "dans toutes les occasions le Sieur de
Vauban a toujours agy selon nos ordres, et soubs nostre
direction". De Clerville said that he had witnessed
many courageous actions on Vauban's part and that he
felt obliged to show his "reconnaissance et l'estime particulière, que nous en faisons" by the issue of this certificate "que nous avons accordé à sa requisition". The
certificate was a little ambiguous, as de Clerville was
careful to say (1) that Vauban had acted only under his

orders and direction, and (2) that the certificate was granted at Vauban's request. De Clerville may have been suspicious of this rapidly rising young engineer who indeed a few years later was to supersede him completely. Of Vauban's life hitherto we know little or nothing beyond what is stated in his *Abrégé*, and it seems to have consisted of a succession of sieges followed by the design and superintendence of fortifications. An anecdote is recorded of his early days which if true shows that Vauban, like others of his time and calling, had looked upon the wine when it was red and sometimes did strange things in consequence. On the occasion of a flying visit to Paris, probably on his way from St. Léger to the Flemish frontier, Vauban after dining too well came out into the street, and met the funeral procession of "un riche financier et chef de maltôtiers,[1] mort d'indigestion" proceeding to the church of Saint Roch. Vauban jumped on to the top of the hearse, mistaking it for a handcart, and shouted "Home" to the attendants. The "nombreux cortège", including the heir, and even the curé conducting the procession, burst out laughing, and regarded the whole thing as an excellent joke. According to the authority for this story, the old Maréchal used to tell it to his grandchildren; and no doubt chuckled over this early effort to show his contempt for financiers and tax-gatherers.

The war with Spain was followed by nine years of peace, and for the first time since 1651 Vauban was able to go home and think of marriage. He became engaged to Jeanne d'Osnay, daughter of Claude d'Osnay, "Ecuier", Baron d'Epiry, and a marriage contract[2] was drawn up between Vauban, the Baron d'Epiry and his daughter Jeanne. In this contract Vauban is described as "Ingénieur ordinaire du Roy, Capitaine Lieutenant du régiment d' Infanterie de Compagnie de M. Le Maréchal de la Ferté Sénectère, et Capitaine d'une Compagnie entretenue en la Garnison de Nancy". The Baron d'Epiry came of an ancient family but had no money, and the

---

[1] Tax-gatherers.   [2] Given in full in Rochas d'Aiglun, *Vauban*, I, pp. 53–4.

marriage contract was apparently intended to provide for him as well as for Vauban and his wife. By the terms of the settlement Vauban and his wife were to have all things in common with the Baron, the Baron was to have the chief control and was to settle 1,000 livres on his daughter, and Vauban "the futur" was to bring into the pool all that he possessed up to the value of 2,000 "livres tournois", for which the Baron was to give him a receipt. The young people were to undertake to pay the Baron's debts up to 1,000 livres, and it was only on this condition that the Baron and his father agreed to the marriage. The contract was signed on March 25, 1660, at the château of Epiry, present Paul Le Prestre and Pierre Le Prestre, cousins of Vauban, Michel René du Courroy, a friend, and "damoiselle Anne Guesdin", wife of Paul Le Prestre. Vauban's mother and sister were not present; perhaps they thought that Sebastien was being cheated in having to pay the Baron's debts. After the wedding Vauban had to return to his garrison duties at Nancy, and his wife was left behind in the Château Epiry, and there, and later on at Bazoches close by, she spent the remainder of her life till her death in 1705. She had two daughters, and one son who died in infancy. Of the daughters, Charlotte, the elder, married Louis de Mesgrigny of whose courtship an amusing but indecent story is told by Jal,[1] and the younger, Jeanne Françoise, born in 1680, married Louis de Bernin de Valentinay d'Ussé at the age of twelve years and three months.

Vauban was seldom with his wife. After he had bought Bazoches in 1675 he came there when he could; at least that is the impression given by his letters to Louvois asking for leave to go there. He was at Bazoches for short visits in 1687, in the winter of 1689–90, and again in 1696–7, but owing to the unfortunate fact that the descendants of Vauban have not allowed his private letters to be published, we know little of the relations of Vauban with his wife and family. In 1702 he made his wife the executrix of his will, and a letter to one of his daughters

[1] See Rochas d'Aiglun, *Vauban*, I, 43.

has survived, in which he says he was sleeping in the open, and that a frog had quartered itself in his shoe, so he was evidently on good terms with his family. Vauban was a just and fairminded man, of abundant kindness and sympathy, and there is no reason to suppose that he was not an affectionate husband and father though, as we shall see later, he allowed himself the licence of his time. From the year of his marriage till the next war broke out with Spain in 1667, there was peace in France, and Vauban was constantly engaged on the frontiers of France, improving existing fortifications and constructing new ones. This work took him up and down France, leaving him no time for anything but flying visits to St. Léger. The remains of his work are to be found on all the frontiers of France, but in order to understand what he actually did it is necessary to make a digression here, and examine the development of military engineering in the sixteenth century and down to the middle of the seventeenth, when Vauban took it in hand, and laid down the lines on which military fortification has developed since that date. The story of Vauban's life is resumed in Chapter V.

CHAPTER II

Effect of gunpowder on fortifications—Ostia—Martini of Siena—Da Vinci —Michelangelo—Dürer—Giuliano da San Gallo—San-Michele at Verona and Venice—The inventor of the bastion—Castriotto—Maggi—Zanchi— Cataneo—Busca—Scamozzi—Floriani—Marolois—Speckle.

THE invention of gunpowder altered the whole problem of the defence of fortified places. In medieval days if the walls of the castle were strong enough and high enough and there was a good moat round it filled with water, as at Bodiam in Sussex, or a dry moat cut out of the solid rock, as at Goodrich Castle high above the Wye, the castle was impregnable except by starvation or treachery. The tower of the Castle of Ham, built by the Constable of Saint-Pol in 1470, had walls ten metres thick,[1] the lofty walls of Cittadella near Vicenza, with their square towers, are a good example of the medieval idea of protecting a city. A great deal of ingenuity and ability was concentrated on defence, but the only method of attack was by arrows, catapults, mangonels, trebuchets and other engines, or by escalade, and these were, in fact, of little use against a well-built castle.[2] In Italy before the end of the fifteenth century attempts were made to improve on this, and the Castello at Ostia, built in 1483–6 for the Cardinal della Rovere, is an early example of this transitional stage. It was designed by Giuliano da San Gallo and Baccio Pouletti. The rapid fall of fortress after fortress in Italy, all supposed to be impregnable, when Charles VIII invaded Italy in 1494, frightened the Italians, and set their quick intelligence to work to see what could be done to meet this alarming menace, and to devise means of repelling the attack, but it took them at least two generations to shake themselves free of the medieval tradition.

It has often been said that famous artists of the Italian

---

[1] Cosseron de Ville-Noisy, *La Fortification*, p. 42.

[2] See Violet le Duc, *Traité sur l'Architecture Militaire au Moyen Age* for medieval methods of defence.

MEDIEVAL WALLS, CITADELLA (15 MILES E.N.E. OF VICENZA)

Renaissance were the first to discover the principles that must govern defence against attack by artillery, and it has been claimed for Francesco de Giorgio Martini of Siena (1439–1502), an admirable artist, that he was the pioneer and even the founder of modern military fortification as distinct from medieval methods. Mr. Selwyn Brinton in his life of this artist refers to Martini's device of the *cappanato*[1] as having revolutionized "then existing methods of defence against artillery fire". Martini did undoubtedly develop the use of mines in warfare, by introducing subterranean galleries for access to the mines, but I cannot find any convincing evidence in support of the claims made for Martini by Mr. Brinton. Martini wrote on military architecture (Book V of his *Trattato*). He was employed in 1478 by Alfonso, Duke of Calabria, in the siege of Castellana about ten miles north of Siena. In 1491 he was invited to report on the earlier fortifications of Lucca (not the existing ones, which were constructed between 1561 and 1650). He was consulted by Alfonso of Calabria at Naples in 1492–5, and after Charles VIII had entered Naples in February 1495, Martini or a mysterious person called "Narcissus the Etruscan" blew up the Castello Nuovo, and Charles and his army were driven out of Naples in November 1495. That Martini was recognized as skilled in fortification is undeniable, and there exists in the ducal library of Turin, a quaint and rather rudimentary drawing of a fort surrounded by a moat or river, and of a mine with its powder and slow match underneath a machicolated tower which is duly collapsing in ruins, but I do not find that Martini had yet grasped the fundamental principles of bastions and enfilading fire. The fort of St. Leo, of which a photograph is given in Mr. Brinton's book,[1] has round towers at the angles, and the wall between, instead of being straight, comes forward to an obtuse angle in the centre, which would have prevented the full use of enfilading fire by

[1] The *Cappanato* is said to have anticipated to a certain extent the covered way, *Le Chemin Couvert* of later fortifications, but there seems to be some uncertainty as to what the "cappanato" really was.

masking the bastions. What Martini shows in his drawing of the fort of the Rocca de Cagli is not a bastion at all. The tendency to find every sort of accomplishment in artists of admitted ability, results from an uncritical enthusiasm, and from the point of view of history is dangerously misleading. Thus Leonardo da Vinci, the admirable Crichton of the arts, has been represented as a great military engineer, and even Colonel Lazard, skilled technician as he is, seems ready to accept this. Speaking of the Italian engineers of the sixteenth century he says: "Leur renommée était grande, il suffit à ce sujet de citer le nom de Léonard de Vinci"—but it does not suffice, nor is it borne out by the evidence. No one is likely to underrate the genius of Leonardo da Vinci. He and many other artists of the Italian renaissance were men of manifold accomplishment and great enthusiasm, but I am rather sceptical about these multiple artists, except in the case of men who, like Baldassare Peruzzi, started with a solid foundation of architectural training.

Leonardo da Vinci was a man of consummate genius, intensely alive to all that he saw, and possessed by a fervent desire "rerum cognoscere causas", or if that knowledge was beyond him, to supply its place by his own ingenious and often ingenuous speculations. Among his multifarious papers are to be found notes and sketches of all kinds, on water and its effects, on machinery for lifting heavy weights, on the flight of birds with a remarkable drawing of an enormous and perfectly useless wing, on guns and cannon, on squaring the circle and so on, but I have looked in vain for evidence of his skill as a military engineer. In the immense mass of his notes I have so far found only two or three drawings which have any bearing on the subject, and only one drawing of any importance. This is a sketch design of a large triangular fort enclosing a citadel, standing in front of a square fortress from which it is separated by a moat. The fortress has round towers at the angles, not bastions, and the triangular fort might be taken as a crude anticipation of a demilune or ravelin[1]

[1] Da Vinci's description is "Modo direvellino anna fortezza". See *Les*

without any consciousness of the use and purpose of a demi-lune. His fort would have been useless, as the citadel in front of it would have effectively blocked the fire of any guns from the main fortress. Da Vinci used the term bastion, but not in the sense in which it was used in the seventeenth century. The bastion as described and drawn by Da Vinci turns out to be only a protective screen made of earth and hay or straw. I come to the conclusion that Da Vinci amused himself with fortification much as he did with many other curious speculations. For instance, he suggested that a method to detect mines was to place two or three dice in the top of a drum, and if mining was going on underneath, the dice would reveal it by waggling. He mentions without comment that one mode of attack was to let loose a swarm of bees, in the pious hope that they would settle in the fortress. He advised that no openings should be made in the lower part of the towers as this would provide the assailants with opportunities to enlarge the holes; and the crenellations on the top of the wall would be a sufficient protection. He was still thinking of the medieval castle, and seems to have been unconscious of the value of flanking fire from casemates in protecting the moat. Yet even in England, casemates were in use before the middle of the sixteenth century. I find them provided in Camber Castle, near Rye, one of the five forts built about 1540 by Henry VIII to protect south-east Kent, Rye and Winchelsea. These forts formed part of a scheme of defence along the south coast, extending, Oman[1] says, from Sandwich in Kent to South Mawes opposite Falmouth in the far south-west. The Camber fort, now ruinous, of which I give a plan, consists of a fort built on an octagon plan, with rudimentary, stilted, half-round bastions in the north-east and south-west angles, and three on the west side facing inland, with entrance to the fort in the centre bastion (five bastions in all). These bastions were in two stories, with four portholes for guns on the ground floor.   In the centre is a keep with an internal diameter of 43 ft. and walls ten feet thick.   This very interesting fort was built to command the entrance to the port of Rye, from which in the sixteenth century it was separated not by fields, as now, but by a broad stretch of sea.[1] I do not doubt that this fort was designed by Italians in the service of Henry VIII, for in 1540 the Italians were recognized in Europe as the leading military engineers of the time, and five forts—Sandown, Deal, Walmer, Sandgate, and Camber—were built between 1538 and 1543 to protect the south-east coast.

The great name of Michelangelo has been brought into the list of military engineers.   Michelangelo helped in the fortification of Florence and the Castle of St. Angelo in Rome, but precisely what he did is not known.   Legends of superhuman capacity grow up round great names, and in course of time these are accepted as historical facts. It is the more necessary, therefore, to ask for the evidence for these far-reaching claims.   Albert Dürer, on the other hand, did study fortification with some approach to scientific method.   He advocated hollow masonry for the walls of ramparts as a means of carrying the platform overhead on which the guns were to be placed, and also of protecting the gunners, but as de Ville-Noisy points out, he had not grasped the theory of enfilading any more than his predecessors.   Moreover, in the sixteenth century the effect of gunpowder was still an unknown quantity. The powder was very bad, and the bronze guns often burst.   At the siege of Castellana, already referred to, there were five bombards with the awe-inspiring names of "The Cruel", "The Desperate", "The Victory" and the "No Nonsense"[2] but Alfonso, the Duke of Calabria, complained to the authorities at Siena that the powder was no use, or if it was good, that it burst the guns.   Alfonso was besieging Castellana with Martini to advise him; and

[1] This is shown in Symonson's map of Rye, 1594. Oman's description of Camber Castle as a "forlorn circular work covering the marshy flat between Rye and Winchelsea" is pretty, but is quite incorrect. For a full account of Camber Castle see the *Victoria History of Sussex*, pp. 185–6.

[2] Brinton, *Martini*, I, 74.

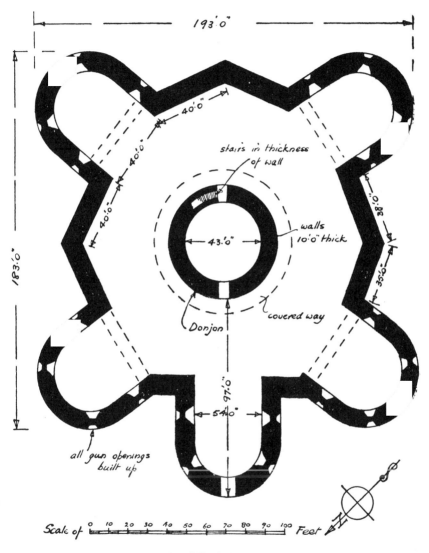

193'0"

183'6"

stairs in thickness
of wall

walls
10'0" thick

43'0"

40'0"

40'0"

40'0"

38'0"

35'6"

covered way

Donjon

97'0"

54'0"

all gun openings
built up

N

Scale of 0 10 20 30 40 50 60 70 80 90 100 Feet

PLAN OF CAMBER CASTLE, NEAR RYE
(*Measured by Reginald Blomfield*, 1937)

Lorenzo de Medici in order to defend Florentine territory, "saw himself compelled to despatch an engineer to Castellana for the purpose of constructing bastions and defences of every kind", and he sent thither Giuliano da San Gallo, who fortified the place, constructing good walls and strong outworks,[1] but San Gallo's first business was to teach the gunners how to fire without being knocked out by the recoil of the guns. In 1483 San Gallo designed the fort at Ostia for Cardinal Rovere, on an irregular plan; and both here and in the remarkable drawing of a triangular fort attributed to Giuliano da San Gallo now in the library at Siena there appears, for the first time, a consciousness of the necessity of protecting forts by flank fire. The courtines[2] are straight and protected by advanced towers, from which fire could be directed parallel to the moat, but the bastion and all that it implies had not yet been discovered. Its invention was due to Michele San-Michele of Verona (1484–1558), a great architect as well as military engineer, who designed the fortifications of Verona with its splendid gateways, the Porta Nuova and the Porta Palio. Vasari, writing in 1568, referring to San-Michele's work at Padua, says that he constructed the bastions "according to the method which was invented by himself, for the idea of constructing bastions with acute angles originated with San-Michele. Before his time they were made of a circular form, by which the difficulty of defending them was much increased. In the present day they have an obtuse angle on the outer side and can be readily defended either by a cavalier[3] erected between two bastions, or by another bastion near at hand, provided the latter be not too far distant and that the ditch have a good breadth. The method of constructing bastions with three squares, to the end that those on the two sides might guard and defend the ditch and the curtains[4] from their open embrasures was

[1] Vasari. Bohn (Foster's translation) II, 489.
[2] The front of the rampart between the bastions.
[3] A cavalier was a tower built on the rampart, in order to get a wider range with guns at a higher level.
[4] i.e. the length of rampart between the bastions.

likewise of San-Michele's invention . . . this method has
since been imitated by all, and supersedes the old manner
of subterranean embrasures called casemates"[1] which
filled with smoke and bad air when the guns were fired,
with risk to the foundations of the walls. In view of this
specific statement by Vasari, San-Michele, not Martini,
must be regarded as the real forerunner of Vauban. In
the Venetian Republic, San-Michele carried out fortifications at Legnano, Porto on the Adige, Peschiera at
the south-east corner of the Lago di Garda, Brescia, where
there still remains a fine bastion in the castello in the new
manner, Zara and Sebenico in Dalmatia, Corfu, Cyprus
and Candia, and finally the great fort opposite the end of
the Lido at Venice.[2]

The Italians were now regarded as the best military
engineers in Europe. Their services were in great request,
and treatises on fortification appeared in rapid succession.
In 1564 Castriotto, "Il Capitan Jacomo, ingegnero del
Christianissimo Re de France", was associated with Girolamo Maggi in a work on the fortification of cities, but in
fact all that Castriotto did was to contribute an account
of fortresses built in France, which forms the fourth part
of a book by Girolamo Maggi. Part I was by Maggi, who
elsewhere discoursed of the Day of Judgment and the end
of the world. Part II was by Captain Francesco Monti-
mellino, who had fortified the Borgo di Roma, and Part
III was on "ordinanze", artillery, by Capitain Giovachino.
The book contains diagrams of courtines with angular
bastions, the flanks of which, that is the returns from the
external faces, are at right angles to the courtine. "Cavaliers" are shown on the ramparts, and in both cases the
diagrams indicate the lines of fire intended. On page 32
a section of a rampart is shown, built with internal buttresses vaulted over to carry the "terre-plein" or platform
of the rampart, the moat, and the "covered way" behind

[1] Vasari, Bohn, Vol. IV, p. 430. Foster's translation.
[2] Vasari gives a vivid description of this work in his life of San-Michele. In
order to test its solidity, the Signori ordered all the heaviest guns of the arsenal
to be brought to the fort and all fired off at once inside the fort, but the fort
stood unmoved, to the shame of the malignant critics.

the glacis sloping down to the open country. On page 44 there is an "orillon", that is a recess at the junction of the flanks of the bastions with the courtine, made for the guns covering the moat, and on page 62 there is shown a courtine with a recess in the centre, and another laid out *en échelon*, both anticipating later methods of Vauban. The treatise also deals with encampments and the disposition of troops. We have here the elements of military engineering for the next two hundred years, treated by soldiers, a very different thing from the amateur efforts of da Vinci, for Castriotto had fought under that stout warrior, Montmorenci, Constable of France, at Saint Quentin, Calais and Thionville. It is not known who designed the fortifications of Lucca, a characteristic example of the most advanced Italian methods in the sixteenth century, begun in 1544 and completed a hundred years later. The walls have ten bastions set about three hundred metres centre to centre, each with faces set out at an obtuse angle and orillons complete. When Vauban said that the governor of a strong place should regard it as his Mistress, and make the round of the ramparts his favourite walk, he might have been thinking of the *arboreto cerchio* of Lucca, the shaded walk on the ramparts.

A book on the fortification of cities was brought out at Venice in 1560 by Battista di Zanchi, which contains plans of octagon forts with bastions and recessed courtines, but the most complete work up to date was that of Girolamo Cataneo of Novara *Delle Arte Militare*, first published in 1559. A third edition was published in 1571, and a French translation with the title of *Le Capitaine de Hierosme Cataneo* was published at Lyons in 1573. Cataneo's work is entirely practical. He begins as usual with some rudimentary geometry, and goes on to deal with the details of fortifications, "boulevards" (ramparts) and foundations, terre-plein,[1] escarpments, parapets, fossé or moat, covered way and glacis. He shows designs for hexagon, pentagon and "star" fortresses, and plans

---

[1] The platform or walk along the top of the rampart.

for camps on mountains and rivers. He deals at some length with guns and bombs, and searchlights, with estimates of the number of guns necessary for a fort, and gives strange names for cannon of different calibre, such as the "colubrina", the "falcon", the "sarre", and the "passervolante",[1] and he gives tables for calculating the area required for a given number of troops. Cataneo was, I think, the first to illustrate the method then in use of advancing to the attack by zigzag trenches. Having got within firing distance by this means, the attacking force set up a screen of gabions, from behind which they blazed away at the fort as well as they could. It was a clumsy method which Vauban completely altered a hundred years later.

Gabriello Busca, referred to in the last footnote, published a book on fortification at Milan in 1619. Busca was an engineer in the employment of the Duke of Savoy, and he fortified Bourg en Bresse, Suza, some thirty miles west of Turin, and Demonte and Montmelian in Savoy. He had a good deal to say on the testing and moving of guns, on attack from behind gabions and screens made of wool, and various mechanical devices, including a gun with many barrels arranged side by side on a wood carriage. These were to be let off in rapid succession in street fighting, a crude anticipation of a mitrailleuse, and Busca says this was actually used by Count Maurice of Nassau in Flanders. Busca, unlike Maggi, had seen actual service, but he wasted his time in discussing subjects such as whether forts are of more use to republics or monarchies, and Palladio's idea of the walls of Troy. The Italians were the recognized authorities on military engineering in the sixteenth and seventeenth centuries, but the French were superseding them. One writer,

[1] In the book by Busca, published at Milan in 1619, a list of guns is given ranging from the double "coulevrine" which took a charge of twelve pounds of powder, to the arquebus which took seven-eighths of an ounce. Between these came the culverine, sarre, fourconneur, ribadoquin, émerillon, mosqueton, mosquet and arquebus, and in addition to these there were guns called bastardes which included the dragon (charge 19 lb.), the basilic and the serpentine (14 lb.), the aspic and the passemur (12 lb.) and the pelican. No wonder Vauban later on complained of the lack of any standard guns.

however, still deserves mention, Vincenzo Scamozzi (1552–1616), the Venetian architect. Some ten miles south of Udine there is a remarkable little town, Palma-Nuova, which was built as a frontier fort of Venetian territory in 1593, from designs by Scamozzi. The town is laid out within a hexagon enclosure with three immense bastions, or rather towers, fifty feet high. This method was already becoming old-fashioned, yet Scamozzi was an authority on fortification and knew all that there was to be known on the subject at the time, for he says that he had visited many fortified places in Spain, France and Germany, and he must have been familiar with the work of San-Michele in Venice. On the title page of his book is an inscription in which he says: "Hoc opus plenum est, mihi crede, laboris, sudoris, pulveris, ex longa peregrinatione, locorum inspectione, librorum evolutione suscepti." One can imagine Scamozzi tramping wearily round Europe in search of information. The result of his labours appeared in an immense book, published in Venice in 1615, the last year of his life, and entitled *L'idea della Architettura Universale*, divided into ten books. In the second book he devotes nine chapters[1] to fortifications, with plans and sections of details. On pages 166–7 there is a typical plan of a fortified place on a river, laid out as a dodecagon with rampart, bastions, moat, covered way and glacis, all according to the approved method; and on page 193 there is an elaborate detail of a bastion figured with letters to give the terms in use. Scamozzi's diagrams and descriptions are elaborate. On the diagrams of the bastions reproduced, A shows the military road running all round on the inner side of the rampart with steps up to the "terre-plein", B the scarp or sloped inner side of the rampart, C the "terre-plein", D Cavaliers, N the moat with a deep, narrow ditch running along the centre as shown in the sections; S the "covered way", and so on. Scamozzi's illustrations represent the farthest point to which the Italian engineers had so far carried the science of fortifications. What they had not yet grasped was the

---

[1] Book II, Chaps. XXII to XXX.

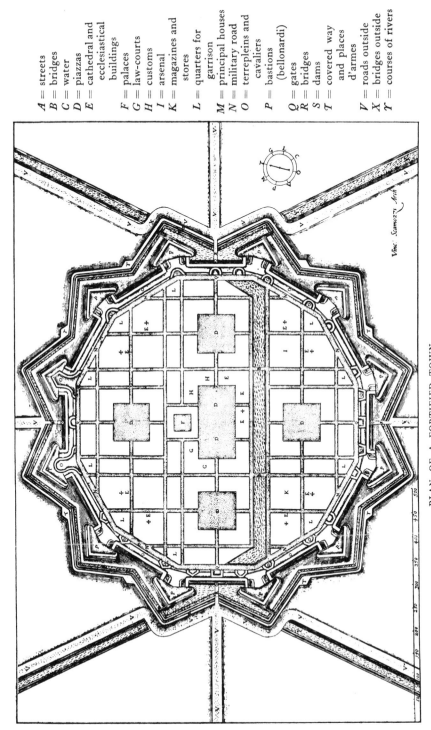

A = streets
B = bridges
C = water
D = piazzas
E = cathedral and
  ecclesiastical
  buildings
F = palaces
G = law-courts
H = customs
I = arsenal
K = magazines and
  stores
L = quarters for
  garrison
M = principal houses
N = military road
O = terrepleins and
  cavaliers
P = bastions
  (bellonardi)
Q = gates
R = bridges
S = dams
T = covered way
  and places
  d'armes
V = roads outside
X = bridges outside
Y = courses of rivers

Vinc. Scamozzi Arch

PLAN OF A FORTIFIED TOWN

From Scamozzi, "L'Idea della Architettura Universale"

importance of outworks, in advance of the main rampart, the demi-lunes, ravelins, tenailles and hornworks of which Vauban was to make such skilful use. Scamozzi does actually refer to ravelins (revellini). He says that they should be the same size as the bastions, and refers to them as having been carried out at Julich in the Duchy of Cleves.[1] The plate of Julich in Fournier's *Architecture Militaire* shows three works which are really hornworks and probably of later date. There are no ravelins in the later French sense of the term.

The last Italian writer on attack and defence was Floriani, whose work was published in 1630. He does not seem to have advanced beyond Scamozzi, to whom less than justice has been done as a military engineer.[2] The Italian engineers disappeared with the decadence of the Italian states. Some of them entered the service of Spain, others that of the Nassau Princes in Holland. Pacciotto, a famous Italian engineer, designed the citadel of Antwerp, a work much admired by Vauban, but in Holland a system of fortifications peculiar to that country had been developed in the long struggle with Spain, and this relied mainly on water as a means of defence. In 1614–15, the year of the publication of Scamozzi's work, a treatise on fortifications by Samuel Marolois (Marolles) was published in Amsterdam. A second volume appeared in 1628, revised and corrected by two mathematicians, one of whom was professor of fortifications at Leyden. In 1638 there appeared a translation of this work by Henry Hexam, dedicated to Sir Harry Vane, Treasurer of the Household of Charles I, with the title "*The Art of Fortification or Art Militaire as well Offensive as Defensive*, compiled and set forth by Samvell Marolois, reviewed, augmented and corrected by Albert Girard, Mathematician, and translated out of French into English by Henry Hexam." In the introduction Hexam says: "The fortifications made in these Low Countries are the strongest, exactest and perfectest which have been made and

---

[1] North of Aix, and near the Belgian frontier.
[2] The French authorities do not mention him at all.

practised." They had been very effective against Alva, and they were skilfully developed by Cohorn, the famous rival of Vauban in the wars of Louis XIV.

In Germany the first really authoritative writer on fortifications was Daniel Speckle, born at Strasbourg in 1536. Speckle had never seen any military service. He had begun as an embroiderer and pattern-maker, and in following his trade had travelled in Denmark, Sweden, Poland, the Netherlands, Austria, and Hungary. At Antwerp he met the engineer responsible for the defence, and Speckle seems to have been an intelligent man who took notes as he went. In 1564 he made a plan of the town for the authorities of Strasbourg; in 1569 he made a map of Alsace for the Emperor Maximilian; and in 1577 prepared a plan for the defence of Strasbourg. Meanwhile, he had been putting together all that he had noted on his travels, and finally, like Scamozzi, published his work on fortifications a few months before his death in 1615. Speckle is regarded by French and German authorities as an important figure in the history of fortification. "Il a parlé à peu près de tout ce que peut intéresser l'ingénieur militaire",[1] but meanwhile the centre of interest had shifted to France, and we must now see how far the French engineers had advanced before the coming of Vauban.

---

[1] Cosseron de Ville-Noisy, *La fortification*, p. 115.

CHAPTER III

Fortifications in France to the middle of the sixteenth century—Jacques Perret; his plans and inventions—Brouage—Jean Errard—A soldier—Fabre—De Ville; follows Italian treatises, but an advance—Importance of his work.

AT the beginning of the seventeenth century, the French engineers were still relying on the Italian authorities for guidance in military fortification. They borrowed what they could and followed them to the best of their ability, but their grasp of the principles that govern military fortification was imperfect. They still relied on ramparts and moats, without any very clear conception or consideration of lines of fire. The earliest French writers were Jacques Perret of Chambéry, and Errard of Bar-le-Duc. Perret, who describes himself as "Gentilhomme Savoysien", brought out a fine folio of plates and descriptions entitled *Des fortifications et artifices, architecture et perspective*, and he dedicated it to the King as "Lieutenant de Dieu sus[1] la terre et le principal ministre de sa Gloire". The King was Henri IV. Moral sentiments from the Psalms surround a grand architectural composition on the title page, and with singular irrelevance they are also engraved round his plans of forts. Perret, I gather, was a Huguenot, and his plates were probably engraved before Henri had said that Paris was well worth a Mass. The first edition of Perret's book appeared in 1594, and it reached a third edition in 1620. It contains eight double plates of plans of forts with descriptive text, followed by fourteen plates of crude designs of houses, and a final plate of his own inventions of "quelques artifices de guerre, comme il a plu à Dieu m'en donner intelligence." The first artifice consisted of five or six arquebuses fixed to an axle on two wheels, and between the barrels were to be fixed lances with grenades attached to the points, and

---

[1] Perret's spelling was erratic, he spells "sur" "sus" in one place, and "sous" in another.

27

sharp partisans "pour offenser gens et chevaux" were to
be attached to the axle. A shield or mantlet was to be
fixed above the axle, to protect the four or eight soldiers
who were to work this remarkable weapon. Perret's idea
seems to have been that after loosing off the arquebuses,
the soldiers were to trundle the machine forward, and
charge the enemy, and it seems that Perret had borrowed
Busca's idea.[1] The second artifice was a moveable screen
for defence against gun fire. It was to be formed of
wool, old mattresses and blankets bound with ropes, and
placed on a platform with wheels 18 in. high. It was to
be 15 ft. long, 7 ft. high and 8 ft. thick, and Perret maintained that this would be kept upright by its bulk and
weight, and that it could be moved from place to place
to resist cannon-balls. The third artifice was an unsinkable boat, and of this Perret said that if there was any
doubt about it, he relied on the authority of Julius
Frontinus[2] and Flavius Vegetius, and that it was by means
of such a boat as this that Cæcilius Metellus had trans-
ported elephants across the Sicilian sea. I do not think
that the ingenious Perret can be taken seriously. His
designs for forts are rudimentary. The first diagram
shows a pentagon fort, with acute-angled bastions set 80
fathoms from point to point of the bastions. These
bastions are shown with "orillons", recesses for guns; the
"courtine" between was to be 44 fathoms, and the ramparts and bastions, including the revetments, were to be
8 fathoms thick and 7 fathoms high above the water of
the moat, a lingering reminiscence of the medieval wall
nearly twice the height that Vauban gave them. The
moat was to be 12 fathoms wide and 2 deep. On the
farther side of the moat there was the covered way with
its parapet, and the glacis sloping down to the open
country. Perret allowed 3 soldiers to each 6 ft. of rampart

---

[1] See p. 23, *ante.*

[2] Sextus Julius Frontinus wrote on the art of war and the aqueducts of Rome
in the reign of Vespasian, and was regarded as a great authority in the sixteenth
century. Flavius Renatus Vegetius was the author of *Rei Militaris instituta*,
dedicated to the Emperor Valentinian III in the fifth century A.D. An English
translation from a French version was published by Caxton in 1489.

BIRD'S-EYE VIEW OF FORTIFIED TOWN WITH 21 BASTIONS AND CITADEL
From Jacques Perret, "Des fortifications et artifices," 1594, 3rd edn., 1620

with one in reserve "pour supporter les inconvenients des morts ou blessez". The soldiers would have been crowded much too close together to be able to aim with their clumsy weapons. The range of the arquebus he put at 80 to 100 fathoms. This system appears in all Perret's designs, and the only variations are in the number of angles. For example, there is one heroic design of a polygonal fortress with 24 angles and 21 bastions, three bastions in one corner being omitted to allow of access by a narrow bridge to a detached hexagon citadel. The diameter of this fortress was to be 1,280 yards,[1] and inside it Perret shows a regular town with streets 36 ft. wide radiating outwards from an octagon "place" in the centre of which there was to be an 8-storey tower. Perret gives fantastic designs for this tower, and for a Governor's palace to house 500 people, a Hospital, an Academy and Law Court. In this vast design of many angles, the angles of the faces of the bastions had to be obtuse, and this was found to be necessary in all polygons of more than 6 angles. With less than that number more or less acute angles were in use.

Perret's designs show the usual practice in the earlier years of the seventeenth century, but they are fantastic, and contain none of the devices of later fortifications, such as demi-lunes, ravelins and hornworks. His text is badly arranged, and does not always agree with the plates; on the other hand, he is lavish in his plates with such sentiments as "Bien heureux est la personne qui vit avec entière et saine conscience, et qui de Dieu les saintes lois ensuit." The conclusion I come to is that Jacques Perret of Chambéry was an eccentric person of an ingenious mind, but not very intimate acquaintance with the problems of military engineering. His designs for buildings were extravagant and even absurd, and it seems that part of the purpose of this handsome folio may have been to introduce Jacques Perret, Gentilhomme Savoysien, to the notice of Henri IV of France and his powerful minister Maximilien de Béthune, Duc de Sully.

[1] About twice the size of Vauban's fortress of Neuf-Brisach, his last work.

Brouage, "L'Aigues mortes de la Saintonge", between Rochfort and Marennes, now almost deserted, is the best example of a fortified place in France of the first half of the seventeenth century, just as Bergues near Dunkerque is of Vauban's fortified places fifty years later. It was built in 1630–40 from designs by Pierre d'Argencourt and was reconditioned by Vauban in 1681. The plan is an irregular square with sides about 400 metres long, with bastions at the four angles and on the south and east sides, a detached work on the west side, and a protected and vaulted entrance on the north side. The walls are 13 metres high, with the arms of Richelieu and a Cardinal's hat cut in relief on the walls here and there. There were 22 "Echauguettes", look outs corbelled out from all the angles of the wall, of which eight still remain. The streets inside the fort are laid out at right-angles. Brouage was abandoned in the reign of Louis XIV, and it was last used as a prison in the time of the French Revolution, for priests and all suspected persons in the neighbourhood, many of whom died in the fort.[1]

Jean Errard of Bar-le-Duc (1554–1610) was a contemporary of Perret, and his work appeared in the same year as Perret's, 1594. Two more editions followed in 1604, and a new and revised edition was issued by Errard's nephew in 1620, entitled *La fortification démontrée et réduite en art par feu J. Errard de Bar-le-Duc, Ingénieur du très Chrétien Roy de France et Navarre.* Errard had seen active service, and designed and superintended the construction of fortifications of importance, at Verdun, Sedan, Montreuil, Calais, Amiens, Laon and Sisteron, and it is for this reason that he played a much more important part in the development of fortification than Perret. Errard insisted that the engineer should have taken part in the attack and defence of fortified places and should understand artillery and the effect of gunfire—a point on which Vauban was to insist very strongly. Above all, in planning fortifications, he must most carefully consider the site, the first note of a warning which later on Vauban

---

[1] Champlain, who founded Quebec in 1608, was born at Brouage.

BROUAGE (CHARENTE INF)

Rynald Blombed

was to repeat again and again, and of a break away from the dogmatic formulas of text books. Errard made the angle of the faces[1] of his bastions a right angle, and advised that the flanks of bastions should return to the courtine at right angles to the faces of the bastions. The objection to this was that the flank fire from bastions was limited to the space between the bastions, and could not be directed outside and beyond them, and also that it made the access from the terre-plein of the rampart to that of the bastion much too narrow. Errard concentrated on the defence of the courtine, rather than on that of the bastions. He suggested a slope on the terre-plein of the rampart so that the defence had not only the regular parapet in front, but was also protected by a modified parapet in the rear, I presume from shots from the other side of the fort.

Errard was followed by an engineer named Fabre, who also had seen active service, and who wrote a book with the title of *Pratiques du Sieur Fabre*, but French writers attach greater importance to the work of the Chevalier de Ville than to that of his predecessors. De Ville was born at Toulouse in 1596, and served in the "Chevau-légers du Roi" at Clérac, Montauban and Nègre-Pélisse. He was in Holland in 1624, in Piedmont in 1625. Two years later he travelled in Greece and Turkey. In 1636 he was at the Siege of Corbie, and in 1637 at Landrecies, then at Castelet, and finally in 1639 at Hesdin with the rank of Maréchal de Camp. He died in 1656. Like Vauban, de Ville wrote from personal experience, and he claims that he had written nothing except what either he or his brother had seen or done; but as he was only 32 when he published his *Traité des Fortifications*, and was only 21 when he began it, this is not possible, and a good deal of this vast folio of 441 pages must have been borrowed from other writers. The title of de Ville's work gives such a comprehensive idea of its purpose[2] that I quote it

---

[1] That is the two sides of the bastion facing outwards.

[2] From Lazard, *Vauban*, p. 15. There is no copy of de Ville in the British Museum. A full account of de Ville will be found in Col. Lazard's work, and Cosseron de Ville-Noisy, *Fortifications*, pp. 127-138.

in full: "Les Fortifications du Chevalier Antoine de Ville. Contenant la manière de fortifier toutes sortes de places— en quelque assiette qu'elles soient. Comme aussi les ponts, passages, entrées de rivières, ports de mer, citadelles. Le tout *à la moderne* avec l'attaque et les moyens de prendre les places, par intelligence, sédition, surprise, et l'ordre des longs sièges, la construction des forts, redoutes, tranchées, batteries, mines et plusieurs inventions nouvelles non jamais escriptes. Plus la défense et l'instruction général pour s'empescher des surprises; les remèdes contre la trahison, l'escalade et diverses inventions nouvelles contre le pétard. La défense contre les longs sièges, des sorties, contremines, retranchements, capitulation, et reddition des places. Le tout représenté en cinquante cinq planches dessinées et gravées par l'auteur. Le descours est prouvé par démonstrations, expériences, raisons communes, et physique, avec les rapports des histoires anciennes et modernes. In folio de 441 pages. Paris 1628," a complete manual, in short, of the military art, and a work of immense industry which became a classic among the military engineers of France. The writer of a little book criticizing the methods of Pagan and Vauban in 1689 says "Le Chevalier de Ville a passé pour le plus habile ingénieur de son temps, et son *Traité des Fortifications* est encore recherché comme le plus utile que ait paru."[1] De Ville must have been an able man. In 1636 he wrote in Latin an account of the siege of Corbie at which Cardinal Richelieu was present, and an account of the siege of Hesdin in French. It was at Hesdin that for the first time a company of sappers was employed to blow up the fortress, all volunteers with a captain in command. De Ville's last work was a treatise on the duties of the Governor of fortified places, published in 1639. Vauban had a good deal to say on this subject fifty years later.

As was inevitable, de Ville borrowed largely from the

---

[1] "Nouvelle manière de fortifier les places tirée des méthodes du Chevalier de Ville, de Comte de Pagan et de M. de Vauban" by Arnold de Ville, probably a descendant of the Chevalier.

Italians, but he had his own contribution to make. He was fully alive to the importance of flanking fire, and relied for defence not only on cannon, but on the arquebus and musket for the defence of parts next the fort, with a range of not more than 200 "pas". This determined the distance from the re-entering angle of one bastion to the salient point of the next and this he put at 150 "pas". In treatises on fortification, a puzzling term the "line of defence" constantly occurs, and apparently different authorities used it differently. De Ville who introduced the term used it for the line of fire from the re-entering angle of a bastion and a courtine to the salient angle of the next bastion. He did not, however, limit the placing of bastions to any hard and fast rule. He allowed them to be nearer together or further apart, according to the nature of the ground, and it was by his common sense and freedom from pedantry that de Ville opened the way for Vauban's splendid practicality.

De Ville's details are interesting. The "terre-plein"[1] was to be 20 to 25 ft. above the surrounding country, with a continuous parapet 4 ft. high, and for further protection he advised an additional small parapet, or a screen of gabions. His moats were to be wide and deep, with a palisade along the centre, and at the foot of the rampart next the moat he advised a "fausse-braye".[2] This was originally a level strip, left to prevent earth or the débris of walls falling into the moat when shattered by gun fire, but when a parapet was provided, the fausse-braye became a means of defence, and in some diagrams, soldiers are shown firing from behind the parapet of the fausse-braye. It was found, however, that owing to its low level, just above the moat, the fausse-braye was too much exposed to fire from the attack, and its use was given up. Vauban never used it. A platform not unlike it, but much higher up on the face of the rampart, known as the "chemin des rondes" was introduced, and was far more effective as it

---

[1] The level part or platform of the rampart.
[2] See illustration from Fournier, p. 82.

commanded not only the moat, but the covered way and the ground beyond it.

De Ville was strongly opposed to casemates on account of the smoke, the bad air when the guns were fired, and the damage done if a shot from the attack entered the casemates. He advised open recesses for guns at the junction of the bastion with the courtine, called "orillons". The real advance made by de Ville was in the attention he paid to the outworks of forts, the "chemin couvert" with its continuous path 5 to 6 pas wide, with its parapet of earth on the outer side, and its "places d'armes" at intervals, wider spaces where the men could assemble. He advised "ravelins", detached works in advance of the ramparts in the moat itself, not only for defence above ground, but also as a protection against mines being carried under the moat. All his recommendations were practical; for instance, he suggested that the ramparts might be formed with alternate layers of earth, well rammed, and bricks, anything rather than the hollow walls of the Italians which were not nearly so strong and prevented the soldiers from seeing anything and knowing what was going on. Colonel Lazard says of de Ville that he was "plus militaire—et écrivain—qu'ingénieur", but that in his advice to engineers: "S'accommoder au terrain . . . il a été vraiment un précurseur".

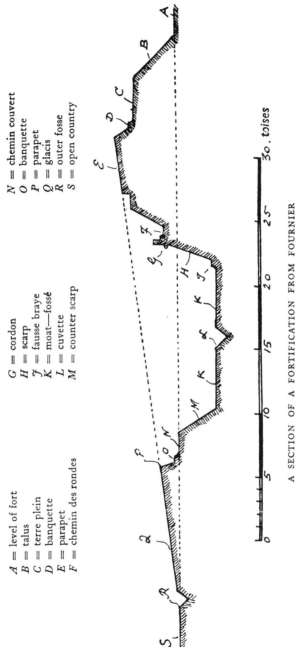

A = level of fort
B = talus
C = terre plein
D = banquette
E = parapet
F = chemin des rondes

G = cordon
H = scarp
J = fausse braye
K = moat—fossé
L = cuvette
M = counter scarp

N = chemin couvert
O = banquette
P = parapet
Q = glacis
R = outer fosse
S = open country

30. toises

A SECTION OF A FORTIFICATION FROM FOURNIER

CHAPTER IV

Fortifications in France—The Comte de Pagan, blinded at Montauban—
Les fortifications de Comte de Pagan—*Le R. P. Georges Fournier, S.J.*
His Traité des fortifications—*Fortifications when Vauban began his career*
*—The Rampart, moat, chemin couvert, bastion, cavalier, courtine, demi-
lune, ravelin, hornwork, counterguard, crownwork, tenaille.*

" L'UN des plus parfaits Gentilshommes de son temps,
le feu Roy[1] en estoit si persuadé, qu'on lui a plusieur fois
entendu dire, que le Comte de Pagan estoit un des plus
honnêtes, des mieux faits, des plus adroits et des plus
vaillans hommes de son Royaume". This is Perrault's[2]
description of Blaise François, Comte de Pagan, born at
Avignon in 1604, who died in Paris 1665. Perrault says
that he entered the army at the age of 12; that he was
at the siege of Caen in 1620, of S. Jean d'Angély, Clérac
and Montauban in 1621, and that at Montauban he was
blinded in one eye by a musquet shot. "Au lieu d'estre
découragé par ce malheur . . . il n'y eut depuis ce temps-
là aucun siège, aucun combat ni aucune occasion, où il
ne se signalait par quelque action ou d'addresse ou de
courage", and Perrault describes a very gallant action of
his during the siege of Suza in Savoy. He was at the siege
of Nancy in 1633, and while serving in Portugal as
quartermaster-general in 1642, lost the sight of his other
eye. He had, however, already published his great work
Les Fortifications de Comte de Pagan in 1640, dedicated to
a kinsman, Hugues de Pagan, Duke of Terra Nova in the
Kingdom of Naples, the original home of his family. His
aim, he says, was not to produce any formal science of
fortification, but to follow the actual practice of famous
captains of war. All Europe, he says, was amazed at the
weakness of existing forts—the strongest of them did not
hold out for more than six weeks, though Vauban would
have thought this much too long for any siege. Pagan

[1] Louis XIII.
[2] *"Les Hommes illustres que ont parus en France pendant ce siècle"*, Paris
1698, par M. Perrault de L'Académie Française.

37

was an able man of wide interests,[1] but in spite of his
military services, and his claim to follow the practice of
great captains, he was a theorist rather than a working
engineer such as Vauban. As a matter of fact, Blaye,[2] on
the right bank of the Gironde, is the only fort known to
have been designed by Pagan, and his reputation rested
chiefly on his book, but he was an original thinker and
introduced two far-reaching changes in the theory of
fortifications, the method of siting bastions and the entrenched camp. Whereas Errard and others had set out
the plan of forts with reference to the interior of the fort,
and added the bastions at the angles of the enclosing
rampart, de Ville determined the positions of the
bastions first, and then joined them by the courtines.
Everything had to be subordinated to finding the best
positions for the bastions. These would be the main
object of attack, and Pagan maintained that it was at this
point that he must multiply his defences by works outside
and beyond the bastions. Hence the complicated system
of demi-lunes and ravelins, tenailles, hornworks and
crownworks which were later developed by Vauban with
such amazing ingenuity and resource. In Chapter XIII
Pagan deals with "Fortifications de Campagne", and here
he anticipated the entrenched camp to which Vauban in
his later years attached the greatest importance, as supplementary to regularly fortified places. Pagan's views were
not accepted by every one—he was thought to have neglected the courtine—but they had great influence on the
time, and were undoubtedly an advance on Errard and
de Ville. A third edition of Pagan's treatise appeared in
1669; and Vauban himself must have studied his work
closely in his younger days, for Pagan's views were those
of an experienced soldier, not those of men writing comfortably in their libraries, for whom Vauban had an

---

[1] Cosseron de Ville-Noisy says that Pagan was the first Frenchman to adopt
and popularize Newton's theory of gravitation, but Pagan died in 1665, the year
in which Newton took his B.A. at Cambridge, and Newton's *Principia* was not
completed and published till 1687.

[2] The citadel of Blaye was begun from Pagan's designs in 1652, and finished
by Vauban in 1685.

undisguised contempt. A writer in the latter part of the seventeenth century said, "M. de Pagan a une experience consommée dans la guerre, et s'est acquis à juste titre la réputation d'être un des plus habiles ingénieurs de notre temps." In this he was very different from the last authority prior to Vauban to whom I shall refer, and this was "Le R. P. Georges Fournier, de la Compagnie de Jésus." In the middle of the seventeenth century, the art of fortification was no longer a mystery to the general public. They were familiar with all its technical terms. In 1652, when the war of the Fronde was beginning, and Condé, fighting Turenne, had taken refuge in Paris with his troops, Paris was upside down, Mademoiselle was firing on the King's troops from the Bastille, and the citizens of Paris were playing at being soldiers. Voltaire says, "Les Parisiens sortaient en campagne ornés de plumes et de rubans," but on the first sight of the royal troops, they bolted like rabbits, and when they reappeared in Paris were received by their fellow citizens with jeers and catcalls. A rhyme of the time described Parisiens ("badauds") as

> Étant dans leurs familles
> Avec leurs femmes et leurs filles
> Ils ne disent parmi les pots
> Que mots de guerre à tout propos—
> Bombardes, canons, coulevrine,
> Demilune, rempart, courtine,
> Porte, terre-plein, bastion,
> Lignes circumvallation,
> Mon tire-bourre, mon écharpe,
> Le parapet, la contrescarpe . . .
> Et d'autres tels mots triomphants
> Qui faisaient peur à leurs enfants.[1]

Some knowledge of military fortification was now considered to be part of a gentleman's education; and as education was chiefly in the hands of the Jesuits, military science or "l'art militaire" was included in the course of studies which they provided for their pupils. Colonel

[1] Lavisse, *Hist. de France*, VII, I, p. 55.

Lazard gives the names of six ecclesiastics who wrote on fortifications; one of them, le Père Nulliet de Châles, was also professor of "Belles-Lettres". Le R. P. Georges Fournier, S.J., is a typical example of these professors, who knew nothing of practical engineering, but were adroit enough to compile treatises from the works of those who did. Fournier composed a very useful little manual dedicated to the Marquis de Hauterive, Captain of Cavalry and Governor of Breda. The first volume appeared in 1647. My copy is the third edition published in Paris in 1671. It measures 4½ in. by 3 in. by 1 in. thick, and is bound in leather much thumbed and pitted by exposure in the trenches, and was no doubt once the faithful companion of some hard-driven engineer in the trenches of the innumerable sieges of Louis XIV. Fournier leads off with appropriate sentiments on the subject of war, that it is to protect the weak, maintain peace and promote the happiness of the people. He condemns duels, and says that the age to begin a military career is fourteen, because that age is full-blooded, and presumably will be none the worse for a little blood-letting; also this will give plenty of time to gain experience. After this introduction we get to business. A chapter is given on technical terms, followed by maxims of fortification and their explanation, detailed notes on the importance of site, flanking and defence, methods of setting out plans, polygons and irregular figures. This is followed by short chapters on guns, on ramparts, the tinting of drawings "pour représenter naïvement une fortification", and the details and dimensions of the various parts of the fortification. There are 42 plans of famous fortresses, 3 calculating tables and 54 plates of details. The forts illustrated lead off with a view of Mont St. Michel, and fancy illustrations of Sestos, "Château de l'Europe", and Abydos, "Château de l'Asie devant Constantinople", but after these come 38 authentic plans including Leghorn, Gravelines, Hesdin, Breda, Arras and other famous forts such as Juliers, a square fort with angle bastions of the sixteenth century, and three elaborate hornworks of a later date. Altogether a complete pocket manual for the young engineer. Vauban had a profound contempt for these "ingénieurs de Cabinet" who had never been under fire or served in the trenches, and he has some very caustic remarks on authorities who delivered themselves on fortifications "sans d'être jetés dans les choses de pratique". Their object, he says, was to lay down rules in the abstract, divested of all the actual conditions of practice. This was no use at all, and the only part of any value in their writings was their historical notes. Those who wrote on fortifications without ever having been in action were to be regarded with suspicion, especially if "ils ont le talent de bien écrire." Not less dangerous are those who, having no practical knowledge, lay it down that there is no need for it, "ne faisant consister toute la perfection d'un homme de guerre que dans le peu de connaissances qu'ils ont." The only engineers to be trusted are those that have practical experience, sound judgment, and who "s'appliquent entièrement à ce qu'ils font". Here we have the man of action in full blast. I think Vauban was a little hard on writers such as Fournier. It is true that Fournier could only claim to have inspected a few forts with the consent of the Governors, such as Hesdin and Metz, and he had never been under fire, but his treatise was entirely practical, and perhaps in those years between 1652 and 1659, when Vauban was learning his business, he may have found the Père Fournier's *Traité* a useful introduction to his work. If not original, it had the merit of stating in simple terms a summary of what de Ville, Errard and others had said on military fortification.

The remains of Vauban's mighty fortifications look complicated till one grasps the general principles which governed them, and the elements which in one form or another constituted the defence. For the sake of clearness it is best to take a section from the interior of the fort to the open country beyond the glacis.[1] The first

---

[1] This is the reverse of the method adopted by Pagan and his successors in setting out the plans of forts. They concentrated on the bastion and its defences,

consideration was of course the site, and the design of the
fort would vary to suit it, but assuming the fort to be
entirely new and constructed on level ground, the general
plan was invariably polygonal, with any number of angles
from the triangle up to the 21 angles shown in Perret's
design for a fortified town. Starting from inside the
fort, first came the military road running all round the
enclosure, with access from it to the different parts of the
rampart. Next came the rampart, with a sloped bank of
45° called the "talus", ascending to the terre-plein, that
is the continuous platform on the top of the rampart from
which the guns were fired. This was protected on the
outer side by a parapet of earth, with or without steps
(banquettes) for the soldiers to stand on when firing.
The top of the parapet was sloped outwards and downwards in order to enable the garrison to fire on the
attacking force beyond the covered way and the glacis
outside the moat. On the outer side of the parapet and
below it, was the "chemin des rondes", a continuous walk
with a parapet on the outer side, and below this the
"battered" face of the rampart running down to the moat
called the "scarp". The face of the rampart from the
top of the parapet to the "chemin des rondes" down to
the moat, was revetted with masonry or brickwork. All
the rest of the rampart was of earth well rammed, covered
with close-growing grass to bind it together.[1] In order
to get a wider range of fire and see what the attack was
doing, short towers, called "cavaliers", were erected on
the rampart; these were superseded later by more solid
constructions called "tours bastionnées", a favourite
device of Vauban and invented by him. At the foot of
the rampart next the moat the earlier engineers constructed a fausse-braye for defensive purposes[2] or a
"berme", a ledge some 4 ft. wide was left. The fossé or

considered from the outside not the inside of the fort. The system is more
easily intelligible if one proceeds from the inside of the fort through the defences
to the open country outside.

[1] Vauban actually specified the grass to be used "four de bourgoane" (Vauban's
spelling) as peculiarly adapted to form wiry and tenacious turf.

[2] This was abandoned by the middle of the seventeenth century.

moat was to be as wide and deep as the earth excavated for the rampart would allow; a usual width was about 90 ft. and 7 or 8 ft. deep, with a deep groove known as the "cuvette" dug in the centre of the moat to obstruct the attack, and intercept mining under the moat. On the further side of the moat was a bank, the counterscarp,[1] usually revetted with brickwork or masonry and on the top of this was the "chemin couvert", the "covered way", carried all along the outer side of the moat, and protected by the parapet formed by the highest part of the glacis. Open spaces were formed at intervals along the covered way, known as "places d'armes" where the soldiers could assemble. Beyond the parapet of the covered way was the glacis, that is the long slope downwards to the open country;[2] a secondary moat was sometimes dug along the outer edges of the glacis.

By the middle of the seventeenth century the defences I have described were found to be inadequate. Engineers began to realize that the defence must be carried further out. The distance from the bottom of the talus to the outside of the glacis in Fournier's section of a fort is 260 ft. In Vauban's fort of Neuf-Brisach it is 702 ft. Low fortifications were constructed in the moat itself, entirely detached from the rampart, demilunes and "ravelins", triangular in plan, reached from the fort by bridges and by "Caponnières", small protected ways, and "tenailles", long works parallel to the ramparts with ends canted outwards to protect the courtine. Readers of *Tristram Shandy* will recollect the argument between Tristram's father and Uncle Toby on the issue: when is a ravelin not a ravelin?

"'The common men,' said my Uncle Toby, 'confound the ravelin and the half moon (demilune) together, though they are very different things, not in their figure or construction, for we make them exactly

---

[1] Fournier.
[2] Pagan gives 36 to 40 toises (216 to 240 feet) as the length of the slope of the glacis.

alike in all points.' . . . 'Where then lies the difference?' quoth my father a little testily. 'In their situa-
tions,' answered my Uncle Toby; 'for when a ravelin,
brother, stands before the curtain, it is a ravelin, and
when a ravelin stands before a bastion, then the ravelin
is not a ravelin, it is a half moon. A half moon likewise
is a half moon and no more, so long as it stands before
the bastion, but was it to change place and get before
the curtain t'would be no longer a half moon: a half
moon in that case is not a half moon, 'tis no more than
a ravelin.' 'I think,' quoth my father, 'that the noble
science of defence has its weak sides as well as others.' "

In point of fact my Uncle Toby was inaccurate. The
ravelin and the demilune were quite distinct. The term
ravelin was applied (1) to small triangular works in front
of the courtine; (2) to small triangular works forming part
of the demilune, but separated from it by parts of the
moat. In this case it was sometimes called a redoubt. In
addition to the tenailles, ravelins and demilunes, further
protective works were constructed beyond the principal
moat, known as "ouvrages à cornes", hornworks, so called
from the angular ends facing the attack. At Luxembourg, the only side open to attack was defended by hornworks, and there were some remarkable hornworks in the
old fortifications of Sedan. The famous "ouvrage
à cornes" at La Rochelle, destroyed before the war to
make way for a new railway station, measured some
200 metres wide by 280 metres long between the horns.
The hornworks in the old fortifications of Strasbourg are
shown on a plan and described in detail in Vol. II, p. 481
of the *British Military Library* (1802), and it is probable
that at that date they were nearly as left by Vauban.[1]
I reproduce this plan as an excellent example of a fully

---

[1] Strasbourg, "la barrière la plus forte de la France", was taken by Louis XIV
in 1681 and fortified by Vauban after its capture. According to the plan in the
British Military Library, Vauban enclosed the whole of the old town with his
fortifications. These were nearly all destroyed by the Germans during the
famous siege of 1870 and afterwards, and all that is left of Vauban's work is a
bastion and two curtains of his pentagon citadel to the south-east of the town.

PLAN OF STRASBOURG

From "The Military Library," 1802

fortified town in the time of Vauban. The hornwork, named "Finkenmott", and figured 38 and 39, is thus described. "It lies in front of the two long faces or false curtains by which both its flanks and terre-plein are flanked. The avant-ditch at the foot of the glacis of this hornwork is a morass produced by the overflowing of the Brensche." The works numbered 58 and 59 are also good

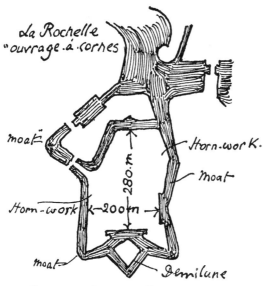

La Rochelle
"ouvrage à cornes"

moat

Horn-work K.

moat

280 m

Horn-work K—200 m

moat

Demilune

"OUVRAGE À CORNES," LA ROCHELLE

examples of a hornwork. Before the days of long-range guns and aeroplanes these fortified places must have been difficult to take. The attack had to cross the outer moat, ascend the glacis, capture the covered way and the horn-works, the demilunes, ravelins and tenailles in the principal moat, and cross the moat before they reached the wall of the rampart itself.

The rampart with its bastions was from the sixteenth century onwards the main line of defence. The earlier Italian engineers had not realized the effects of gunfire, or that a dead inert substance such as earth was a more effective defence against it than masonry or brickwork.

They faced their ramparts with solid masonry, backed by piers set some 15 ft. centre to centre, and vaulted over to carry the platform, the rampart. It was found that gunfire shattered the masonry and brickwork and the scattered fragments were dangerous. In the seventeenth century these hollow ramparts were given up, and the ramparts were formed of solid earth with masonry or brickwork used only on the outer side for revetments and parapets and for buttresses. On the inner side a bank was formed rising some 12 to 15 ft. above the ground level of the fort, and the rampart measured at the base some 66 ft. thick and at the upper part above the terre-plein 24 to 36 ft.[1] The terre-plein was about 30 ft. wide with a slight slope. The parapet varied in height. Errard made it 4 ft., which was too low, and the usual height was 6 ft., with one or more banquettes, steps, on which the soldiers stood when firing. The parapet was formed entirely of earth, not less than 18 or more than 24 ft. thick, with turf well rammed in layers with branches of willow or osier between, and covered with turf; the top of the parapet was given a slope of 1 foot outwards and downwards, sufficient to admit of the line of fire reaching the attack on the further side of the moat. Vauban gave the height of the rampart from the moat to the top of the parapet as 4 toises (24 ft.). From the outer edge of the parapet, a steep bank descended to the "Chemin des Rondes", protected by a low parapet of masonry or brickwork, forming the upper part of the revetment of the rampart. Vauban's rule for the batter (incline) of the revetment was one-sixth of the total height.

The moat was always an essential element of the defence. It was in fact the channel left after the amount of earth necessary to form the rampart had been excavated, and various widths and depths were given by the authorities. Pagan would have it 96 ft. wide (16 toises) and 24 ft. deep for the principal moat next the rampart, and 72 ft. wide by 12 to 15 ft. deep for the moat beyond

[1] Vauban and Pagan.

the glacis. Fournier gives 45 to 75 ft. for the width and
15 to 25 ft. depth of the principal moat, but this of course
varied according to the point at which the width was
taken. Vauban made the width 96 ft., the depth he
made 18 to 20 ft. below the ground level of the interior
of the fort. He objected to the outer moat that it got
in the way of sorties from the fort. The authorities were
uncertain whether the moat should be dry or full of water.
If full of water it was a useful obstacle to the attack, but
as against this, the stagnant water, with the whole fort
draining into it, became very unwholesome, and led to
epidemics in the garrison. Vauban disliked it for this
reason, though he used the water moat when he had to,
as for instance the fine moat on the east side of what is
left of the ramparts of Ypres, north and south of the
Menin Gate.

Why the "chemin couvert" was so called, I do not
know, for it was never covered, and was in fact a plain
roadway for the movement of troops in defence some
20 to 30 ft. wide, behind the parapet of the glacis.
Vauban says that the covered ways at Philippeville were
"aussi unis et aussi propres que le plancher d'une chambre",[1] and he gives as an instance of the care taken of the
fort that on one occasion, a drunken man having clam-
bered on to the parapet, some dozen "Suisses" set upon
him and "le massacrèrent impitoyablement" and only
handed over his body when they had been treated to
four "pots de bière". The chemin couvert was, in fact,
an outer line of defence, from which the garrison could
fire, and, if the attack was too strong, retreat to the fort.

The bastion was always regarded as the most important
part of the defence; but here again there was a difference
of opinion among the authorities. The two front sides
of the bastion known as the "faces" ended on the outside
in an arris or point, the parts from the inner ends of the
"faces" back to the courtine were known as the "flanks",
with the recesses for guns called "orillons" in the re-
entering angles at the junction with the courtines. The

---

[1] Philippeville, near Namur, once a fortress, now a lonely village.

points at issue were: (1) whether the "faces" of the bastion should meet at the salient at a right angle or at an acute or obtuse one; (2) whether the "flanks" should be set at a right angle to the faces of the bastion, which would bring them to an acute angle with the courtine, or whether they should be set at a right angle to the courtine. The objection to any but an obtuse angle for the faces of the bastion, was that any more acute angle reduced the width of the entrance to the bastion from the "terre-plein", known as the "gorge". The objection to a right angle return of the flanks to the courtine was that it exposed the flanks. Fournier, who had no practical experience of sieges, laid it down that the angle of the faces of the bastion should be a right angle, never obtuse and never so acute as 60°, the width of the "gorge" not less than 42 paces, the length of the flanks of the bastion 21 paces. The Dutch, he says, made the faces of their bastions some 48 toises (288 ft.) long, the French varied, but he mentions a bastion at Hesdin, the faces of which measured over 300 ft. Vauban's practice was to make the angle of the bastion obtuse, which gave it ample width, and to return the flanks at right angles to the face (not the courtine) as this gave better protection to the guns placed in the "épaules" or "orillons". At one time it had been the practice to place two or more guns one above the other in these "orillons", but this was found to be unworkable owing to the smoke and the foul air resulting from the firing of the lower guns in an enclosed space, and this must have also been an objection to guns fired from the "cavaliers", the little towers 10 to 18 ft. high[1] built on the terre-plein at intervals. When Vauban introduced his larger towers, known as "tours bastionnées", as in the fort of Neuf-Brisach (1697), he provided large central flues for the escape of the smoke and bad air.

The length of the courtine, that is, the wall of the rampart between two bastions, was given by Pagan as 60 toises (360 ft.). Vauban's practice was to regulate it by the number of the bastions and the conditions of the

[1] Fournier.

site, but the determining factor, apart from local conditions, was always the range of the musquet, which
Fournier and others put at 120 to 150 toises, say 240 to
300 yards. The courtine on the east side of Maubeuge
must be not less than some 600 yards between the bastions. There is now a gap in the courtine recently made,
which may have been occupied by a work of some sort,
but owing to the nature of the ground I was unable to
measure the length between the bastions. I find from
an old plan of the town that the courtine on the south
side measured 400 yards, an unusual length, but it was
protected by a tenaille of great size and elaborate detail.
The whole of this has disappeared. Fournier insisted
that the defence must rely in the last instance on
the musquet rather than cannon, because cannon were
expensive, necessitated too many men, were early
knocked out, and could not keep up a continuous fire.
We shall find later on that Vauban complained bitterly
of the inadequate arms supplied to the troops and the
confusion caused by the lack of any standardized guns.

CHAPTER V

Vauban's fortifications.

THE tendency of French military engineers in the second half of the seventeenth century was to push the defence ever further out into the country by outworks not only in the moat but beyond it. Hornworks, for example, were used freely in the defences of Maestricht and Sedan,[1] and when Vauban had to fortify Tournai he left the old walls and towers, constructed his demilunes with hornworks in front of them, and second demilunes in front of the hornworks. The most famous of Vauban's fortifications were the town and citadel of Lille, begun early in his career in 1668, Neuf-Brisach—actually his last work —and Maubeuge. Lille was captured in 1667, and Vauban was at once instructed to prepare plans for its fortification. He was granted in November 1667 pay of 500 francs a month, the services of two men, and forage for his horses—a somewhat exiguous allowance. The King approved Vauban's designs, a contract for the work was made with Simon Volant of Lille, and the work was begun in 1668 and pushed on with all possible speed, for Volant had 6,000 men at work on the citadel and walls. In 1669 Vauban was begging Louvois to agree to his designs for the gateways, Lille being his "Fille ainée dans la fortification". In 1672 Vauban was able to send Louvois a plan of Lille, citadel and all, and in 1674 he reported that the inhabitants were busy building their houses in the new town. By this time the new Lille seems to have been nearly completed. Vauban had surrounded it with new fortifications and had built the citadel on the north-west side, a vast pentagon fort with bastions and the usual detached works, all surrounded by water; and within the walls a great "place", 180 paces across, large barracks, a Governor's house, a church, an arsenal, and other details—

[1] See plan of Sedan from *Atlas Portatif*, p. 91.

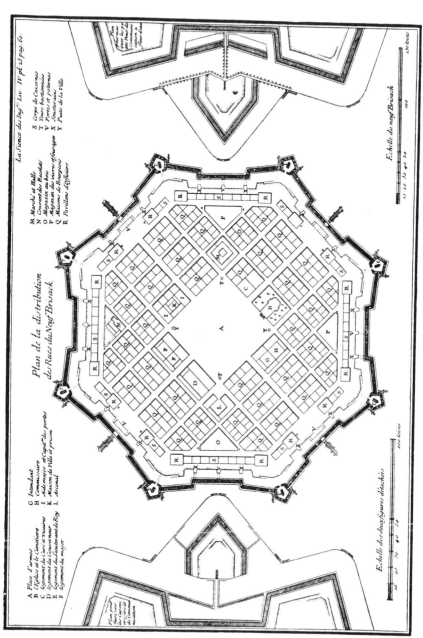

Plan de la distribution
des Rues du Neuf Brisach

La Science des Ing.rs Liv. IV pl. 28 pag. 60.

A Place d'armes
B L'Eglise et le Cimetiere
C logement du Curé à Vicaires
D logement du Gouverneur
E logement du Lieutenant du Roy
F logement du major

G Intendant
H Commissaire
I Aide major et capit.ne des portes
K Maison de Ville et prison
L Arsenal

M Marché et Halle
N Couvent des Recolets
O Magasin au bois
P Magasin des vivres et fourages
Q Maisons de Bourgeois
R Pavillons d'Officiers

S Corps de Casernes
T Tours bastionnées
V Magasin au bois
X Fonderie
Y Puits de la Ville

Echelle des bourg.s figures détachées

Echelle du neuf Brisach

PLAN OF NEUF-BRISACH

From Belidor, "La Science des Ingénieurs," 1729

the largest and most completely equipped citadel yet built in France. A later inscription to the right of the main entrance describes the citadel as

Le chef-d'œuvre
de Sebastien le Prestre
de Vauban
1633–1707
Reine des citadelles
commencé en 1667
pour garder à toujours
à la France
Lille et la Flandre Wallonne
et défendre contre tout envahisseur
Le Pré carré
des provinces recouvrées
par Louis XIV

The architecture of the buildings inside the citadel is simple and straightforward, but heavy-handed. Vauban was one of the greatest engineers that have ever lived, but he was not an architect, and though it is often forgotten nowadays, there is an art of architecture with the high ideals and all the sensibility to beauty that the term implies.[1]

Neuf-Brisach represents the latest development of Vauban's methods. The plan is an octagon with bastions and elaborate outworks. It is fully described in Belidor's *La Science des Ingénieurs dans la conduite des travaux de fortification*, published in Paris in 1729. Belidor was a Commissioner of Artillery, Professor of mathematics in the school of the Artillery, a member of the Royal Societies of England and Prussia, and corresponding member of the Académie des Sciences of France. Ignoring Pagan, de Ville and earlier writers, Belidor says that no scientific treatises on fortification had yet been written, for as for publications issued under the name of Vauban, they were quite worthless and Vauban had always repudiated these works. Belidor's own treatise had the

---

[1] The best plan of the Citadel of Lille is given in Baedeker's *Belgium and Holland*. Recent guide-books continue to show fortifications here, at Dunkerque and elsewhere which have been destroyed.

formal approval of Antoine le Prestre de Vauban, who died at Béthune in 1761, a distinguished soldier, Lieutenant-General, Grand Cross of the Order of Saint Louis, Governor of Béthune, director of fortification in Artois and a nephew of the great Vauban. It was also approved by three engineers, Demus, Vallory and Gittard, directors of fortifications and Chevaliers of the Order of Saint Louis. All agreed that Belidor's work was "traitée avec précision et netteté" and was "très avantageux au service du Roi".

Belidor's Vth book was devoted to the decoration of civil and military buildings, and is in fact a treatise on the orders for the instruction of engineers, with excellent plates. This was submitted for approval to Robert de Cotte who had succeeded J. H. Mansart as Premier Architecte du Roi. De Cotte gave it as his opinion that there was nothing that was not treated "avec beaucoup de méthode et de capacité"—a somewhat supercilious judgment on the architectural efforts of the Professor of Mathematics. Though Vauban had never published anything on fortification, Belidor must have made free use of his notes, and must have had access to his detailed instructions; indeed the model specification given in Belidor's VIth book followed closely, if not literally, the specification for the fortress of Neuf-Brisach. Belidor insists on the importance of never losing sight of the end in the multiplicity of details of fortification, and he says of Vauban "c'étoit une des grandes qualités de M. le Maréchal de Vauban" that though incessantly occupied with "tout ce que pouvait contribuer à la sureté de l'État et au bonheur des peuples, il a pu descendre à l'examen d'une infinité des petits sujets."[1] Books IV and VI are devoted to the details of fortification as practised by Vauban, and as executed in his last work, the great fort of Neuf-Brisach on the Rhine. Book VI, pages 5 to 80, contains a model specification for a "place neuve telle que le Neuf Brisac", with plans and sections of the works. These were on a very considerable scale. The diameter of the octagon of the fort, measured across from centre to

---

[1] For instance the mole-catcher at Dunkerque, see p. 85.

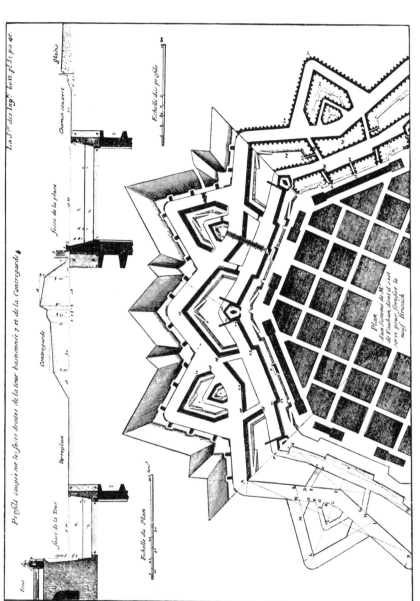

PLAN OF DETAIL OF NEUF-BRISACH

From Belidor, "La Science des Ingénieurs," 1729

centre of the courtines, was six hundred yards. The length given for the sides of the polygon, measured from angle to angle is 360 yards, and the courtines between the tours bastionnées at the angles were to measure 250 yards. It seems that the range of the musquet was still what it had been seventy years earlier, for in 1647 Fournier gave the effective range of the musquet as 120 toises (240 yards)—the walls of the rampart were to be 30 ft. high from the top of the footings in the moat to the "cordon", the half round stone band running all round the ramparts. The wall was to be 10 ft. 2 ins. thick at the base reduced to 5 ft. at the level of the "cordon", and strengthened by solid internal buttresses set 15 ft., c. to c., vaulted overhead and filled in solid with earth. The parapet of earth turfed was to be 18 ft. thick at the top, which was to be 4 ft. 6 ins. above the banquette or firing step. Belidor specifies two rows of trees to be planted on the terreplein or platform of the rampart, with another row at the foot of the bank rising to the rampart from the ground level of the interior of the fort. Instead of the old-fashioned bastion, at the angles of the ramparts there were to be "tours bastionnéés", with outer faces 17 ft. 5 ins. wide, flanks or returns 36 ft. wide and the "gorge" or base line of the pentagon facing to the inside of the fort 42 ft. wide.[1] The walls of the towers were to be 13 ft. thick above the footings, diminishing to 8 ft. at top and were to be in two storeys with a flat roof, parapet and embrasures for guns. Inside there was to be a central chamber containing a powder magazine surrounded by a vaulted corridor and a staircase leading to the roof, and Vauban also provided vent flues to carry off the smoke and fumes of the guns. The "tour bastionnée" was an invention to which Vauban attached great importance.

Vauban, however, relied on the outworks of his forts more than on the traditional rampart, bastion, moat, covered way, and glacis. He trusted to his tenailles, demilunes and counter-guards, redoubts, ravelins and

[1] These dimensions, by the way, do not agree with those of the plans of a "tour bastionnée" on Plate 53, Book VI., which show a much larger building.

hornworks to defend his fort. In the section which
Belidor gives of Neuf-Brisach, we find first the rampart,
then the moat, the tenaille, the moat again, the redoubt
surrounded by the moat being part of the demilune group,
the demilune, the moat again, the covered way and its
parapet, and the glacis 380 yards from the rampart to the
outer line of the glacis. Elsewhere not content with
this, Vauban would sometimes construct hornworks and
detached forts beyond the glacis. All the outworks
mentioned were to be revetted with brickwork or masonry
up to the level of the base of the parapet, and on all of
these except the tenailles, a strip of earth 10 ft. wide
called a "berme" was to be left, on which was to be
planted a "haie-vive" of whitethorn. Behind this came the
earth parapet and banquette 15 ft. thick, 12ft. to 15 ft.
high at the salient angles, with a slope towards the fort of
one foot. All these outworks were connected with the
fort by wood bridges over the moat, and also by "caponnières", narrow vaulted passages under it. The inner
triangular work, forming an inner part of the demilune,
is called "reduit"[1] by Belidor, but he also gives plans of
another "reduit" or redoubt, which was a detached fortified post, square in plan, in two storeys with flat roof and
parapet; one plan is 48 ft. square, the other 60 ft. square.
These correspond to the "reduits" described by Fournier
as places erected for a last stand by the garrison or to
coerce rebellious citizens within the fort.

Belidor gives details of bridges over the moat, and the
bridge next the entrances to the fort, the pont-levis and
the bascule, a hinged bridge worked by counter-weights,
and an ingenious device of Belidor which he calls the
"sinusoide", an example of which, still in existence, I
saw at Peronne in October 1918. He deals at length with
the entrance gates to forts, the portcullis and the "orgues",
a gate which simply dropped from above, crushing or
decapitating anybody who got in the way, and an inner
gate 4 ins. thick to resist petards and bombs; the gate still
in existence at the main entry at Maubeuge is of solid oak

---

[1] See also p. 60 for ravelins and demilunes.

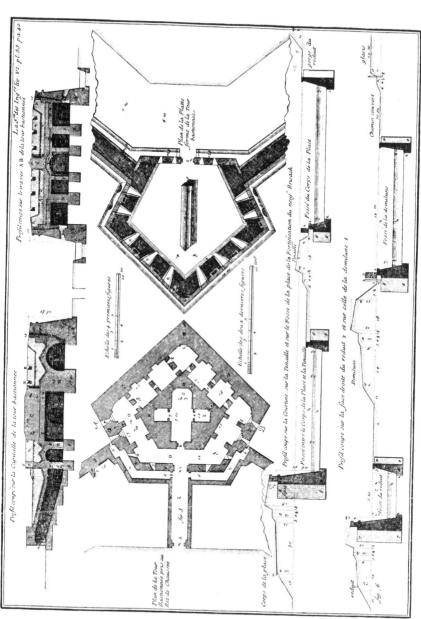

DETAILS OF TOUR BASTIONNÉE, NEUF-BRISACH

From Belidor, "La Science des Ingénieurs," 1729

6 ins. thick. The entrance was to be "garni de toutes ses fermetures, ponts-levis, orgues et bascules". Inside the entrance was a vaulted archway above which were chambers for the machinery of the gates and bridge. Beyond this a vaulted roadway, one storey high, led to a "peristyle" or vestibule 38 ft. by 21 ft. 6 ins., to the right and left of which were guard rooms, a prison and stairs to the ramparts, and above the guard rooms quarters for the guard. The gatehouse at Maubeuge is an excellent illustration. This was the final development of the elaborate gatehouses of the Italians of the sixteenth century.

The actual entrance gates were to be only 9 ft. 9 ins. wide and 13 ft. high, but they were to be set in an architectural frontispiece 50 ft. wide, and here Vauban and his colleagues fairly let themselves go, as for instance the gateways at Strasbourg and more particularly Lille, costly affairs, rather clumsily designed, sometimes with Doric or Tuscan columns and entablatures, panels of florid sculpture, and elaborate trophies. The most famous of these is the "Porte de Paris" at Lille, attributed to Vauban and also to Simon Volant or Vollant, the architect contractor for the citadel and the fortifications. It is a very ambitious affair with a very small gateway set in an enormous rusticated arch, with pairs of engaged Doric columns, entablature and all, on either side, and three sets of trophies overhead. The Tournai gate at Lille, with its two archways and pairs of Doric columns dividing and flanking them, was simpler and better. Indeed, it suggested a dim reminiscence of the Porta del Palio at Verona. At Strasbourg Louvois insisted on Vauban's omitting his ornaments, his "triglyphes, metopes et denticules" and that the cost of his two gateways must not exceed 12,000 écus. Vauban replied that he might save 500, but the gateways would be "très simples et même très vilaines". Besides, he pointed out, Strasbourg was the entrance to Germany, and the Germans, "qui sont extrêmement curieux et ordinairement bons connoisseurs" could judge the magnificence of the King

and the value of the place by these gates. Belidor
himself gives several designs of his own invention for
the gateways of forts, and notes almost with regret that
since the introduction of elaborate outworks, these
gateways were simpler than they used to be. "Aujourd'-
hui que la force des places consiste dans les ouvrages
détachés, on fait les portes beaucoup plus simples."
The entrances to Vauban's great forts seem to me
to be the worst thing about them. The frontispieces
are rather rudimentary compositions of the orders, too
ambitious, too elaborate, out of scale, and out of character
with the purpose of the fort, and it is curious that French
admirers of Vauban should have taken these gateways as
the most signal evidence of his ability.[1] It is true that
Vauban himself took the design of his gateways seriously,
and was hurt when Louvois insisted on cutting down the
expenditures. Vauban thought that this would make his
gateways too plain. Yet having regard to their purpose,
this is just what they should have been. Greater knowledge of architecture and a deeper understanding of the
functions of that art would have saved him from these
deviations into the commonplace and the unessential.
Vauban was a magnificent engineer, none finer, but he
was an amateur in architectural design, and he does not
seem to have realized that when he undertook architectural design he was in a strange country. The massive
simplicity of the Ramparts of Oléron, Gravelines, Bergues,
le Quesnoy and Maubeuge is more impressive, and more
suggestive of a great mind and a strenuous historic past,
than any of Vauban's gateways.

Maubeuge, south of Mons, and Le Quesnoy, south-
east of Valenciennes, are notable examples of Vauban's
methods. Maubeuge he considered to be one of the best of
his designs for a fortified town. When he sent his designs
to Louvois in 1683 he wrote: "S'il y a quelque chose
dans la fortification qui mérite l'admiration des hommes

---

[1] In a paper in praise of Vauban in *L'Architecture* for August 1934, views are
given of the gateways of Neuf-Brisach, Vieux-Brisach, Metz, Phalsbourg, Strasbourg, Selestat, Landau, La Rochelle, Saint Martin de Ré, Maubeuge and Lille.

PORTE DE PARIS, LILLE

Designed by Simon Volant under Vauban, 1682

on peut dire qu'il se trouve dans cette place plus que dans aucune du Royaume"—on account of the depth of its moats and "la belle symétrie et solidité de son revête-ment, la beauté de ses batteries", and more particularly its "grandes esplanades", that is, the open spaces clear of all buildings left round the fortifications. The road from Mons passes through an outer gate, protected by triangular works on either side, crosses the moat, now dry, and enters the town by another gate and a vaulted passage, above part of which on the town side is a large gatehouse of two storeys constructed of hard stone and brick, with an attic storey and dormers. In the centre is a projecting frontis-piece with three arches on the ground floor, three win-dows over, and a heavy pediment. The gatehouse stands in the centre of the courtine, with large bastions at either end; all in fine brickwork and on a large scale. The walls are some 25 ft. high from the moat, and the moat by the bridge leading to the Porte de Fleurus is seventy-five paces wide. Over the principal entrance there is the usual sonorous inscription glorifying the work of Louis XIV.

Ludovicus Magnus
Rex Christianissimus
Belgicis Sequanis Germanicis
Triumphator semper Augustus
ut adversus Hannoniae metropolim validum
vicinumque propugnaculum
objiceret
urbem hanc operibus munitionibusque
firmavit
Anno MDCLXXXV[1]

"Rex Christianissimus" is significant. In this year, 1685, Louis XIV revoked the Edict of Nantes, egged on by the Jesuits and Mme. de Maintenon, and was now posing as the champion of Christianity. Vauban might well be proud of his work at Maubeuge, and in the late war it

---

[1] Louis the Great, the most Christian King, ever the mighty victor of the Belgians, the Sequani [Franche-Comté] and the Germans, strengthened this city with fortifications and arms in order to oppose a near and strong bulwark of defence against the capital of Hainault [Mons].

actually held out against the Germans under von Kluck from August 25th till September 7th, 1914. Yet "heu pietas heu prisca fides", on a recent visit to Maubeuge I found workmen busily cutting through the magnificent walls of Vauban's ramparts in order to form a bye-pass road. The French are supposed to take care of their historical monuments, but when their practical interests are concerned they are deadly, and can tolerate with unruffled equanimity an outrage such as this.

Le Quesnoy, being a small and relatively unimportant town, has so far survived with little injury. It is a very picturesque and remarkable example of Vauban's work, with outer and inner fortifications, and on one side of the town the brick rampart rises sheer from a great sheet of water, half a mile long and a third of a mile wide, which laps the foot of the wall; above the rampart is the usual grass parapet, with a row of poplars along the top. On a bright day, when the reflections are clear and vivid, the effect is very beautiful and unlike any other fortress. At one end a causeway runs out from the town, and beyond this what was once part of the water piece is now a dry hollow of considerable size covered with birches and saplings, and this part must have been the scene of a notable exploit in the late war described in Conan Doyle's *British Campaign in France and Flanders*. Le Quesnoy had been captured by the Germans in March 1918 after a very gallant defence by Captain Combe with a hundred men. In November 1918 the New Zealanders with Byng's Third Army were sent to attack the place. "Le Quesnoy", Conan Doyle says, "was now completely isolated, but its ancient walls and gateways were strongly defended by all modern devices, and machine guns clattered through slits where a bow may once have been bent. The enemy refused to surrender. . . . A forlorn hope of New Zealanders then approached with scaling ladders in the good old style and swarmed up the walls. There was only one ladder and three successive walls, but in some miraculous fashion the whole of the 4th New Zealanders' battalion reached the top of the rampart with the loss of one

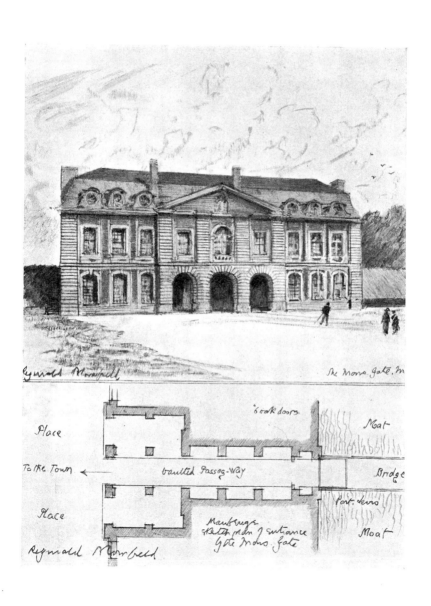

THE MONS GATE, MAUBEUGE (NORD)

man. This was accomplished by sweeping the walls
round with such a fire that the defenders could not peep
over. On seeing that they had reached the rampart the
German Commander at last hoisted the white flag." The
dry bed beyond the causeway would be the place where
the New Zealanders scaled the wall. The grass parapet was
several feet higher than the wall, and by keeping a steady
fire on the top of the parapet the New Zealanders were able
to scale the wall and then rush the grass bank at the top.
It was a gallant feat of arms that would have warmed the
heart of Vauban—ever watchful for opportunities of
attack, and dauntless in driving them home. Conan
Doyle, by the way, let his imagination run away with
him. There are no arrow slits in the walls of Le Quesnoy,
which were built from Vauban's designs.

Vauban's unfailing resource is shown in his designs for
fortified places in mountainous districts such as Mont
Louis in the Pyrenees, Briançon, and Mont Dauphin and
Château Queyras on the Savoy frontier. Château
Queyras is a small fort standing on a rock in a mountain
valley, commanding the junction of two roads into Italy.
Vauban here had to make the best he could of an older
fort at a height of over 4,000 feet above the sea. Briançon
is a little town on a rocky plateau above the Durance, protected on the upper sides by the citadel and the gorge of
the river, and on the two lower sides by Vauban's fortifications. The town was burnt out in 1692, and Vauban
was instructed to prepare plans for rebuilding. He found
that the site was irregular, rocky, and constricted, not a
flat plain as at Neuf-Brisach. Writing to Le Pelletier, the
Minister of War, in 1693, he pointed out the difficulties
"dans un lieu où toutes les règles sont à bout, et naturellement interdites par la mauvaise situation du lieu, qui est
horriblement bossillée et commandée à vue d'oiseau
presque de tous côtés, ce qui oblige à remplir et bossiller
très fréquemment les remparts de traverses, de chutes, de
retombées et d'adossements, ce qui ne peut se faire
comme il faut, qu'avec de grandes dépenses, beaucoup
d'adresse et d' industrie, qui est ce dont nous manquons

le plus." Instead of attempting to coerce nature by pedantic adherence to formulas and stereotyped designs, Vauban followed the natural contours and outline of the site and produced this remarkable little fortified place with its citadel high above the town, its Governor's house and its massive ugly church on a bastion overlooking the road to Grenoble. Here, at Mont Dauphin and elsewhere Vauban's guiding principle was that of Bacon's famous maxim—"Natura non nisi parendo vincitur."

Vauban did not invent the details which I have described. It was in his use of them that his extraordinary ability was shown, his eye for ground, his resource and his quick and decisive judgment. No formula ever stood in his way. "L'art de fortifier," he said, "ne consiste pas dans des règles et des systèmes, mais uniquement dans le bon sens et dans l'expérience" and he pointed out how foolish it was to apply dogmatic systems to unsuitable and unusual sites "où toutes les règles sont à bout".

Ingenious French writers, intent on classification, have attributed to Vauban three manners, and Colonel Lazard,[1] though he does not endorse this view, gives examples from the models in the "Musée des Plans Reliefs". The "first manner" shows the rampart, bastion and moat, with a tenaille in front of the courtine, a demilune in front of the tenaille, the covered way and glacis. The "second manner" shows a small bastioned tower instead of the ordinary bastion at the angles of the rampart, a narrow moat between the ramparts, and the tenaille and a greatly enlarged bastion, detached from the rampart. Outside this came the principal moat, demilune, chemin couvert and glacis. The only variation in the third manner is that the tenaille instead of having two angles on the plan is now planned as a single obtuse angle, that along the top of the escarpment, both of the demilunes and the detached bastions a "haie-vive", a quickset hedge, was to be planted, and a redoubt (or ravelin), a small triangular work, was to be formed, on the base line of the demilune. Vauban, however, would have disclaimed

[1] *Vauban*, p. 376. Plates XVI and XVII.

BRIANÇON (HAUTES ALPES)

PORTE DE TOURNAI, LILLE

Destroyed 1890–95. *Designed by Simon Volant under Vauban*

any such attempt to systematize his work. "Il a toujours dit, et il a fait voir par sa pratique qu'il n'avoit point de manière. Chaque place différente lui en fournissoit une nouvelle, selon les différentes circonstances de grandeur, de sa situation, de son terrain".[1] Vauban hated being bound by formulas. He possessed immense stores of practical knowledge acquired by hard-won experience in the trenches, and he relied on this, not on books. He was always the man of action, not the arm-chair theorist, and it is a notable fact that some of his fortifications were still capable of resistance even in the late war. Colonel Lazard says that Longwy, fortified by Vauban in 1678, was attacked by the Germans in August 1914 and, with Vauban's work hardly altered at all, was able to resist the German attack for nearly a fortnight. Vauban sometimes took less time than this to capture fortresses for Louis XIV.

Most of Vauban's work has disappeared, superseded by later fortifications, or swept away by the town planner and improver, but there is still enough left to enable one to realize its scale and importance; but Vauban, the "preneur des villes", was not less great in attack than he was in defence. There was a saying of the time:

> Ville assiégée par Vauban ville prise;
> Ville défendue par Vauban ville imprenable.

Here we have to rely on what we are told, but the evidence is entirely convincing, and there can be no doubt that Louis XIV owed all or nearly all his successful sieges to the skill of Vauban and the new methods of attack that he introduced, namely attack by trenches parallel to the rampart, instead of by the older method of approach by zigzag trenches on lines at right angles to the fort attacked. It was also due to Vauban that the lives of soldiers were not thrown away in useless attacks, as they were through the incompetence of French generals, and on the enemy's side by the indomitable obstinacy of Cohorn, who insisted on direct assaults, regardless of loss of life. Vauban's

[1] Fontenelle, *Eloge.*

lines and parallels have disappeared as was inevitable; we do not know, for instance, how near to the place attacked he brought his front line of trenches. Fifty years later, Tristram Shandy, hardly an authority, says, "My uncle Toby when laying out his trenches in his garden" [for one of his mimic sieges] "found that not a single inch was left for his first parallel, which should be at least 300 toises from the main body of the place", but as in a normally fortified place the distance to the glacis would have been not less than 300 toises, this will not do. The front line must of course have been well within the effective range of the guns of the attack, and it appears from Vauban's mémoire on the defence of Paris, that he put the range of guns at 1,000 to 1,200 toises, say 2,000 yards. The vitally important point in Vauban's method of attack, was that by means of lines parallel to the place attacked, instead of at right angles, he was able to make simultaneous attacks from different points, instead of the old-fashioned method of direct attacks, made from behind a screen of gabions at one point, which enabled the defence to concentrate its fire on that one point. At the siege of Namur in 1692, Cohorn, who was defending the place, attributed its capture to Vauban's method of attack, "de la manière dont on l'avait embrassé de toutes parts, il avait fallu se rendre.[1] La verité est que notre tranchée est quelque chose de prodigieux. Embrassant à la fois plusieurs montagnes et plusieurs vallées, avec une infinité de tours et retours autant presque qu'il y a de rues à Paris." Racine, who was at Namur as official historiographer, wrote to Boileau in June, describing the siege, which had begun in May, and said, "M. de Vauban avec son canon et ses bombes a fait lui seul toute l'expédition". He had placed his batteries on high ground above and at the back of the citadel and also on the ground to the west. Racine reported that in less than sixteen hours Vauban had carried the enemy's chemin couvert with its palissades, had filled up a moat 60 ft. wide and 8 ft. deep, had taken a demilune opposite the courtine between two

[1] Racine's description.

The Ramparts, Le Quesnoy.

Reynold Mombrun

THE RAMPARTS, LE QUESNOY (NORD)

bastions. "En un mot, Namur a vu tous ses dehors emportés . . . sans qu'il ait couté au Roi plus de trente hommes," and Racine reported that the fire of the French guns was so deadly that the outworks of the fort, the demilunes, redoubts and ravelins were found to be full of bodies, "dont le canon a emporté les têtes, comme si on les avait coupées avec des sabres".[1] Racine's account is very sketchy, though he uses technical terms as terms of common use. It seems that the principal attack was directed against a strongly fortified post on the high ground to the west of the citadel, and Cohorn's last desperate stand was made in the Fort Guillaume which had been built by him for William of Orange only the year before, "un grand ouvrage à cornes, avec quelques redans dans le milieu de la courtine", a fort so cleverly concealed that you could not see it till you were right on to it. Cohorn swore that he would do or die in this fort.[2] However, after incessant bombardment the fort surrendered and its capture meant the capture of the citadel and with the citadel of the town. The attack was made with a very strong force, and Louis XIV was present in person. But the whole conduct of the operations was in Vauban's hands, and all that the King and Dukes and Maréchals de France had to do was to stand by and cheer.

---

[1] Racine to Boileau, June 24, 1692.
[2] Now named Fort Cohorn in his honour.

WE left Vauban at the end of Chapter I and now return to him. He had married in 1660 and spent the next seven years partly at home at St. Léger-Foucherest, but the greater part of it in running up and down France in discharge of his duties as "Ingénieur ordinaire du Roi".

Louvois succeeded his father as Minister of War in 1666, and from this date onwards there followed Vauban's amazing correspondence with Louvois which sheds a vivid light not only on the methods of the wars of Louis XIV, but on the personalities both of Louvois and Vauban. Louvois believed in Vauban, and in spite of his arbitrary ways was Vauban's best friend, as he showed in the troublesome affair of Alt-Brisach. In the years 1664–6 Vauban was employed on the fortifications of Alt-Brisach, that picturesque old town on the upper Rhine, south-east of Colmar, and here he got entangled in an affair which might have ruined his career. A certain Colbert de Saint Marc, a distant kinsman of the great Colbert, was Intendant of Alsace, and wanted to get rid of Vauban. In 1666 he wrote to Colbert suggesting the removal of Vauban, on the ground that though intelligent, he did not understand masonry and starved the work. Vauban had to leave Brisach for the campaign in Flanders in 1667, and had left in charge a certain Saint André, an old soldier. Colbert de Saint Marc took the opportunity of concocting some false accounts, with the help of Saint André, which were presented to Vauban for signature on his return. Vauban, nothing doubting, signed them in good faith without examination, but it appeared soon afterwards that the prices charged were higher than the contract prices, and that work had been charged which had never been executed. Vauban was technically responsible, and when the accounts were brought before the Cour des Comptes, the fraud was discovered, and if it had not been for the high opinion of Vauban held by Colbert (the Minister), and the strenuous loyalty of Louvois, it would have gone hard with Vauban. As it was, he was entirely exonerated, though it was not till 1671 that the false accounts signed by Vauban were returned to him to be burnt, and Louvois was able to write to him that after "deux ans de solicitations", he had kept his promise to Vauban to rescue him from an affair that might have ruined him and his family. In August 1671 a letter was sent from Fontainebleau signed by the King, and countersigned by Colbert, exonerating Vauban from all charges. As for Colbert de Saint Marc, Colbert wrote to him in 1669, "Il y a six ans entiers que je souffre de vous une conduite la plus bizarre et la plus extraordinaire dont on ait jamais entendu parler." Saint Marc was dismissed, and Vauban says that when Saint Marc left Brisach in 1671, he made the Custom House pay him 1,000 écus, sold all the wine in the cellars of the Governor's House to the local cabaretiers, carried off the furniture, and never paid a farthing of his debts to any one. The certificate that De Clerville gave Vauban in 1666 was probably connected with this troublesome affair at Alt-Brisach.

In 1667 Louis XIV began the series of wars which, with brief intervals of peace and ever diminishing success, were to occupy the rest of his reign. The "casus belli" was the succession to the Netherlands on the death of Philip IV of Spain in 1667. Louis XIV claimed the Netherlands on behalf of his wife Maria Theresa, daughter of Philip by his first wife, and Charles II of Spain, the son of Philip by his second wife, claimed it as part of his kingdom. Louis XIV took the field in person in 1667 with 35,000 men, invaded Flanders and captured various places, Dunkerque and Bergues, and Lille after a nine days' siege. The King was so pleased with Vauban's conduct, that he gave him a commission as Lieutenant in the Royal Guards, allowed him

5

to sell his commission in the Regiment of Picardy, and granted him a pension of 2,400 livres. Vauban, who had no private means said frankly that he had no money, and had the courage to ask the King's permission to sell the lieutenancy in the Guards, and though this request was considered "fort extraordinaire", the King agreed, and Vauban realized 20,000 livres by the sale. He had already obtained for himself and his family the patent of nobility which was a condition of entering the Guards.[1]

After the death of Mazarin, the administration of fortresses was divided between Colbert who took the west side of France, and Louvois who took the east. Colbert, as we have seen, had full confidence in Vauban and treated him with much consideration, but his most loyal and constant backer was François Michel Le Tellier, Marquis de Louvois, and after the capture of Lille in 1667, Louvois began to do all in his power to push Vauban to the front. Vauban was made Governor of the Citadel of Lille, and was instructed by Louvois to prepare designs for its fortifications. De Clerville, the engineer, who was much Vauban's senior, had already made designs, but these were not liked by the King, and Louvois was very anxious to put Vauban in De Clerville's place. A meeting was arranged at Lille between de Clerville, Vauban and others, and Louvois' instructions were that de Clerville was to be allowed to talk because he liked talking, but none of his suggestions were to be carried out till confirmed by the Governor of the town of Lille. In 1667 Louvois wrote to the Intendant of Flanders, "Vous pouvez laisser discourir M. le Chevalier de Clerville, sur tout ce qu'il aime à faire dans les places. Comme il parle fort bien, et qu'il y prend plaisir, vous pouvez le laisser dire, mais ne faites jamais rien de tout ce qu'il dit que vous n'en ayez ordre d'ici, ou que le Lieutenant-général[2] le désire absolument." De Clerville was a distinguished soldier, but Louvois did not like him, and Vauban who was much younger than de Clerville had no opinion of his ability. In 1668 Vauban was writing to Louvois "Je m'étonne que

---

[1] See p. 2.   [2] The Marquis d'Humières.

pour un grand homme comme est M. le Chevalier de Clerville, il emploie tant de belles paroles pour dire si peu de choses." Apparently, de Clerville resembled Kaye, Bishop of Lincoln, of whom Sydney Smith said that he "could talk at greater length and say nothing, than·any man that has ever been". The intrigue proceeded on lines familiar to professional men, and in due course Vauban's design was preferred and the work was entrusted to him. De Clerville was very angry but could do nothing, and ten years later died a broken man on the island of Oléron, where he had been put on the shelf as Governor. The contract of the work at Lille was given to Simon Vollant, a master mason or architect contractor of Lille, who did so well that the King gave him the rank of "ingénieur et architecte de ses armées", and after completing the work at Lille, Vollant was entrusted with the fortifications of Menin and other places, although in 1671 Louvois had written to Vauban, "Vollant est un fou et un visionnaire." Apparently he had suffered from false alarms, and Vauban was to reassure him by saying that the worst that could happen to him, was that for the rest of his life he would have to continue in his present appointment. The famous gateway at Lille known as the "Porte de Paris" is claimed for Vauban as one of his designs, but it is more likely to have been designed by Vollant.[1]

All sorts of difficulties arose at Lille. Louvois had received unfavourable reports of the ground at Lille, and was frightened of running sand ("sable bouillant ou mouvant"). Vauban assured him that piles were not necessary, that the belfries in Lille were built without piling, and "qui porte un clocher peut porter les Pyrénées".[2] Then there were troubles with the men. The masons ran away, because they found that much of the stone they were set to quarry was useless for building, so that they could not complete the work allotted to them in the day and earn their pay for it. At first Vauban

---

[1] *See* p. 55.
[2] A rather doubtful assertion. At the Menin Gate where we found running sand, I used reinforced concrete piles 16 ins. by 16 ins. and 36 ft. long, to carry the raft for the foundations.

tried to deal with this by kindness, and ordered the fore-
man "quand il en verrait quelqu'un tomber en délire par
la pure faute du travail, de lui remettre le cœur au ventre
par l'onction de quelques pièces de 15 sols dans la paume de
la main". The desertions, however, continued, so Vauban
now borrowed two mounted guards from the Governor
of Lille, "avec chacun un ordre en porte, et un nerf de
bœuf[1] à la main", and if any failed to answer the evening
roll call, the guards were to go next morning to their
lodgings, and "les amèneront par les oreilles sur l'ouvrage".
There was no such thing as striking work for Louis XIV;
death or the galleys was the usual penalty. The only
thing to do was to run away. In 1671 Vauban wrote
again to Louvois to complain of "la quantité de la
friponneries que se perpètrent tous les jours sur les
travaux par les soldats". It seems that the soldiers even
went for the contractors, took them by the throat and
beat them. There seems to have been little systematic
discipline in the French army in 1671, but the employment of soldiers both here and later in the aqueduct of
Maintenon was an abuse of the terms on which the
men served: they had enlisted as soldiers, not as navvies
and bricklayers.

Vauban reported to Louvois nearly every week and
sometimes nearly every other day, and he wrote with a
direct and vivid frankness which makes his letters extraordinarily interesting. Vauban never minced matters. As early
as 1668 he wrote to Louvois, that he preferred "la verité,
quoique mal polie, à une lâche complaisance" and at that
time Vauban was only a junior officer of thirty-five, and
Louvois was Minister of War and the most powerful man
in France, after the King and Colbert. Three years later,
when certain officers at Lille had complained that Vauban
had been too hard on the soldiers, Vauban demanded a
full and searching inquiry, and was ready to take whatever came to him. In a fine and characteristic letter to
Louvois, he said "J'ose bien dire, que sur le fait d'une
probité très exacte, et d'une fidélité sincère, je crains ni

[1] A cutting whip.

RAMPARTS, OLÉRON (ÎLE D')

le Roi, ni vous, ni tout le genre humain ensemble. La fortune m'a fait naître le plus pauvre gentilhomme de France, mais en récompense elle m'a honoré d'un cœur sincère, si exempt de toutes sortes de friponneries, qu'il n'en peut soutenir l' imagination sans horreur." In others than Vauban one might suspect that the writer did protest too much, but Vauban was transparently honest; he had, Fontenelle said, a passion for truth "presque impudente et incapable de ménagement". Nor did he shrink from complaining when he thought it necessary. He wrote to Louvois from Nancy in 1673 "que depuis de mon retour de l'armée j'ai toujours voyagé, ou plutôt toujours couru, de place en place, essayant tout ce que l'hiver et le mauvais temps ont de rude et de fâcheux, avec 7 ou 8 chevaux, et 6 ou 7 hommes, dont trois mangent ordinairement avec moi, que depuis ce temps-là, je n'ai point autre gîte que les cabarets, que sont les lieux de monde les plus propres à se ruiner à petit bruit et sans façon, specialement en Flandre, où ils excellent sur tous les autres pays en cherté et mauvaise chère." All this, he continued, meant heavy expense, and the Cabarets insisted on cash down. He was tired out, for six months he had not received a farthing's pay, he had heard nothing more of his "pension" and M. Bailly, to whom he had sold his commission as lieutenant in the Guards, did not pay the balance due. As for his own affairs, they were completely neglected, and he therefore asked for three weeks' leave to go home. "Souvenez vous, s'il vous plait, qu'en 6 ans de temps, je n'y ait été que trois jours, encore m'en avez vous bien grondé." Louvois replied that he would see to it, but that leave was out of the question. Vauban returned to the charge, half humorously, in January 1675. "Est il possible," he wrote to Louvois, "que vous ne puissez m'exempter de tant des corvées . . . faut il que je suis prédestiné à être toujours gueux, et à n'avoir jamais de repos ni hiver ni été?" Vauban suffered from a chronic cold, robust though he was. In 1671 he wrote, "L'incommodité de mon rhume était tellement aggravée par la fatigue du cheval, que j'ai failli en créver par les chemins, et la vérité est que j'ai été obligé de mettre plus de cinquante fois pied à terre, à cause des maux de tête, et des éblouissements que le toussement me causait." Elsewhere he says "Les fréquents voyages me ruinent." In spite of this he says he was able to write a mémoire of 150 pages, with more than thirty drawings on the conduct of sieges, "un livre rempli de la plus fine marchandise que soit dans ma boutique". Louvois was impatient to have this book, but Vauban replied that he could not do more than he could. He had no time, and could not write three words without blotting them, and that if Louvois would only stop his persecutions he would add another drawing, that neither his secretary nor his draughtsmen always understood his notes, and "Quand je trace, je n'écris pas, et quand j'écris je ne saurai dessiner", and that with the best intentions he could not do everything at once. To which Louvois replied that his handwriting was deplorable, and that if he did not have all his letters written by his secretary, he would cut off the secretary's pay. In 1678 Louvois, writing from S. Germain, was in one of his irritable moods. He scolded Vauban for his contractors, said that the prices were too high, that in his designs for some redoubts "vous donnez un peu dans l'étoffe, et il faut essayer de les faire moins magnifiques". As for his proposal to build redoubts at Dunkerque in order to prevent the enemy fishing in the Mouère, this was "un peu burlesque" and he laughed at it. But this was Louvois' way. Louvois and Vauban thoroughly understood and trusted each other, and an attractive side of Louvois' character is shown in his correspondence with Vauban. He was, as a rule, a harsh arrogant man, and his heavy irony does not compare with Vauban's excellent sense of humour, but he was a loyal and understanding friend who never failed Vauban in backing his schemes and seeing them through. He had a real regard for his engineer. In 1668 Vauban was ill at Chaumont. Louvois wanted to see him at once, but implored Vauban not to risk his health; he was not "précipiter votre départ, de crainte que vous ne rétombiez malade", and later on both the King and Louvois were constantly forbidding Vauban to risk his life in the trenches. In 1672 Louis XIV declared war on Holland. Turenne with an army of 180,000 men invaded Flanders, and the King himself took nominal command at the sieges, informing Colbert that he believed it to be in the interest of his designs and likely to promote his prestige, if he attacked four places on the Rhine, Rhinberg, Wesel, Bürick and Orsoy. He took the nominal command in person at all four sieges. In the earlier and prosperous years of his reign Louis XIV was fond of sieges; he greatly preferred them to pitched battles at which he never appeared. He seems to have regarded sieges as rather exciting court picnics. With him went some of his courtiers; he dined off silver plate and insisted on the formal ceremonial of the Court. He knew something about sieges and fortifications, but he was not a fighting man, and to go into action himself like Henri IV was the very last thing that he intended to do. The programme was always the same. Vauban prepared the plans of attack; these were submitted to the King who duly appended his signature in the manner of "Angelica fecit", if he was present; if not, the plan was sent to Louvois for the King's approval, but it was common knowledge that Vauban was the man behind these successful sieges. Even the ladies of the Court had heard of him as the "preneur des villes".

Vauban himself was under no illusion as to these sieges of paltry little places, "toutes ces bicoques[1] de sièges", as he called them. Writing to Louvois in 1675 he said that they were of no real use, whereas if important places such as Condé, Valenciennes and Cambrai were attacked, "Leur prise assurerait vos conquêtes et ferait le Pré Carré tant désirable, sans quoi le Roi ne pourra jamais rien faire de considérable, et plût à Dieu qu'au lieu de s'amuser à toutes ces bicoques de sièges on eût songé à s'accommoder sérieusement de cette place." "S'être amusé à

---

[2] "Bicoque", "a paltry little town"; Boyer, a twopenny-halfpenny affair.

toutes ces bicoques de sièges" is a terse and scathing description of many of the sieges undertaken by Louis XIV. He
liked to pose as the invincible hero and return to his
ladies with the laurels of his easy victories won by some-
body else. Utrecht was taken with twenty-two smaller
places, and the "rot" was not stopped till the Dutch
opened their sluices and flooded out the French army.
Vauban returned to his duties as Governor of the citadel
of Lille, and ended up the year with a difference of
opinion with d'Artagnan, our old friend of "The Three
Musqueteers". D'Artagnan, who was temporary Governor of Lille, had given orders in the citadel of which
Vauban was Governor. Vauban complained to Louvois,
and added that if he had only been appointed Governor
of the citadel in order to draw 2,000 livres per annum, he
would sooner resign at once. Louvois reassured him by
saying that d'Artagnan's term of office would end in a
month's time. In actual fact d'Artagnan was killed at
the siege of Maestricht in the following year.

The great event of 1673 was the famous siege of Maestricht. "En 1673, il fit sous les ordres du Roi le siège
de Maestricht, qui fut terrible. Ce fut là qu'il commença
pour la première fois, à mettre en usage la réforme qu'il
a depuis executée si heureusement dans les attaques de
places. Celle-ci fut réduite à capituler en 13 jours de
tranchée ouverte. Ce siège fut fort sanglant, à cause des
incongruités qui arrivèrent par faute de gens qu'il ne veut
pas nommer."[1] The reform in attack which Vauban
introduced here for the first time, was the attack by successive lines of trenches parallel to the place attacked.
Hitherto the method of attack had been to form a zigzag
trench of approach at right angles to the glacis to a point
within gunfire of the fort. Here the attacking force
emerged, and opened fire on the fort from behind a
temporary screen of gabions. This, of course, left the
attack exposed to the fire of the fort, and the gabions
were a flimsy defence against gunfire. Moreover, all the
movements of the attack were visible from the rampart.

[1] *Abrégé.*

The new method of attack was to advance "avec de grandes lignes parallèles, qui étaient larges et spacieuses, de sorte que par les moyens des banquettes[1] qu'il y avait, on pouvait aller à l'ennemi avec un fort grand front".[2] By this means the place could be attacked from all sides, or at any rate all along the front. The garrison of Maestricht did not know what to make of this new method of attack, and surrendered after a siege of 13 days. The "incongruités" mentioned in the *Abrégé* were the blunders of the higher command, in insisting on a direct attack on the "chemin couvert" and the demilunes in the moat. Vauban always condemned this direct attack, as wasteful of life; and at the siege of Maestricht lives were thrown away by the use of the direct attack in the wrong place. Vauban noted that the French soldier had an ingrained dislike for taking cover. In a note on the siege of Maestricht he wrote, "Je ne sais, si on doit appeler ostentation, vanité ou paresse, la facilité que nous avons à nous mettre à découvert hors de la tranchée sans necessité. Ceci est un péché original dont les Français ne ses guériront jamais." Maestricht was attacked unsuccessfully three years later by the Prince of Orange in 1676, and Louvois who had seen the plan of attack, said he had never seen such a ridiculous scheme in his life, such "âneries". The engineer had made his attack from a re-entering angle, where he was exposed to fire from every side. In 1673 money was still plentiful in France, or rather the King had not yet realized the dangerous state of the finances. "Tout était payé grassement, et la libéralité du Roi s'étendait jusqu'à faire donner des cent écus pour une simple contusion." Louis XIV was so pleased with the capture of Maestricht that he gave Vauban 4,000 louis. Vauban attributed the success to the fact that "le travail fut dirigé par une seule tête, qui en reçevait les ordres immédiats du Roi et n'en rendait compte qu'à lui seul."

[1] "Banquette"—a step.
[2] Description written by Louis XIV. See Lazard *Vauban*, p. 156. Louis XIV was keenly interested in siege operations, and actually had some knowledge of them.

After preparing plans for the fortification of Maestricht, Vauban was sent to Nancy and Alt-Brisach to deal with the consolidation of the frontier and was greatly exercised about the faulty state of the frontier defence. There were wide gaps in the line. Fortresses so far had been considered as isolated units, without regard to their relation to one another as parts of an organized line of defence. Vauban conceived of France as one great estate, which he wished to enclose in a ring fence strong enough to resist any attack. In a letter to Louvois in January 1673 he used these remarkable words: "Sérieusement, Monseigneur, le Roi devrait un peu songer à faire son *Pré Carré*. Cette confusion de places amies et ennemies pêle-mêles ne me plait point. Vous êtes obligé d'en entretenir trois pour une, vos peuples en sont tourmentés, vos dépenses de beaucoup augmentées, et vos forces de beaucoup diminuées, et j'ajoute qu'il est presque impossible que vous puissiez toutes mettre en état et les munir . . . c'est pourquoi . . . prêchez toujours la quadrature non pas du cercle, mais du Pré." Throughout his career from this time forward, all Vauban's schemes for frontier defence were dominated by this idea of the "Pré Carré". Certain places might be given up, but others such as Brisach, Strasbourg and Luxembourg were essential to the security of France. When urging the desirability of the siege of Condé, his argument was that the capture of this place would save the King a number of useless garrisons, "et ferait un Pré Carré en Flandre, que vingt années de guerre ne pourraient pas lui arracher". Vauban foresaw that France would soon be attacked on every side, and he advised Louvois "si nous voulons durer longtemps contre tant d'enemis, il faut songer à se reserrer".

In 1674 war was declared with Spain, and Vauban was placed in charge of the siege of Besançon in Franche-Comté. The picturesque town of Besançon stands on a rocky peninsula surrounded on three sides by the River Doubs, but commanded by higher ground all round. Vauban pointed out to Louvois that the place, which was held by a strong Spanish garrison, could not be taken by direct assault, and that the only thing to do was to attack it by artillery from Mont Chandane, on the other side of the river. "Il sera besoin d'une grande artillerie," and he asked for 36 guns, from 12 to 24 charge, 4 mortars and other guns, "mais, aussi il ne faut pas se flatter", for the garrison were stout fellows. However, after a siege of 19 days, Besançon surrendered, and Vauban set about the reconditioning of the ramparts and the citadel and the construction of a small fort on Mont Chandane. Vauban had taken Besançon by gunfire from Mont Chandane. Curiously enough he wrote a long letter to Louvois three years later from Dunkerque, objecting strongly to anything but a small redoubt on Mont Chandane and Mont Brézille, both of which commanded Besançon, on the ground that these forts could easily be taken by the enemy and would enable him to carry the town. For once in a way Vauban's argument seems to be illogical.

Vauban was appointed a Brigadier of infantry in 1674 and on his way to inspect some work at Bergues "Il pensa être tué" at La Bassée, by a party of the enemy, who killed his escort, wounded his nephew, broke the arm of his groom, and took his secretary prisoner. Vauban appears to have escaped, the *Abrégé* does not say how. On hearing of this Louvois wrote to Vauban by the King's order forbidding him to expose himself to any such risks in future. The King, Colbert and Louvois knew his value. Colbert writing to the Intendant of Rochfort in 1674, described Vauban as "le plus habile et plus entendu qu'aucun ingénieur qui ait jamais été en France". In spite of this, his pay was still in arrear. In February 1674, in a long letter to Louvois, he pointed out that his pay as Governor of the Citadel of Lille since the preceding April was still due, and his pay as engineer since May of the year before, and that he did not want to have to ask Colbert, "attendu je suis ni d'humeur ni accommodé à mendier mon pain à sa porte." Vauban's want of money was chronic, and for some reason he was unwilling to address himself to Colbert. This is the more strange, since Colbert had the very highest opinion of

Vauban's ability, as is shown by the episode of Niquet at Metz.

In 1675 Vauban called Louvois' attention to the importance of the "trois évêchés", Metz, Toul and Verdun. He had placed in charge an engineer named Niquet, who it seems could never accept instructions without criticizing them, and now had the audacity to make some changes in Vauban's designs. He was at once ordered by Colbert to carry out Vauban's designs without any alteration of any kind. Colbert was very angry. He wrote to the Intendant of Metz that if a handful of earth was moved contrary to Vauban's orders, Niquet would be recalled there and then, and to Niquet he wrote, that the letter which Niquet had sent him, "ne tend qu'à faire votre panégyrique", and that if he dared "rémuer une pelletée de terre", unless so instructed by Vauban, he would be dismissed at once. "Sachez que ce n'est point à vous à toucher aux ouvrages de Sieur de Vauban sans ordre exprès, et vous devez encore travailler à étudier dix ans sous lui, auparavant que vous poussiez concevoir une aussi bonne opinion de vous." Colbert and Louvois did not mince matters in writing to their subordinates. Niquet, who seems to have been a clever but uncomfortable and obstinate person, nearly always managed to come into collision with Vauban, but the latter, who could endure any one but knaves and "fripons", bore with him again and saved him from dismissal. Later on, Vauban came to have a high opinion of Niquet, and in 1690, when it was proposed to form a canal from Arles to the Port de Bouc, Vauban advised that Niquet was the one man capable of the work.

Vauban wrote freely to Louvois on the futility of sieges conducted without method, to which that Minister replied "J'ai reçu avec submission vos réprimandes." One hardly expected this genial irony from Louvois. However, the sieges continued. Condé, Bouchain, Aire and Valenciennes were taken and Vauban was promoted to the rank of Maréchal de Camp. For the siege of Condé on the Scheldt, Louvois had a floating battery constructed, which was tried on the grand canal at Versailles. Louvois assured Vauban that it was unsinkable and that he would have it brought overland to Condé, but we hear nothing more of this floating "redoute". However, Condé fell after a siege of five days, Bouchain in May after nine days, and Aire in July after ten days. In December Vauban wrote to Louvois from Verdun: "J'arrivai hier soir de Stenay, par le plus mauvais temps et le plus froid temps de monde. Toute la terre n'était qu'une glace, sur laquelle je faillis vingt fois à me casser mon cou. Les crampons n'y font rien, et les chevaux sont toujours prêts à tomber. Si ce temps-là continue, le Roi n'aura pas grande satisfaction des ouvrages de cet hiver, et je serai fort heureux, quant à moi, si j'en suis quitte pour quelque bout de nez ou d'oreille gelés."

Cambrai, Guillain and Valenciennes were taken after short sieges in the spring of 1677, Valenciennes, "autant par la bonne disposition des attaques (Vauban), que par le bonheur extrême qui accompagnait le Roi dans toutes ses entreprises."[1] Valenciennes was a very strong place. Voltaire[2] says: "Il fallait d' abord attaquer deux demilunes; derrière ces demilunes était un grand ouvrage à couronne, palissadé et fraisé, entouré d'un fossé, coupé de plusieurs traverses: dans cet ouvrage à couronne était encore un autre ouvrage, entouré d'un autre fossé. Il fallait après s'être rendu maître de tous ces retranchements franchir un bras de l'Escaut: le bras franchi, on trouvait encore un autre ouvrage qu'on nomme pâté; derrière ce pâté coulait le grand cours de l'Escaut profonde et rapide, qui sert de fossé à la muraille; enfin la muraille était soutenue par de larges remparts. Tous les ouvrages étaient couverts de canons."

Contrary to the usual practice, and against the advice of Louvois and all the five Maréchals de France, the

---

[1] *Abrégé*—a left-handed compliment, and Vauban writing thirty years later, must have had his tongue in his cheek when he wrote of the King's good luck.

[2] *Siècle de Louis XIV*. Voltaire seems to be wrong in placing the crownwork behind the demilune, as it should have been in front of it, but he always wrote in haste. The ramparts at Valenciennes were converted into boulevards at the end of the last century.

attack was made not at night, but in broad daylight. Vauban insisted that this was less costly of life, since it prevented the troops from getting mixed and shooting each other in mistake for the enemy; also that the enemy would not expect an attack by day. Moreover "la nuit favoure la timidité." "Le Roi se rendit aux raisons de Vauban malgré Louvois et cinq Maréchaux de France." The King was so pleased with the capture of Valenciennes that he gave Vauban a gratification of 25,000 écus, "de son mouvement, sans l'avoir demandée ni prétendue." This seems to have been in addition to the payment to Vauban of 75,000 livres "en considération de ses services et pour lui donner moyen de les continuer".[1] I find from the "Comptes des Bâtiments du Roi" that in this year, (1677) J. H. Mansart, the King's architect, was being paid at the rate of only 6,000 francs per annum "à lui accordés en considération des services et de la conduite qu'il a des bâtiments de S.M.", 6,000 fr. for Clagny, and 500 fr. for attendance at "conferences". Perrault only received 4,000 fr. for his designs for the Louvre and the Arc de Triomphe, and Le Brun "premier peintre du Roi" 8,000 francs. These figures suggest the immense importance attached to Vauban's ability by the King and his Ministers.

Cambrai, Ghent and Ypres were taken in 1677-8, but Louvois was getting anxious about the reckless way in which Vauban exposed himself at sieges, and wrote to Humières, the Commander in Chief in Flanders, telling him to take special care of Vauban, and that it was the King's wish that Vauban should not be allowed to go into the trenches. "Vous savez assez le déplaisir que sa Majesté aurait, s'il arrivait quelque inconvénient à mondit Sieur de Vauban." It is needless to say that Vauban persisted in taking risks and spent hours daily in the trenches, to make sure that they were being properly carried

[1] Probably arrears of pay. In 1694, writing to Barbezieux, who had succeeded his father as Minister of War, Vauban says: "On m'a payé jusqu'ici, par le extraordinaire de la guerre, pour le soin des fortifications dont je suis chargé 15,000 livres. Ce sont des appointements que feu M. votre père m'avait reglés, il y a longtemps."

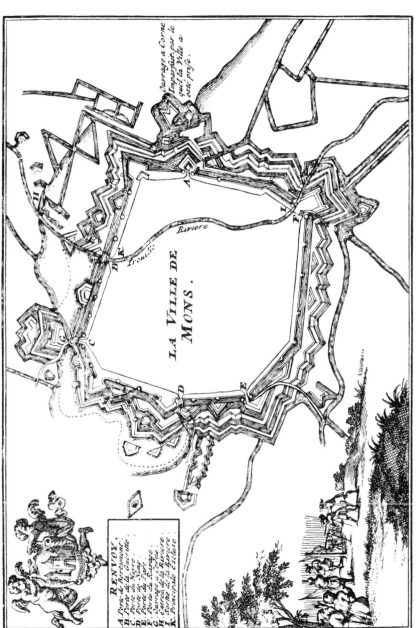

Ouvrage à Corne
Imparfait, par le
quel la Ville a
esté prise.

Riviere

Troulle

LA VILLE DE
MONS.

RENVOY.

A Porte de Bertaimont.
B Porte de la Gueritte.
C Porte du Parc.
D Porte du Nort.
E Porte de Fart.
F Porte du Rivage.
G Ouvrage à Corne.
H Sortie de la Riviere.
I Sortie de la Riviere.
K Principale Eclusse.

PLAN OF THE TOWN OF MONS
From "Atlas Portatif," 1702

out, though he was as well aware of the danger as Louvois or the King. Mons and Namur were taken in the spring of 1678, and the war ended with the Peace of Nymeguen (1678). Spain gave up a number of important places in the Netherlands, S. Omer, Cassel, Ypres, Condé, Cambrai, Valenciennes and others. France surrendered Charleroi, Ath, Ghent, Oudenarde, Maestricht and other places in Flanders, but retained Nancy, Fribourg, and la Franche-Comté. Vauban was seeing the realization of his idea of the "Pré Carré, and he was at length appointed Commissaire Général des fortifications de France". After the capture of Ypres he accompanied Louvois on a tour of inspection of the forts on the northern frontier, and spent the rest of 1678 in making "les beaux et grands projets des villes de Menin et de Maubeuge, qui sont exécutés depuis, qui furent suivis de celui de Longwy d'où il se rendait à la cour", one of his very rare appearances at a court, where he must have been completely out of his element, for he had none of the grace and elegance of the courtier, and in his inner heart had a complete contempt for the French aristocracy. He was now in the full enjoyment of his career. He was forty-five, in vigorous health, recognized as the first engineer in France, implicitly trusted by the King and his ministers and on excellent terms with his men. In 1677 when a question arose about some redoubts at Thionville, Vauban wrote to Louvois that he could do what he liked about the redoubts, all he asked was that Louvois should not commit him with his men, "qui me regardent comme leur supérieur et avec qui je vis comme des frères". If the peace of Nymeguen marks the apogee of the reign of Louis XIV, I think it also marks the happiest time in Vauban's career.

CHAPTER VII

Vauban's Mémoires on forts to be relinquished; and on the training of engineers and selection of officers—Dunkerque and the new harbour—Vauban's gateways —The pirates of Algiers—The siege of Luxembourg—Vauban's pay and expenses.

THE peace of Nymeguen ended the war with Spain, and for the next ten years (1678–88) there was peace in the land, and Vauban was able to take steps to realize his ideal of the consolidation of the frontiers of France. In 1678, he drew up a "mémoire" on the places on the Flemish frontier that ought to be fortified, from Dunkerque on the north-west coast to Dinant on the Meuse, including Bergues, Furnes, Le Kenocq, Ypres, Menin, Lille, Tournai, Montagne, Condé, Valenciennes, Le Quesnoy, Maubeuge, Philippeville and Dinant. In addition to these he gave a list of places of secondary importance, Gravelines, S. Omer, Aire, Béthune, Arras, Douai, Bouchain, Cambray, Landrecies, Avesnes, Marienburg and Charleville. He also proposed a canal to run from Ypres to the Lys, and from the Lys to the Scheldt, fortified with redoubts, or as we might call them, blockhouses. Vauban also drew up at Louvois' request a "mémoire" on "Les fonctions des différents officiers employés dans les fortifications", one of the earliest of his very able papers. Vauban found that much of the heavy cost of fortifications was due to faults of design and organization, careless supervision, and ignorance of building construction. Surveyors, he said, must know their business, and if it was necessary to demolish private property, the owner should be compensated, "étant juste que le propriétaire à qui on prend les biens sans les lui demander, et pour un prix très médiocre, ne soit pas frustré de son revenu annuel, par l'attente trop longue de son principal"—a point too often forgotten in slum clearances to-day. In all his reports and mémoires to these powerful war Ministers, Vauban always insisted on justice for people who could not speak for themselves.

In regard to young men who aspired to be engineers, he said they must be trained for the work, possess some knowledge of mathematics, geometry, trigonometry, surveying, geography, civil architecture and drawing. If passed at a first examination, they should be sent for a year or two to some big work then in construction, and after this again examined. If passed, they should be given brevets as second engineers; if not passed, they should be turned over to the infantry. Vauban gave many other wise suggestions as to the training and organization of engineers, but the most notable is his insistence that no favour should be shown. In every branch of the service "Il faut que le mérite seul et la capacité des gens leur attire des emplois." Vauban anticipated "la carrière ouverte au talent" of Napoleon, for it seems that the French army of the time of Louis XIV was honeycombed by intrigue, purchase and patronage. Vauban cut at the root of this, but the Court was too strong for him. It was his fate both here, and in all his aims and ideals, to be about a hundred years ahead of his time. Vauban returns to this point in a paper on the appointment of officers. Privates, he says, should not be excluded from appointment as officers. "Il faut pour faire d'excellentes troupes, tendre non seulement les mains au mérite, mais aller au devant. En quelque sujet qu'il se rencontre, il est toujours excellent. Dieu le Père et le Créateur de tous les hommes, se moque de nos distinctions et loge le bon esprit où il lui plait. Tous les hommes sont les mêmes devant lui. Le bon esprit et le courage sont de tout pays et de toutes conditions. Il faut les prendre où on les trouve. C'est une marchandise rare et précieuse." It is one of the many attractive points in Vauban, that in the most flunkey-ridden court in Europe, he regarded men as men and not as clothes-horses.

Colbert was responsible for the forts and defence of France from Dunkerque all along the west coast of France, and in his anxiety to promote trade was much concerned

6

about the harbours. Vauban had made designs for the fortifications of Dunkerque as early as 1668, "le plus grand, le plus beau dessin de fortification du monde", but the harbour of Dunkerque was quite inadequate and very weakly protected. In 1678–9 Colbert called in Vauban, and Vauban produced a most able scheme, with an estimate of cost of three million livres. Colbert accepted it at once and wrote to Vauban, "Je ne puis m'empêcher de vous témoigner la joie que j'ai de l'espérance que vous avez, que ce travail réussira à la satisfaction du Roi, au bien et à l'avantage de son service." Colbert hoped that the harbour would now be able to take in ships up to 700 or 800 tons. Vauban began the work in 1678. Before he altered it, the old harbour of Dunkerque came right up to the walls of the town; it was quite shallow and could only be entered at high tide. In le Père Fournier's *Traité* there is a plate which shows a harbour behind a sand-bank on the sea side, with a high bank or causeway at the north end and the entrance from the south. Both for trade and as a harbour for ships of war this was of little use, and Vauban dealt with it in a masterly way. He gave up the existing harbour as useless, and formed an entirely new harbour, with basins for ships and quays next the town, and to the south-west of it, and for access to it, formed a broad channel with high embankments about 2,000 yards long, right through the sand which had formed the bed of the old harbour. He formed two forts at the sea entrance, and about two-thirds of the way from the town he constructed another fort called "the Risban".[1] In order to clear the sand away, he built dams above the town to collect all the water from the adjacent marshes by means of four canals; from time to time the sluices were opened to enable the head of water to drive the sand out to sea. This method devised by Vauban to keep the channel clear is still in use with water drawn from the marshes east of Dunkerque known as "Les Moères". The walls of the channel or canal were revetted, with a roadway along the top. Fournier gives

[1] A lighthouse now stands on the site of the Risban.

VIEW OF DUNKERQUE
From Fournier, "Traité des Fortifications"

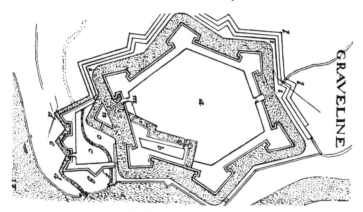

PLAN OF GRAVELINES
From Fournier, "Traité des Fortifications"

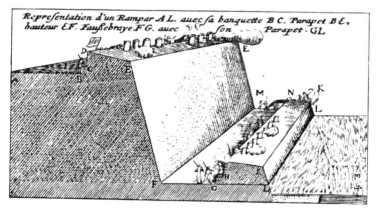

SECTION OF A RAMPART
From Fournier, "Traité des Fortifications"

a view of Dunkerque as it was in 1647, and the *Atlas Portatif* gives a plan of the town and harbour as altered by Vauban, and except that there are five docks now occupying the space called the "Esplanade de la Citadelle" and part of the original harbour as far as the Risban, the general lines of Vauban's design for Dunkerque can still be traced. The entrance to the port still follows the line of Vauban's channel, and two of the "bassins" occupy the same position as they did in Vauban's scheme. The accounts of it given by Colonel Lazard and M. Halévy are not quite accurate. Col. Lazard says that Vauban had to deepen and widen the "Canal", but no canal existed before Vauban made it. M. Halévy describes the Risban as having been made in the sea 1,000 yards from the town. Vauban's own description is that it was built "plus de cinq-cents toises avant, dans le mer, sur un banc de sable mouvant, qu'il a fallu pour ainsi dire fixer."[1] The map of Dunkerque in the *Atlas Portatif*, shows exactly what Vauban did. He built the Risban close to the south bank, on piles driven into the sand, which was covered by the sea at high water. A lighthouse has since been built on the site of the Risban.

Vauban was so proud of his work that he thought it should have a Latin inscription in accordance with the prevailing fashion of the time, and a learned friend, the Baron de Woerden, whose business it was to provide inscriptions in Flanders, produced the grandiloquent inscription given at the bottom of page 84.

Meanwhile Vauban had been reconstructing the fortifications of the town. Hitherto its only defence had been a wall with little circular towers at intervals. As Dunkerque was now to be one of the most important harbours in the north of France, and as it was liable to attack by the English from the sea, and the Dutch from the land, it was essential that it should be strongly fortified. Vauban formed an entirely new system of defence with rampart, bastions, moats, demilunes and hornworks with a separate suburb for the sailors of the fleet. Vauban's

---

[1] The Risban stood on the south bank of the canal.

fortifications were partly dismantled in 1713 as one of the conditions of the Treaty of Utrecht, but were reconstructed by Louis XV. It seems that their final destruction was comparatively recent, as in the plans given in Joanne (1907) and later guide-books elaborate works are shown on the north side between Dunkerque and Malo les Bains. These have all disappeared except a fragment of a brick wall at the north-west corner of the town, with the largest "cordon" I have ever seen, consisting of a half-round moulding 9 in. in diameter with a 6-in. fillet under, a total depth of 15 in. Dunkerque is a disappointing place. There is little trace of its history in the present town. I tried to visit the site of the Risban, but though I could see the lighthouse in the distance, after three attempts to drive there through a maze of docks, railways, and little bridges, I found myself each time at my starting point, the Gare Maritime, and gave it up. There is a large, unattractive church, two or more

---

Quod olim apud Batavos, structa arce Britannica,
injicere oceano claustrum
Caesar Augustus
Terrarum orbe perdomito, frustra tentavit,
Ludovicus Magnus
Terrarum orbe recens per se pacato
Arte Naturam superante confecit.
In maritimi imperii pignus et auspicium
Aeternam hanc in volubili solo salique molem
Subjugato mare,
Propugnando portui, summovendo hosti
Rex nil nisi magni nominis dignum meditans
Imposuit 1681.[1]

[1] Halévy, *Vauban*, p. 48. M. Halévy considers this too beautiful to translate. He may have been defeated as I am, by the meaning of "Structa arce Britannica". The inscription is to the effect that "what Caesar, having conquered the world, and built the Arx Britannica, tried in vain to do among the Batavians, Louis the Great after pacifying the world, has done, with an art that conquers nature. As a pledge and omen of the rule of the sea, the King has set this eternal monument on moving earth and salt, conquering the sea, for the defence of the harbour, and the removal of the enemy, ever thinking of what is worthy of his name."

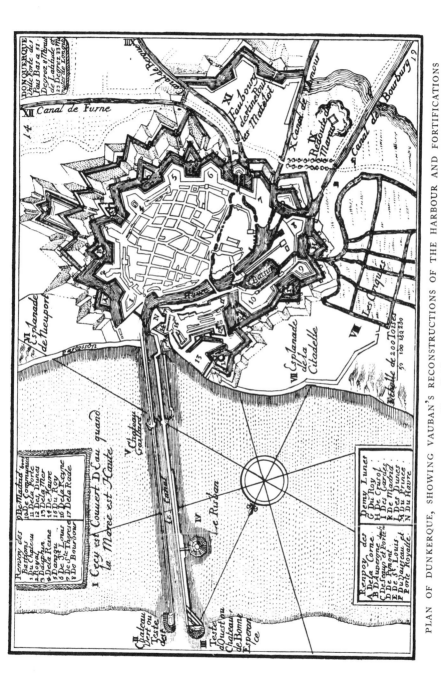

PLAN OF DUNKERQUE, SHOWING VAUBAN'S RECONSTRUCTIONS OF THE HARBOUR AND FORTIFICATIONS

From "Atlas Portatif," 1702

bays of which at the west end were destroyed in the
seventeenth century to make way for a road. In the
centre of the town there is a large Place, with a bronze
figure of Jean Bart, the privateer, in sea-boots and an
enormous hat brandishing a tiny sword, the work, as I
expected, of that deplorable artist David of Angers, surely
the worst artist that ever modelled a figure to com-
memorate a hero. The little town of Bergues a few
miles south of Dunkerque is far more interesting and
attractive. Here much of Vauban's fortifications remains
almost intact, and a comparison of the plans of Dunkerque and Bergues shows Vauban's amazing versatility
of design. Vauban's care for detail is illustrated in a
letter written three years later. It seems that moles had
been undermining the walls, and a mole-catcher had been
appointed, but the man, Vauban says, was "un espèce de
vaurien qui se n'applique pas et qui ne sait qu'aller à la
chasse". So Vauban recommended another man who
undertook to destroy not only the moles, but field mice,
"les mulots qui font presque autant de mal que les
taupes".

From Dunkerque in the north, Vauban moved to
Toulon in the south to settle the defences and enlarge
the harbour, and summoned Niquet from Metz to
superintend the work in spite of his inveterate habit
of insubordination. That indomitable person again
thought he could improve on Vauban's designs. Colbert
was furious. He wrote to Niquet that the King would
not stand his ridiculous and intolerable vanity, "qui
vous a rendu depuis si longtemps insupportable dans
tous les lieux où vous avez travaillé". Colbert referred
to his conduct at Metz and Verdun, and said that
Niquet was causing "Mille désordres" in the work at
Toulon, and that if this continued, he would be dismissed
the service and do three years in prison. Niquet was
actually imprisoned at Toulon, but Colbert seems to have
relented, no doubt owing to the generous action of Vauban who defended him, and later on, in 1682, spoke well
of Niquet's work both at Toulon and Antibes, and said

that though slow he was sure, and attentive to his work.

From Toulon Vauban was ordered to Cette, and Louis XIV was so anxious about him, that he forbade him to go on a galley to Cette, and insisted, in spite of Vauban's protest, on his going by land. He inspected various places in the south-east of France, and in 1679 designed the fortifications of Port-Vendres and the remarkable fort of Mont Louis high up in the Pyrenees, to complete the defence on the Spanish frontier begun ten years earlier at Villefranche de Conflent. There seems to have been some trouble in connexion with these forts on the Spanish frontier. The *Abrégé* for 1679 says that Vauban "fit le projet de la fortification de Mont Louis, et de tous les autres pièces nouvelles de cette province même de celui de Port-Vendres, qui n'eut pas de suite par la jalousie du ministre de ce temps." Vauban seldom allowed himself comments of this kind, and one would like to know who the minister was. In view of their friendly relations, it is unlikely that he referred to Louvois.

In this year, writing to Louvois from Perpignan, he put in one of his many appeals on behalf of his staff, not because they were relations or friends, "ni par envie que j'ai de partager avec eux—c'est parce que tous sont capables, fidèles et appliqués": because living was expensive in the south and they must have horses to get to their work. Yet here was one of them, Rousselot, who had not received a farthing of pay or allowance since last year, and another, La Londe, had only been paid 50 écus. Vauban complained that he was too often ignored by Louvois: "Je suis un bon garçon qui va droit au bien du service, sans m'amener à la vétille.[1] Mais on ne fait plaisir de me négliger et de me compter pour moins que je suis."

The year 1680–81 was a comparatively quiet year. Vauban inspected S. Malo, Dieppe, Cherbourg and Boulogne, the Ile de Ré, Oléron, La Rochelle, Rochfort,

---

[1] Vétille—"a thing of nothing". Boyer.

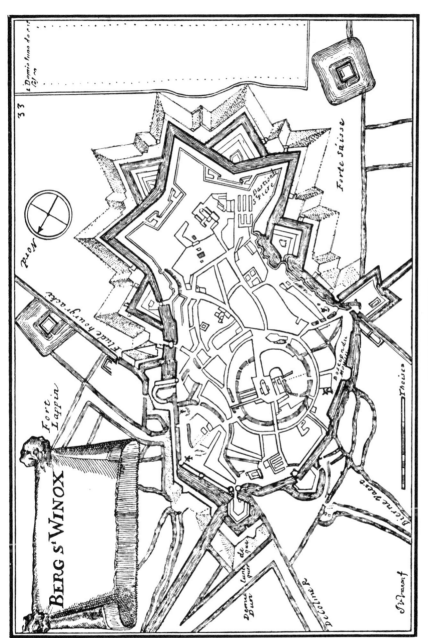

PLAN OF BERGUES

From "Atlas Portatif," 1702

and that strange little fortress of Brouage standing in lonely solitude in the marshes of the Charente.[1] He was then sent across France to the Alsace frontier. Strasbourg had surrendered to Louis XIV in 1681, as soon as it heard that the French army was within two leagues of the town, and Vauban was at once instructed to prepare plans, for Strasbourg was held to be one of the most important places on the French frontier. The usual correspondence with Louvois began. Vauban sent him his "projets, un gros volume d'écriture" with 17 drawings, and at the same time asked that the soldiers should be relieved from work on Sundays. "Je suis persuadé que si on les abandonne les dimanches, ils en feront tout autant en six jours qu'en sept." Louvois replied with 112 detail criticisms of Vauban's designs, and complained that Vauban was wasting the King's money on magnificent gateways which were of no use in defence.[2] "Les dessins de portes que vous avez envoyés pour la citadelle, sont trop grands et trop magnifiques. Il faut encore trouver moyen de les réduire considérablement. Sa Majesté fait construire trop de places, pour continuer à y faire de belles portes qui ne font rien à la bonté de la Place." He was probably thinking of the unsuitable design of the Porte de Paris and the Porte de la Citadelle at Lille. Vauban was undoubtedly extravagant; he had a single eye for the work without regard to the cost, and Colbert had written to the Intendant of Rouen, warning him that Vauban was "accoutumé à des dépenses prodigieuses dans les fortifications des places".

The two gates in question at Strasbourg, were the Porte de Saverne, and the Porte Moyenne des Pêcheurs. The Porte de Saverne consisted of an elliptical archway, flanked by pairs of rusticated Tuscan columns, with an entablature surmounted by obelisks, with large seated

---

[1] Brouage to which I have referred on p. 30, was in the sixteenth and seventeenth centuries the rival of La Rochelle and had a garrison of 6,000 men. The course of the river was blocked by the prince of Condé in 1587, but Richelieu restored it, and it was still an important place in the reign of Louis XIV, but nothing more was done to it, and Vauban must have reported that it was useless as a fort. [2] See p. 70.

figures on either side and a large trophy in the centre. The Porte des Pêcheurs was a much more modest affair, an elliptical arch flanked by pilasters supporting an entablature and a triangular pediment. This was destroyed after 1870, and the Porte de Saverne was knocked to pieces by the German guns in the same year. Vauban was not exempt from a misconception sometimes held by engineers, that they can design architecture, but in his time this was supposed to be within the province of the military engineer. Le Père Fournier advised that gateways to forts were to be of the Tuscan order, "ferme, solide, et qui jette par ses ornemens plutot de l'horreur à ceux qui la regardent, que de l'admiration pour sa gentillesse".

For the fortifications of Strasbourg, Vauban designed an irregular plan[1] to suit the site, with many bastions, a square citadel with a hornwork in the north-east corner, to the south-west a detached pentagon fort, and across the Rhine to the west, another detached fort to the same plan as the citadel. He also used an unusual section for the defence. First there was the normal rampart with parapet, but the chemin des rondes, instead of being high up on the counterscarp, was dropped to the foot of the rampart, like the old fausse-braye, and was protected by a narrow moat and a secondary rampart lower than the main rampart, beyond which was the principal moat very wide, then the chemin couvert with glacis as usual.[2] Louvois seems to have been in a bad temper for he complained that Vauban was wasting his time at Strasbourg, and that he ought to have gone to Casal, the capital of the Duchy of Montferrat, which the Duke of Mantua had handed over to Louis XIV in 1681 in consideration of 2,400,000 livres.

During the years of peace before the next war broke out Vauban was running up and down France, inspecting old fortifications, designing new, settling points of

---

[1] See p. 44.
[2] Description from a print of the time illustrated in the August 1934 number of *L'Architecture*.

administration, never idle, never given leave, for Louvois was a hard taskmaster, and Vauban was indispensable. Here is a characteristic letter to Louvois written from Lyons in 1682, advising him of his return from Toulon and Antibes, "desquels j'ai fait des projets de marine et des fortifications proportionnés à l'importance de ces places et aux ennemis qu'ils auront à craindre, reconcilié tout le monde les uns avec les autres, et enfin arrêté un dessin d'arsenal dont nous sommes tous contents, Intendant, ingénieurs, officiers de marine et maîtres charpentiers." Louvois sometimes accompanied Vauban on his tours of inspection, and one would like to have heard what they said to each other, for both men were free with their tongues, and called a spade a spade.

In 1682 Vauban was again at Toulon, and was so concerned with what he heard of the damage done to French trade in the Mediterranean by the pirates of Algiers, that he wrote a mémoire to Louvois on the best method of dealing with the pirates. It was no use, he said, attacking Algiers from the sea. Ramparts on land were a better defence than the wooden sides of ships, and gun fire from fixed platforms on land was likely to be more effective than fire from ships tossing in the sea. He suggested that the best course was to do what the English did, keep the pirates locked up in the harbour of Algiers by means of squadrons of five or six ships of the 4th and 5th class, with a few light frigates, as he called them, from Dunkerque. Vauban's advice was not taken, and the Algiers pirates continued to infest the Mediterranean for another hundred and thirty years, till in 1816 Lord Exmouth bombarded Algiers, destroyed its harbour and blew this hornet's nest into the sea.

Spain had failed to carry out the conditions of the peace of Nymeguen, and her troops had been raiding on the French frontier, so in 1683 Louis XIV besieged and captured Courtrai and Dixmude. D'Humières was again instructed to see that Vauban did not expose himself to danger, but nothing would prevent Vauban from going to any part of the trenches that he thought necessary, no

matter whether he was under fire or not. The trenches
were his "job", and he was going to see that they were
properly carried out. D'Humières wrote to Louvois that
there was no holding Vauban, that he had promised to
stay in his quarters to receive reports from his engineers,
but that Vauban had gone out notwithstanding, "Vous
savez qu'on ne gouverne pas comme on voudrait."

The siege of Luxembourg was begun in 1684. Luxembourg stands on high ground surrounded on three sides
by deep valleys, along which run two streams, the Alysette
and the Petrusse. The only side open to attack was the
north-west side, rocky ground defended by rampart and
hornworks,[1] and the fortress was supposed to be impregnable. It was held by a garrison of 2,600 Spanish
troops, 600 cavalry and a local force of 400, under the
command of the Prince de Chimay. The French army
consisted of 20,000 foot with 7,000 cavalry, 42 cannon
and 21 mortars, under the command of the Maréchal de
Créquy, and Vauban had a small force of 60 sappers and
miners, an overwhelming force, but Luxembourg was
strong, and the garrison put up a very gallant defence.
Vauban reported that in May the trenches were to be
opened in four different places, and that this, with the
help of the cavalry, would prevent the defence from
putting "le nez hors de la contrescarpe".[2] In three or four
days he hoped to be master of the lower town, after
which only the birds of heaven would be able to enter or
leave the town. "Et tous seront renfermés et amoncelés
dans la ville haute, où nous les écraserons à plaisir," and
make "un terrible ravage." Vauban was so pleased with
his plan, that he wrote "La disposition est la plus belle
que j'aie faite de ma vie. Les ingénieurs sont tous
instruits, et les troupes savent ce qu'elles ont à faire."
On May 11, Vauban reported that the trenches were
going on well, and that a few mistakes due to the "trop
grande obscurité de la nuit" had been corrected. On
May 14th he reports that they had got so near to the

---

[1] Now a public park.
[2] That is, beyond the covered way behind the glacis.

chemin couvert of the defence, that they were within twelve or fifteen paces of one of its angles, and one of the engineers had tried to take "l'angle tenaillé". The attack was held up by the fire of two mortars, and three of Vauban's engineers were "roués de coups de guerre comme s'ils avaient eu cent coups de bâton" but no bones were broken. An attempt was made at midnight to draw the enemy, and tempt them to start their mines to blow up the glacis. The enemy, however, refused to be drawn. "Cependant de tout ce tintamarre" no one was hurt, and except for one or two grenadiers, and young d'Humières, son of the Maréchal, who was killed, "Le tout se serait passé en risée." On May 16 Vauban reports that the "cavaliers" he had put up had answered their purpose. These were built up with gabions two metres high, so that the angles of the bastions could be attacked. Vauban reported that they had taken the head of the chemin couvert, but found it very difficult to cut trenches through the rock, so much so that when day broke, the soldiers had only a foot and half of cover as the result of a night's work, but that in daylight they found the rock was in layers like stone slates, and the work was easier. Vauban reported that the bombs had done excellent work, killed many people in the fort, that "les bombes tournaient tous les dedans des ouvrages sens dessus dessous", and that fifteen mortars were worth sixty cannon. On May 22, however, he wrote that the guns burst, and the powder was foul, to which Louvois replied that the reason for firearms bursting was that, for campaigning purposes, they had to be light, and these would not stand the strain of continuous firing and overcharges of powder. On May 26, Vauban reported that he hoped Luxembourg would fall in seven or eight days. On May 28, three breaches which had been made in the hornworks, were attacked by three columns, each of 1,800 men, and on the 30th "il y eut . . . action fort jolie et bien dirigée". A battalion of fusiliers with four companies of grenadiers had effected a lodgement close to the moat, on which Vauban intended to place a battery of three guns and to make a mine close to the moat. The siege, he reported, would soon be finished, and he himself was so tired out, that if he was not given two or three days' leave, he would be "un homme confisqué". He had already told Louvois that he could not write at length, owing to the necessity "de faire tous les jours regulièrement deux voyages à la tranchée, de six à sept heures chacun". On the night of May 31, the "chamade", the signal of surrender, was heard, and a messenger was sent at once to Louis XIV. A Te Deum was ordered to celebrate the success, but the news was premature, as the Prince de Chimay had only intended to ask for a truce of eight days. This was not granted, and on June 3 Luxembourg surrendered. It had been a memorable siege. The Spaniards had fought bravely, and Vauban mentions the Prince de Chimay, and the Comte de Tilly, apparently a Huguenot, "un fort honnête homme", as among the bravest of the defence, and it appears that there were many "officiers réformés" in the Garrison.[1] The Spaniards lost heavily, the French losses were small, but included the Duc de Choiseul, killed by a bomb, and young d'Humiéres, who insisted on showing his head above the parapet, though repeatedly warned not to do so. Vauban himself had nearly lost his life. In one of his reconnaissances of the enemy's defence, he and his attendants had got too close, and were challenged by a sentry. Vauban instead of running away signalled to the sentry not to fire, and advanced towards him as if he was one of his officers. The story is that the sentry accepted him as such, and let Vauban continue to stroll about the glacis taking his notes. I am a little sceptical of this story. One would have thought that Vauban's uniform or his dress would have given him away, but Vauban was quite reckless. Louvois had written to him at Luxembourg "Contenez-vous mieux que vous n'avez fait pas le passé." There was no need for him to amuse himself by taking pot shots at the enemy—"carabiner des dessus des cannonades". However, the siege soon ended, and

[1] See note at end of this chapter on "officiers réformés".

PLAN OF LUXEMBOURG

From "Atlas Portatif," 1702

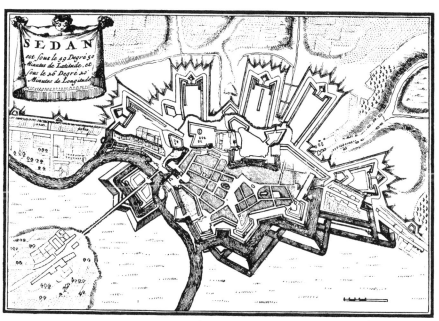

PLAN OF SEDAN. (NOTE THE HORNWORKS)

From "Atlas Portatif," 1702

Vauban wrote to Louvois on June 4, "Voilà enfin ce terrible Luxembourg réduit au point que vous désirez. . . . C'est la plus belle et glorieuse conquête qu'il (le Roi) ait jamais faite en sa vie, et celle qui lui assure le mieux ses affaires de tous côtés." Louvois, who had been rather ill-tempered, complaining that Vauban had not sent him the necessary plans, now wrote, "Je vous embrasse de tout mon cœur et suis tout à vous," and what was more to the purpose, sent with it a "gratification" from the King of 8,000 pistoles. The usual correspondence followed as to fortresses, and Louvois suggested in November that as Vauban would not listen to any one, he had better come to Paris and listen to a few operas, after which they could meet and discuss the fortifications of Belfort.

Vauban seems to have been well paid for his work, though he would not admit it in his letters to Louvois. Fontenelle, in his éloge, said that Vauban never asked for anything. Had he been able to see Vauban's correspondence with Louvois he would not have said this, for in nearly all his letters, Vauban asks for something. Most of his requests were either purely professional, or recommendations of deserving officers for promotion, pleas for justice to the oppressed and help for those who needed it, but Vauban did not hesitate on occasions to ask things for himself, chiefly, it is true, for the payment of arrears long due, but sometimes for his own personal interests. When, for example, a rich abbey with a revenue of 40,000 livres a year fell vacant, Vauban did not hesitate to ask for it, as one of the most zealous subjects of the King, and one "qui fait humainement ce que je peux pour mériter le pain qu'il a la bonté de me donner". Louvois, however, had already given the abbey to his son Barbezieux, but promised Vauban that if any more abbeys were going, he would not forget him. Yet these personal requests were in a way characteristic of Vauban's frank and ingenuous temperament. He wanted something to which he believed himself to be entitled, and the simplest thing to do was to ask for it right away, for he knew that Louvois was quite capable of refusing. What with the 8,000 pistoles given after Luxembourg, and similar "gratifications" from the King, and the sale of his commission and appointments, Vauban, though never a rich man, must have made a good deal of money one way and another. He had made 20,000 livres by the sale of his commission in the Guards. The King had given him 4,000 écus after the siege of Maestricht in 1674. In 1683 when he was made Governor of the citadel of Lille for the second time, he sold the Governorship of Douai, to which he had been appointed three years before, for 150,000 livres, for in the reign of Louis XIV it seems that nearly all these appointments could be bought and sold. In addition to these various sums, Vauban had his pay as chief Engineer, but he also had heavy expenses. He had bought the Château of Bazoches near St. Léger in 1675, and had added a wing to the château, with a gallery in which he could hang up his large scale maps and drawings on the rare occasions when he was able to work at home, for Bazoches was his nominal home for the rest of his life, in so far as he had any home at all. Also he had to keep up two establishments, and so long as the old Baron d'Epiry, his father-in-law, was alive, he had to support him and pay his debts. Vauban was constantly complaining to Louvois that he had no money and that the expense of his campaigns was intolerable. Yet considering that Vauban had begun his career without any money except his pay, he had not done badly, since at the age of forty-three he was able to buy, recondition and add to a house of the size and importance of Bazoches. Vauban had bought this place from the Comte de Melun for 69,000 livres, with 5,500 livres to the Comte de Nevers for the feudal rights, which gave him a definite rank in the local aristocracy, but he was scarcely ever at Bazoches. He complained of this to Louvois, and in 1688 said he had only been home twice in the last three years, and this only for about a fortnight, without the time to do any business, and he asked leave to visit "Sa pauvre famille". He did manage to visit Bazoches in April, and again in August 1687, flying visits, when he found time enough to set down some of the notes which he had made on active service, and his thoughts on things in general, including the very drastic suggestions of the paper entitled "Pensées d'un homme qui n'avait grand' chose à faire," a curious title, for Vauban's brain was never idle. In 1687 he sent Louvois the draft of a mémoire, the contents of which are unknown, to which Louvois replied with more than his usual brutality. Lazard suggests that this may have been an early draft of his proposals for the reform of taxation. Louvois in his reply said, "Quant au mémoire . . . je vous renvoie avec cette lettre, afin que vous puissiez le supprimer." If it was not that Vauban was more skilful in fortification than this "mémoire" would lead one to believe, he would not be fit to serve even the King of Narsingue[1] whose engineer could neither read, write, nor draw. For himself, Louvois said he would have been ashamed even to have thought what Vauban had put in writing. He had never known Vauban blunder so badly hitherto, and could only suppose that "l'air de Bazoches vous avez bouché l'esprit," and that the best thing he could do was to prevent Vauban staying any longer at Bazoches. It was a ferocious answer to ideas which Vauban had much at heart, but Louvois may have been anxious to save Vauban from committing himself too far, knowing the furious enmities which his proposals would excite at court and among the financiers. Yet it was the final development of his ideas on the reform of taxation that was the last heroic act of Vauban's life.

[1] Say, King of Ruritania.

Note.—Vauban had a high opinion of the "officiers réformés." In 1671, writing to Louvois from Lille he gives a characteristic description of a "Capitaine réformé" named Latouche, who had had thirty years' service and been a Major in the Régiment d'Enghien. Peace had reduced him to service in one of the free companies of Brisach, since disbanded. He had never been near Paris or the Court, but no man had done better service in the German Wars. He was, Vauban continues, a resolute soldier, who knew all about Germany, and was the "Meilleur Partisan du Royaume"—rather given to drink and no longer young, but still vigorous. Vauban had little use for the young elegants from the Court who regarded military service as a joke. The officers that he wanted were hard-bitten veterans, like Latouche, who knew their job.

CHAPTER VIII

Vauban and "la conservation des hommes"—Lack of engineers—The aqueduct of Maintenon—Vauban's proposals not accepted—The King insists on the aqueduct—Complete failure of the scheme—The Canal du Midi and Niquet—Vauban's criticisms—Other canals and navigation of rivers, 1685-7.

THE siege of Luxembourg had impressed strongly on Vauban two very serious defects in the French Army, the want of military knowledge in the officers, and the lack of an organized corps of engineers. The officers of Louis XIV were gallant enough, but their idea of attack seems to have been to wave their swords in the air, and order their men to charge, without the least regard to the cost in lives. In one of his occasional papers, Vauban complains bitterly of officers who threw their men away, and then came back and boasted that they had lost one hundred men in taking some minor point of the defence, which could easily have been taken with a loss of ten men or less. Vauban's view was "la conservation de cent de ses sujets, lui (le Roi) doit être beaucoup plus considérable que la perte de mille de ses enemis." Fontenelle said that one of Vauban's main objects was "la conservation des hommes", and when Vauban reported his invention of "Cavaliers de Tranchée" to Louvois, he said that one of its merits was that it saved great losses, as it gave the men cover. At the back of Vauban's mind there was always this anxiety to save his men as much as possible and to see that they were properly armed, fed and paid. Even when he was opening the siege of Luxembourg, he ended his letter of May 8 to Louvois with entreaties that his engineers might receive their pay for the preceding month, "parce qu'ils sont d'une gueuserie qui n'est pas croyable". A month later he again asked that the engineers should be paid. "Car la plupart sont jeunes gens de petite paie, qui ont été obligés de faire leurs équipages à la hâte, et d'acheter le fourrage aussi bien que moi pendant tout le siège, qui nous est revenu à 24 et 25.1. per cheval, ce qu'il fait qu'ils n'ont pas un sou, et qu'ils seront obligés d'aller à pied, si vous n'avez cette bonté pour eux. Ils le méritent autant mieux, qu'ils ont été les victimes de l'armeé, et cela d'une manière si courageuse et si délibérée, que ce n'aurait pas un affaire de se faire tuer jusqu'au dernier, sans qui pas un d'eux s'en fût plaint, tante l'émulation était grande parmi eux." It was this constant regard for his men that made them love him and made them ready to follow him anywhere. He and his men were a band of brothers. Writing from Dunkerque in 1677 he had in referring to them said, "Avec qui je vis comme de frères." Vauban again and again called attention to the dangers to which the engineers were exposed, greater than those of the infantry, and he was unwearied in urging their claims not only to arrears of pay, but to recognition as a very important part of the army.[1] So far Vauban had only had a few trained engineers to help him in his sieges and a small number of sappers and miners. He had to rely on soldiers for the greater part of his work, and the soldiers knew nothing about the work, did it very badly and hated it. Vauban insisted that a special corps of engineers ought to be established with trained officers and a colonel in command, and that for the ranks men should be definitely enlisted and trained as sappers. Sieges till the time of Vauban were conducted, anyhow, on pedantic lines, and without much approach to scientific method. Moreover, there did not yet exist any properly organized companies of sappers and miners to carry out the instructions of the engineers, and the engineers attached to besieging forces were so few in number that owing to deaths, wounds and exposure, they were seldom able to gain experience by seeing a siege through from start to finish. Vauban says that at the siege of Montmédy on the Meuse between Sedan and Luxembourg in 1657, in a besieging army of 10,000 men there were only 4 engineers, and of these 3

---

[1] Vauban reported that at the siege of Luxembourg, out of his scanty band of engineers, thirty-five had been killed or wounded, in most cases by grenades.

had been killed within five days of opening the trenches, that he himself was the only engineer left, and that he had to carry on though he had received 7 slight wounds "et plusieurs autres coups dans ses habits".[1] The siege of Montmédy lasted forty-two days, 1,300 of the besieging force were killed, 1,800 wounded and an unknown quantity of sick and wounded were left in miserable makeshift hospitals. Yet the garrison which defended Montmédy consisted of only 700 men. Much the same thing happened in 1654 at the siege of Stenay, a few miles west of Montmédy. Vauban who was present at both these sieges, and spoke from personal knowledge, might well say, "Il faut avouer que c'étoit acheter les places bien cher." The truth was that till Vauban came, there was nobody in the French army who understood "grande finesse" as Vauban puts it. People wrote freely and voluminously on fortifications and defence, but nobody seems to have studied the not less important matter of attack. There seems to have been no organization, and the attack was made on the old-fashioned lines laid down in the text-books, with the result of long sieges and great loss of life. Vauban complained that general officers interfered with the lines laid down by the engineers, and exposed their men to quite unnecessary risks. "Il n'est rien de si commun parmi nous, que cette brutalité, qui dépeuple nos troupes des vieux soldats, et fait qu'un guerre de dix années épuise tout un Royaume." Vauban spoke from an experience of 50 sieges, and after a lifetime spent in the service of Louis XIV. In 1657 he was a young man of twenty-four still learning his business in the trenches, and it was to take many years of hard campaigning on the frontiers of France, and ceaseless efforts to drive the necessity of reforms into the heads of recalcitrant ministers, before he could realize any part of his ideal, the reorganization of the French army. After the siege of Luxembourg, Vauban wrote a long letter to Louvois in which he said, "Si la guerre continue, il faudra que vous ayez la bonté de procurer auprès du Roi, la

---

[1] *L'attaque des places.* Written in 1705.

compagnie des sapeurs que je vous ai tant de fois de-mandée, autrement il m'est impossible à réduire la conduite des sièges dans l'ordre que je pourrais la mettre, si j'étais assisté de gens instruits, et toujours sous ma main, au lieu que je suis obligé de me servir de gens ramassés, la plupart desquels je ni connais, ni ne me connaissent et ne m'entendent point." He asked for a company not less than two hundred strong. Vauban as usual had to wait for what he asked, but his proposal was the first step to the ultimate establishment of that brilliant engineering service, the "Génie" of the army of France.

Vauban had hoped to be made a Lieutenant-General after Luxembourg, and it was generally believed that he had in fact been promoted. In a letter dated May 26, 1684, Boileau wrote to Racine: "Vous avez raison d'esti-mer, comme vous le faites, M. de Vauban. C'est un des hommes de notre siècle, à mon avis, qui a le plus pro-digieux mérite, et pour vous dire en un mot ce que je pense de lui, je crois qu'il y a plus d'un Maréchal de France, qui quand il le rencontre, rougit de se voir Maréchal de France." Many of Vauban's friends wrote to congratulate him; but the news was premature. Vauban was not promoted till four years later, and he suggested to Louvois that if he was not promoted, he ought at any rate to be refunded the postage of the 80 to 100 letters that he had received, congratulating him on his supposed promotion.

Peace between France, and Spain, the United Provinces and the Emperor, was declared in 1684, and it was sup-posed to be assured for the next twenty years. It lasted for just four, till the war of the League of Augsbourg (1688–97). Vauban was now called upon to deal with a problem of civil engineering. Colbert had died in 1683, and Louvois, who succeeded him, readily fell in with the King's prodigal ambitions. Though the frontier defences of France were still incomplete, though the deficit in the treasury was increasing, Louis XIV did not hesitate to squander enormous sums on Versailles and Marly, and embarked on the most insensate and disastrous of all his follies, the Aqueduct of Maintenon. The new palace of Versailles had been begun in 1669, and after nearly twenty years Louis XIV and Mansart his architect realized that the water supply was wholly inadequate, not only for the gardens but for the enormous palace and its dependencies. Vauban was called in, and "En 1685 et 1686 il fut occupé à faire le projet de ce grand et magnifique ouvrage de l'aqueduc de Maintenon." After many surveys to find sources of supply, it was decided to divert the waters of the Eure at Pontgouin, a point some eighty kilometres south of Versailles.[1] It appears from the Comptes des Bâtiments du Roi that La Hire, a famous mathematician and Member of the Académie des Sciences, was paid 2,116 livres in March 1684 for taking levels at Vaucresson and Fontainebleau and also on the Eure. He took further levels in 1685. The Eure was surveyed from its source down to the point at which a canal was to be made to convey the water to Versailles; four of Vauban's draughts-men were paid 600 livres for drawings, and a plan of the Eure was made and engraved, for no such thing as "sun prints" existed, and the only way to multiply drawings was to make many tracings, or have them engraved and printed. The Surveyors seem still to have been doubtful about their levels. Three more members of the Academy were paid 2,800 livres in 1686 for taking fresh levels and making a map of the new canal from S. Prest to Bailleau, and finally, a map of the whole course of the new water supply from Pontgouin to Versailles was engraved with the levels marked on the map. The distance was given as 87 kilometres with a fall of 27 metres.

Canals were dug in 1685, the Canal de Jouy,[2] Canal de Nogent le Roy between Dreux and Maintenon, and the Canal d'Epernon between Maintenon and Rambouillet. These canals joined before reaching Maintenon, and everything seemed straightforward till the valley of Maintenon was reached, and the question arose how the

---

[1] Rochas d'Aiglun says twenty-five kilometres, but he describes Maintenon as about half-way to Versailles, and Maintenon is forty kilometres as the crow flies from Versailles.

[2] About ten kilometres north of Chartres.

water was to be taken across the valley. Vauban wanted to siphon the water up to the necessary level on the Versailles side, by means of a water tower, but Louis XIV was determined to have a gigantic aqueduct across the valley, surpassing the Pont du Gard and anything that the Romans had built, something to meet the King's conception of himself as an Olympian to whom Nature herself must bow. Louvois acted as the King's mouthpiece, and being quite ignorant of science, consulted the Académie des Sciences as to the best means of defeating what he called "La fausseté" of Vauban's proposal. In February 1685 he wrote to Vauban that he had deceived himself "grossièrement" in his calculations, and then gave what he meant for a scientific demonstration to show that Vauban was all wrong, but Louvois got hopelessly muddled with his figures. He first asserted that to stand the pressure of the water, the walls of Vauban's towers would have to be 5,443 ft. thick, and the smallest leak would bring the whole thing down in a dozen hours. Apparently he meant hundreds not thousands, for in a second letter he reduced the thickness to 550 ft., and it is quite clear that whether advised by the Academy or not, he did not know what he was talking about. Vauban proposed that iron pipes should be used for the siphon, to which Louvois replied that the cost would be prohibitive, giving the wholly arbitrary figure of 18,375,000 francs. Finally, he had to give the true reason. "Il est inutile que vous pensiez à un aqueduc rampant, dont le Roi ne veut pas entendre parler. Si le mémoire ci-joint n'est pas suffisant pour vous en faire comprendre la raison, la volonté du maître doit vous empêcher de plus parler." This was Louvois at his worst. First the absurd attempt to prove scientifically points of which he was wholly ignorant, and then the crushing of the expert, by informing him that the aqueduct was the King's wish, and that that was the end of it. The decision of Louis XIV was dictated by his boundless vanity, and nobody seems to have considered what would happen to the people who relied on the water of the Eure, when the Eure was diverted to Versailles. So the aqueduct was begun. In 1686 Le Sieur Robelin, one of Vauban's engineers, was appointed Director of the "grand aqueduc de Maintenon" with a salary of 6,000 francs a year and a house at Maintenon, and a division of 20,000 men[1] under the command of the Marquis de Huxelles was encamped in the marshes of Maintenon to build the acqueduct. It was a gigantic affair. The total length was to have been 4,600 metres, but only the lower arcade was built, 975 metres long, with 47 arches varying in height from 13 to 15 metres. In the years 1685–87 nearly six million francs had been spent, and when in 1688 in consequence of the war of the League of Augsbourg, the aqueduct was abandoned, the total cost amounted to 8,613,000 francs,[2] all wasted, for not a drop of water reached Versailles from the Eure, and Versailles had to depend on the famous machine de Marly, which for another 100 years wheezed and groaned as it pumped up water from the Seine, was constantly getting out of order, and involved an aqueduct 643 metres long and 23 metres high. The cost in men and money of the Aqueduct of Maintenon had been enormous, and so many of the soldiers died of malaria, that by the King's order nobody was allowed to speak of it. The ruins of the Aqueduct still stand in the valley of Maintenon, a grim monument of the vanity and futility of Louis XIV.

Not only was Vauban's advice about the aqueduct ignored, but he was very badly served. The War Ministry at Paris appears to have been quite indifferent to the quality of work done. In 1685 Vauban was at Belle-île, the large island south of Quibéron, "brûlé du soleil ou balayé par tous les vents", the scene of many an attempted raid. Vauban was at work on the fortifications but was in serious difficulty with the dishonest and incompetent contractors sent him from Paris. In a letter to Louvois from Belle-île in 1685 he said the contractors were all wrong. "Il est certain que toutes ces ruptures de

---

[1] Mme. de Sévigné, writing to her daughter, spoke in her liberal way of "une armée de quarante mille hommes".

[2] *Comptes des Bâtiments du Roi.* Vols. 2 and 5.

marchés, manquements de paroles, et renouvellement d'adjudications, ne servent qu'à vous attirer tous les misérables qui ne savent où donner de la tête, les fripons, et les ignorants pour entrepreneurs". The contractors went bankrupt before their contract was half completed, and Vauban implored Louvois to accept no contractor who was not "solvable et intelligent." Any architect who has had to work with a contractor on the verge of failure will know what Vauban had to put up with. Here were some of them. Gouteroux, contractor in 1684, was "un peu trigaud".[1] Caris, who succeeded Gouteroux, was a "fripon": he had made the embrasures of "moellon piqué"[2] when they should have been in dressed stone or brick. Collin, a new contractor, was a young man of twenty-seven, "fort adonné au vin, et du surplus un peu bretteur[3] et polisson". He had borrowed money all the way from Paris to Belle-île; he had given no sureties; yet he was in charge of the men's wages. "Ne voilà-t-il un joli entrepreneur et de belles ressources?" This letter throws a clear light on the troubles Vauban had to contend with. Louvois replied cheerfully that "nonobstant votre mauvaise humeur, je n'en suis pas moins tout à vous."

Vauban devoted a good deal of attention to the whole subject of waterways and canals. In the year 1666, a certain Baron Pierre Paul Riquet, had begun, largely at his own expense, the famous Canal du Midi. The idea of joining the Atlantic to the Mediterranean, by way of the Garonne to Toulouse, and thence by a canal to the Mediterranean, had been first suggested by Sully, the Minister of Henri IV. Riquet, who was not an engineer, began the canal, but died six months before it was finished, and the work was completed by his son, and was formally taken over by the Intendant of Guyenne and Languedoc in 1681. As left by Riquet, it was 279 kilometres in length with a width of 20 metres and a depth of 2. The cost had been seventeen million livres.[4] At that date the canal

---

[1] Tricky.   [2] Rough undressed stone.   [3] Quarrelsome.
[4] Rochas d'Aiglun. *Vauban*, 1, 540.

began at Toulouse and proceeded eastward by Carcassonne and Beziers, to Cette on the coast of the Mediterranean. In 1687 Vauban "fit la visite du Canal de la Communication des Mers, et du port de Cette, et tous les projets nécessaires pour mettre ce grand et bel ouvrage dans ses perfections, qui ont été depuis exécutés, du moins la plus grande partie". The last sentence is inaccurate for many of Vauban's suggestions were not carried out till long afterwards. Vauban wrote a long mémoire on the Canal de Languedoc (Canal du Midi) in 1691, and criticized it severely, though he admitted that it was "le plus beau et le plus noble ouvrage de cette espèce qui ait été entrepris de nos jours". A serious mistake he thought had been made in ending the canal at Cette. In his opinion the canal should have continued from the Etang de Thau (a large inland waterpiece twelve miles long, north of Cette), "jusqu'à la radelle des Aigues Mortes", thence by an old canal to Sauveréal, and by the use of the "Petit Rhône" to Arles, and from Arles to the Porte de Bouc in the gulf of Foz in the Mediterranean. He thought the canal was not deep enough to admit boats of any size, he would have it deepened to twelve feet, and instead of starting the canal at Toulouse, he would have made the entrance much lower down the Garonne at Cadillac, some twenty-two miles south-east of Bordeaux, or even at Bordeaux itself, in order to simplify transport and avoid double handling. Vauban pointed out all the advantages to trade that would result from his proposals, among many others the re-establishment of "Les foires de Beaucaire, qui sont les plus belles du Royaume si célèbres partout, et à présent à demi ruinés par l'infidelité des embouchures de Rhône", and he gave a list of between seventy and eighty places the trade of which would profit by this canal. Vauban prophesied that if the measures he suggested were taken, the canal would be as secure 200 years hence as it was that day.

Vauban prepared his plans and sent them to Seignelay, who had succeeded his father Colbert, on the death of the latter. Seignelay duly examined the plans and wrote to Vauban that they appeared to him to show "un grand sens—et une imagination singulière, et d'une forte application". He also informed Vauban that the King had granted him a "gratification" of 12,000 livres. It seems that some of his proposals were put in hand at once, for Niquet was put in charge and as usual differed from Vauban, saying of his designs that "il n'était d'avis de les exécuter." Vauban simply said, "N'être pas d'avis n'est pas une raison". However, he did not remove Niquet, who superintended this and other works at Aigues Mortes, Beaucaire and Arles, in connection with the Canal works. Seignelay, writing to Vauban in 1686, described these as being "de la dernière importance pour la Commerce". Vauban set down his ideas five years later in the "Mémoire sur le Canal de Languedoc". He seems to have been keenly interested in the possibilities of rivers and canals in 1699, and wrote a mémoire on "Navigation des rivières". Both of these mémoires were included in his *Oisivetés*. Rochas d'Aiglun says that he even had ideas of joining the seas by way of Burgundy, and of joining the Loire to the Saône, and the Saône to the Seine. Vauban's intellectual activity was inexhaustible.

CHAPTER IX

Mont-Royal and Landau—War of the League of Augsbourg—Siege of Philisbourg—The Dauphin at the siege—Mannheim—Frankenthal—Seignelay—Les Oisivetés—Notes on building—Mémoire on the importance of Paris to France and proposals for its defence.

THE year 1687 was one of the very few years in which Vauban had any time to himself. In April he was writing to his friend Catinat,[1] from Bazoches, on a point of statistics. The population of Italy Vauban believed to be about 8 millions; that of France 14 to 15 millions, though the resources of the country could maintain a population of 21 to 24 millions. Vauban loved statistics. He was never tired of collecting them and making drastic proposals for reform on the results. He agreed with Catinat that there were too many fortresses in France wasting money that was wanted elsewhere, and said that he was leaving Bazoches in a few days, to see about the construction of a new fortress, against his better judgment. The new fortress was Mont-Royal, to be built on an island in the Moselle. Vauban sent Louvois his plans for the fort, together with a mémoire, the contents of which are not known.[2] Vauban had advised against the construction both of Mont-Royal and Landau. They added, he said, to the number of places to be held without adding to the strength of the frontier. However, he was overruled by Louvois, the King had expressed a wish for their construction, so that settled it. Mont-Royal was a pentagon in plan, with courtines of the unusual length of 400 to 500 metres, and here for the first time Vauban constructed his favourite bastioned towers in the centre of each courtine. These towers were a development of the old "Cavalier" on the rampart, the purpose of which had been intended for outlook beyond the glacis, rather than

---

[1] Catinat, originally an avocat, became one of the best of the generals of Louis XIV and a Maréchal de France (1693). Voltaire describes him as "homme capable de tout et fait pour tous les emplois".

[2] See p. 95.

for artillery fire. The "Tours bastionnées" were of solid masonry, carried up two storeys, each storey provided with casemates for guns, and a flat roof with emplacements for more guns, and "Merlons", embrasures in the parapet for the guns. On the angles of the bastions were "Guérites", sentry boxes, corbelled out from the walls. There are good examples of these at Brouage; they are shown in plates by Belidor, and Colonel Lazard gives a reproduction of a beautiful working drawing,[1] to scale, of a tour bastionnée for Besançon made and signed by Vauban at Bazoches in 1687. This was pentagonal in plan, with very solid outer walls, pierced with openings for guns on the four outer sides. A broad passage inside ran round the central newel stairs. The Mont-Royal fort was on a considerable scale. It included an arsenal, bakery, magazines for powder, cisterns, officers' quarters and barracks for a garrison of 4,000 men. It took five years to build, but the whole of it was destroyed ten years later in accordance with the Treaty of Ryswyck. Landau on the Queiche in Alsace, a few miles north-west of Karlsruhe, is described in the *Atlas Portatif* as "fortifié d'une nouvelle manière". It was an entirely new fortress laid out on an octagon plan, with bastions at the angles, tenailles, demilunes, moat, covered way, places d'armes and glacis, with a large redoubt surrounded by the moat on the north side and two large hornworks also surrounded by the moat on the north-east and south-east angles. The fortifications are destroyed, and Landau was handed over to Germany after 1815.

Landau, Fort Louis on the Rhine, Mont-Royal on the Moselle and Hunninguen were the answer of Louis XIV to the League of Augsbourg founded by the Protestant powers after the revocation of the Edict of Nantes in 1685. In 1688 Louis XIV made one of his many miscalculations, in thinking that William of Orange would be entangled in England. He accordingly invaded and ravaged the Palatinate, and so began the War of the League of Augsbourg in 1688. The Emperor of Austria, the

---

[1] *Vauban*, p. 200, plates VIII and IX.

Kings of Spain and Sweden, the Elector of Bavaria, the
Elector Palatine, the Elector of Brandenbourg and the
Duke of Holstein were ranged against France, a strange and
formidable combination, joined in 1689 by England and
Holland, and the only neighbours of France who were not
its bitter enemies were the Swiss, who did not count one
way or the other. Louis XIV began the war in a futile
and tentative way. Vauban wrote to Louvois in September 1688. "On a débuté assez grossièrement avant-hier
matin, pour vouloir entrer dans Offembourg avec un
détachement de 400 hommes, que ayant marché toute la
nuit et bien fait japper et hurler tous les chiens des
villages où l'on passe", found all the gates shut against
them, and had to return without having done anything
but supply "matière aux gazettes de faire de beaux discours". Vauban had a profound contempt for the Press,
and his description, "bien fait japper et hurler tous les
chiens des villages" is delightful. The first serious opera-
tion was the siege of Philisbourg on the Rhine, north of
Strasbourg and south of Landau. The army was under
the nominal command of the Dauphin, his first appearance attended by a Maréchal de France and eight
Lieutenant-Generals, including Catinat. Philisbourg had
been strongly fortified by the French thirty years before,
but had been lost in one of the bewildering quarrels of
Louis XIV with his neighbours, and Louvois was particularly anxious that the Dauphin should start his first
campaign with a brilliant success. Vauban began to lay out
his lines and place his batteries at the end of September.
The guns were brought by river, and the Dauphin arrived
on October 6, with a company of young noblemen from
the Court including Louvois' eldest son Barbezieux, who
had come to see the sport and get in everybody's way.
The trenches were opened on October 8, and the attack
began in three places. Vauban's men had drained the
marsh which protected part of Philisbourg, so that the
outer moat was dry, and the attacking force was able to
reach the glacis without difficulty. Vauban reported to
Louvois that he was able to bring Monseigneur to a point

only sixty paces from the covered way, and here to enable him to see what was going on, Vauban mounted the Prince on a stand, while he held on to his coat-tails in order to pull him down when necessary. After a short time, the Prince got down and returned to his quarters with the young bloods of his company, very greatly to Vauban's relief. Vauban reported that the Prince showed no sign of fatigue, though he had tramped half a league along the trenches in "fort grosses bottes", and that he was so much interested in the trenches, "effriandé à la tranchée", that the only way to prevent his going there again was to tell him that he would be up to his knees in mud. Not the least of Vauban's troubles was his responsibility for the King and princes, who would insist on appearing at these sieges. The Dauphin, who was then twenty-six, was an unsatisfactory young man who spent his time in eating, drinking, "la chasse", and sleeping. Louis XIV tried in vain to interest him in politics, but he was too fat and lazy, and after the death of his wife in 1690, he took up with a certain Mdlle. Choin of whom Saint Simon gives a very unsatisfactory description. He died, "être épais et obscur", in 1711. Though Vauban speaks of him kindly, he did nothing to distinguish himself here or at the siege of Mannheim, which followed that of Philisbourg, or anywhere else. Stahremberg, the governor of Philisbourg, surrendered on October 28, after a siege of just three weeks. The French had lost heavily, and Vauban had lost nine killed and fifteen wounded out of his very small company of engineers, whom he called "les Martyrs de l'Infanterie". But the Dauphin was so pleased with the capture of Philisbourg, that he gave Vauban four cannons and a thousand livres as a mark of esteem for his "mérite singulier". Vauban sent the cannons to Bazoches to decorate his garden, and as the King sent him another 2,000 pistoles, Vauban did very well, but what pleased him most was a personal letter from the King, who wrote: "Vous savez il y a longtemps ce que je pense de vous, et la confiance que j'ai en votre savoir et en votre affection . . . je ne saurai finir sans vous commander absolument de vous conserver absolument pour le bien de mon service". Louis XIV knew very well that his Maréchals and Generals might make a fine show, but that without Vauban, they were useless at these sieges. In 1688 he was at length given the promotion to Lieutenant-General which he had expected four years earlier.

Philisbourg was one of the most notable of Vauban's sieges. He used here his "cavaliers de tranchée". Hitherto when the attacking force got as near as they could with their trench, they set up a temporary screen of gabions to protect their guns. Vauban's "cavalier de tranchée"[1] was a much more solid affair, a temporary rampart built up in front of the nearest trench, with steps up on the outer side to enable the attack to obtain a line of fire on the covered way and beyond it. At the siege of Philisbourg Vauban also introduced his device of the "tir à ricochet",[1] the ricochet shot. Vauban had noted that in attacks on fortified places the shot either hit the revetment of the rampart, or buried itself in the earth of the parapet above the chemin des rondes, or went clean over everything. In any case it did not do much harm to the garrison. In order to remedy this, Vauban hit on the idea of reducing the charge, and as one might say, "lobbing" the shot on to the rampart or inside the fort, where it might either make another minor effort, or land among the buildings and men inside the fort—an anticipation of the idea of the Stokes' mortars used in the late war. The general staff did not think much of this, because the guns did not make noise enough, but Vauban said that it was most efficient in breaking up the hornworks of the fort. His only complaint was that the guns were very bad and broke like pottery. Mannheim fell in November 1688, the garrison having forced the Governor to surrender by presenting "vingt bouts de fusil dans le ventre, le menaçant de le tuer, s'il ne se rendait pas". It appears that for seventeen months the garrison had received no

---

[1] See Lazard, *Vauban*, p. 211, Fig. 18, for a plan showing Vauban's method of approach by parallel trenches, also a diagram showing Vauban's "tir à ricochet".

pay, and was completely out of hand. While Vauban and his men were quietly cutting a way into the citadel at night, the German soldiers, "au fond, de fort bonnes gens" were making merry on the further side of the fort with "fanfares, trompettes, timbales et hautbois", playing airs from French operas; and this went on "tout autant qu'ils ont trouvé le vin bon, c'est à dire, toute la nuit". It is an engaging picture, drawn with Vauban's inimitable touch. After the surrender, the soldiers wanted to kill the Governor, and he had to be guarded by a detachment from the regiment of Picardy, Vauban's own regiment. Some of these sieges were little more than formal affairs, with no serious attempt at defence.

Frankenthal, for instance, fell after a siege of thirty-eight hours, and Vauban regretted that he had here no opportunity of trying the effect of his "batterie à ricochet". His comment on Frankenthal was that as a fortress it was absurd. It had a very strong position at the meeting of the Neckar and the Rhine, and in Vauban's view had it been properly fortified, it might have defied Monseigneur and all the Princes of Europe. Moreover, Vauban said the Prince Palatine had been an idiot to have two fortresses such as Mannheim and Frankenthal close together, as it meant the defence of two places instead of one.

The next two years Vauban spent in going the rounds of the frontier forts. In 1689 he visited Dunkerque, Bergues and Ypres, and found the fortifications at Ypres "dans un grand désordre". He wrote from S. Malo to Seignelay, pointing out that it was false economy, "mauvais ménage" to starve fortifications, and he took the liberty, he says, of telling him once for all that the only true economy was to build solidly, and to give a fair price, but nothing more for the work done. Anything else was "mesquinerie", with the result that the work was badly done, and in consequence the King lost more than he gained by saving money in the wrong place. Vauban mentioned instances of Seignelay's false economy. "Mais je veux vous épargner." Seignelay was young and inexperienced and Vauban's attitude was that of an elder brother rather than that of an officer addressing the Minister of Marine. Seignelay was said to be a cultivated man with literary tastes, but he would never have occupied the position he did, had he not been the son of the great Colbert.[1] Then as now knowledge and experience were not considered essential for very important government offices.

Vauban was at Ypres in the autumn and was very seriously ill. Ypres was an unhealthy place, lying in the flat low lands of Flanders, and Vauban, who did not spare himself, "étant presque toujours présent sur les travaux" caught "une grave maladie dont il pensa mourir". In January 1690 Louvois wrote to him to take quinine and come to Paris to see the doctors, where he would find "plus habiles médecins" than were to be found in Lille. Vauban, however, seems to have gone to Bazoches, where he recovered by drinking milk for twenty consecutive days and also by drinking asses' milk, a remedy suggested by a private soldier. In March he reported that, except for weakness in the legs, he was doing well and in June he was able to appear at Court, and proceed, by instructions of the King, on a tour through Flanders, then to Sedan, Luxembourg, Thionville and Mont-Royal, after which he might return to Bazoches. It seems that the King had arranged this as an easy tour such as a convalescent could undertake, and in this and indeed on most occasions Louis XIV showed a real consideration for Vauban.

On his return to Bazoches Vauban occupied his time in writing some important papers which are included in *Les Oisivetés de M. de Vauban*. Vauban must have been writing notes and mémoires all his life, though they increased in number and importance in his later years, ending with the Dîme Royale, the last of his papers and the most remarkable. Vauban had collected all his papers, and had them copied, illustrated and bound up in twelve volumes. These

---

[1] Seignelay, born in 1651, succeeded his father as Minister of Marine in 1676. He died in 1690.

BERGUES, S. GATE (NORD)

papers were separated after his death, the technical papers going to the "Section technique du Génie", where they now are. The rest were divided between Vauban's two daughters, and those that went to the elder daughter, private and domestic papers probably of the greatest interest, have come by inheritance to one of her descendants, who unfortunately refuses to have them published, so that little is really known about Vauban's private life.[1] Colonel Rochas d'Aiglun collected and printed large extracts from the *Oisivetés* and most of Vauban's official correspondence in his *Vauban, sa famille et ses écrits*, a book that is admirably edited and invaluable to any student of Vauban's life and work.[2] The *Oisivetés* contain papers on all sorts of subjects, some of which I shall deal with later. Rochas d'Aiglun classifies them under nine heads:

(1) Attaque et défense des places.
(2) Réorganization de l'armée.
(3) Art des constructions.
(4) Vie Rurale.
(5) Les Colonies et la Marine.
(6) Mémoires politiques.
(7) Rivières et Canaux.
(8) Statistiques et descriptions de pays.
(9) Pensées diverses.

One of the earliest of his papers was "Plusieurs Maximes bonnes à observer pour tous ceux qui font bastir", probably written when he was adding to his château at Bazoches, a treatise containing excellent advice on building construction, which reminds me of the volumes on *Building Construction* published by Rivingtons, which used to be the text book of architectural students fifty years ago. As I have pointed out before, the roles of engineers and architects were not yet clearly differentiated, and if I may use the phrase, Vauban rather fancied himself as an

---

[1] A full account of the history of the *Oisivetés* is given in Rochas d'Aiglun *Vauban*, I, p. 81 to 100.

[2] *Vauban, sa famille et ses écrits*, by Lieut.-Col. de Rochas d'Aiglun, 2 volumes, Paris, 1910. As only 300 copies were published, it is a rare book.

architect. He knew the orders as well as another, and, proud of his knowledge, probably thoroughly enjoyed himself in the luxury of designing the gateways of his forts; but unlike the Italians of the sixteenth century, he had not started with a sound grounding in the art of architecture. His knowledge was limited to the orders and their paraphernalia, for which quantities of illustrated text-books were available. Apart from this, his ideas of design were not much more than those of a competent builder with good common sense and an exceptional knowledge of building construction, and it is no use expecting from Vauban masterpieces of design, such as the Porta del Palio or the Porta Nuova at Verona. The church at Briançon and the gatehouses at Maubeuge show the level of Vauban's architectural attainments. His real strength lay not here, but in the massive simplicity of his mighty walls, and his splendid planning.

In 1689, Vauban wrote two treatises, one on the importance of Paris to France, the other a splendid plea for the recall of the Huguenots. The mémoire on Paris points out that Paris is "le vrai cœur du Royaume, la mère commune des Français, et l'abrégé de la France", but that its defences were lamentably weak. He therefore proposed to restore the old fortifications and bring them up-to-date, and to make a second line of defence, at the distance of a cannon's range, "c'est à dire, à mille ou douze cents toises de distance", including in it all the high ground such as Belleville and Montmartre. There should be two citadels, one where the Seine enters Paris, and the other where the river leaves it. These were to be fully equipped, "but," Vauban added, "il ne faudrait pas craindre que Paris se portât jamais à rien qui pût blesser son devoir". For once Vauban was at fault. He had forgotten the Fronde, and he could not foresee 1789. Arsenals and magazines were to be built and the city provisioned for a year. Corn was to be brought when the price was low and stored. This would enable the farmer to pay his rent, and in dear years "le pauvre peuple serait toujours soulagé dans ses misères". Vauban reckoned that

2,100,000 "setiers[1] de blé" would last 700,000 to 800,000 people for one year. Forage for cavalry, wine, brandy, beer, salt and provisions of all kinds were to be stored in readiness for a siege. Vauban believed that Paris would be impregnable, the new outer line of defence would keep the enemies' guns three quarters of a league distant, and to invest Paris an army of not less than 200,000 men would be necessary, but he rather discounts his scheme by saying that all the people in the neighbourhood would take refuge in Paris, as if they did, the stores could not provide for them as well as the citizens. To clinch his proposals, Vauban used the unsound old argument that money would not go out of the country. In conclusion, Vauban says he made these proposals for the consideration of thoughtful people. They would take ten or twelve years to be carried out and this could only be done "dans une paix profonde". Vauban appears to have made two designs for the enceinte of Paris, and returned to the subject after the defeat of Blenheim, but the "paix profonde" never came in Vauban's time, and when it did, France was bankrupt.

---

[1] A "setier" of grain was 12 bushels.

CHAPTER X

THE mémoire on the recall of the Huguenots was, with the exception of that on the Dîme Royale, the bravest paper that Vauban ever wrote. In 1685 Louis XIV, at the instigation of Mme. de Maintenon and the Jesuits, had revoked the Edict of Nantes. Mme. de Maintenon was all-powerful and her hostility could almost certainly wreck the future of those who incurred it. Yet Vauban took this risk at the height of his career, only four years after the revocation of the Edict. He was so deeply impressed with the injustice to the Huguenots and the injury to France, that he felt compelled to say quite plainly what he thought about this disastrous blunder. Yet he was temperate enough at first. This measure, he said, so excellent in intention, had failed. "Le projet si saint et si juste . . . loin de produire l'effet qu'on en devait attendre, a causé et peut encore causer une infinité de maux très dommageables à l'État". Thus (1) it has lost France 80,000 to 100,000 people of all sorts, who have left the country, and taken with them 30,000,000 livres in cash. (2) It has seriously injured the arts and manufactures of France, many excellent craftsmen having fled. (3) It has ruined trade. (4) It has strengthened the navies of France's enemies by giving them eight or nine thousand of the best sailors in France.[1] (5) It has strengthened their armies, by handing over to the enemy five or six hundred officers and ten to twelve thousand men, all veteran soldiers. As to the conversions, Vauban did not think that they were genuine, and believed that those who had abjured were probably more Huguenot than ever. Everybody in foreign countries had heard of the persecutions, and the Huguenots' martyrology had

[1] From ports such as La Rochelle.

provided excellent copy for the enemies of France. Among the refugees were "bonnes plumes", men who could write, and these writers bitterly attacked France and the King. The more the Huguenots were coerced, the more obstinate they would be, and they would either have to be exterminated as rebels,[1] or maintained by the State as lunatics. If the law was enforced, more would leave the country, and to send those who resisted to the galleys, or cut off their heads, would only add to the martyrology, and would increase the numbers of the Huguenots, as had happened after the massacre of S. Bartholomew in 1572, when the number of Huguenots in France was increased by 110,000. Again the Revocation would endanger the country in case of war and would break up the State. He did not believe, he continued, that the Revocation had produced a single genuine convert. In a letter to Le Pelletier written from Lyons in 1693, Vauban, referring to Pont Saint-Esprit, said: "Du côté de Languedoc, elle a les Cevennes et le Vivarais —pays pavé de nouveaux convertis, qui sont catholiques comme je suis mahométain". He therefore suggested that the revocation should be cancelled outright, that the Huguenots should be limited to the numbers that existed in 1670, and that they should be allowed the free exercise of their religion, on payment of thirty sous a head. The obstinacy of the Huguenots was, he said, of great assistance to the Prince of Orange, and it was no use deceiving themselves as to the state of France. "Le dedans du royaume est ruiné, tout souffre, tout pâtit et tout gémit," and if no one said that this was so, it was only because they were held back by their personal respect for the King. Yet now that the King was in full enjoyment of his power and universally respected, the time had come to make concessions, as an act not of compulsion but of generosity. It might be hard for a great Prince to go back on what he had done, yet he would know that what might be right at one time might be wrong at another, and circumstances had changed. When this measure was

---

[1] This was attempted fifteen years later in the war in the Cevennes.

passed, the King had reckoned on a peace of twenty years. The peace had only lasted five, and it would be against all good sense and judgment to persist in this policy. He appealed to the King on the ground that France was in danger, and also that the King himself would not wish that any of his subjects should be constrained in their religion. It was a gallant plea on behalf of a brutally persecuted people, though 30 sous a head for the free exercise of one's religion may seem an odd suggestion, and the statement that the King did not want to interfere with the religion of his subjects, was a plain and obvious contradiction of the facts.

Vauban proposed the re-enactment of the Edict of Nantes to enable all persons to follow either the Roman Catholic or the Protestant religion. The Protestants were to be free to re-establish their temples, and there was to be a general amnesty for all who had left the country on account of their religion, and even for those who had served in enemies' forces against France, such as the Comte de Tilly, and the "officiers réformés" in the garrison at Luxembourg. Their property and all rights were to be restored, and all who had been imprisoned or sent to the galleys were to be freed. Vauban even went so far as to draft the actual wording of the announcement of the proposed change. This action would, he said, conciliate the Protestant Princes of Brandenbourg, Saxe, Limburg, Hesse, and the Swiss cantons, and it would place a dagger in the heart of the Prince of Orange, "mettrait le poignard dans le sein du Prince d'Orange," of whom elsewhere Vauban said that he hoped it would please God to remove that "fin et rusé politique", the Usurper, who was the scandal of Christianity, the sworn enemy of France and Religion, and the disturber of the peace of Europe. Vauban had already recognized in William of Orange the most dangerous enemy of France. Vauban maintained that his proposals, if adopted, would check the power of Austria, and lay the foundations of a permanent peace, "parcequ'elle couperait la principale racine[1]

[1] The defence of Protestantism.

qui unit les confédérés". The declaration must be clear and explicit "dans toutes les formes requises sans y laisser de queue", and if the Pope objected, all that the King need do, was to tell him to mind his own business and inform His Holiness that this was "une affaire temporelle et purement politique, où il va du salut d'un État", and that the King must provide for the safety of his kingdom.

Vauban returned to the subject of the recall of the Huguenots in 1692 and said that he saw no reason to change anything that he had said three years before. The converts, he noted, did not go to the churches, or if they did, committed sacrilege by taking the sacraments in which they did not believe, and they were being disloyal to France. To exterminate them would be horrible, whereas to make them contented would be honest and charitable. The Frenchman, he said, was not a good hater, and many were disgusted with the harsh treatment of the Huguenots. Vauban as usual reinforces his appeal by statistics. There were, he said, half a million Huguenots in France. Deduct 10,000 for genuine converts and 10,000 for invalids. Deduct from the 480,000, 360,000 for women and girls, children under 17 and men over 50. From the 120,000 left deduct half or two-thirds for other occupations, and for those who did not wish to be soldiers, which would leave 60,000 men capable of bearing arms. At least one-third of these would join the army, and as for the 40,000 men left over, as they would be "sans tête et sans corps", one need have no anxiety about them.

It was a curious way of dealing with the subject. There can be no doubt of Vauban's genuine sympathy with the Huguenots. He himself was a professed Roman Catholic, but one's impression is that this did not weigh heavily with him, and on general principles he had an ingrained dislike for dogmatism. He did not, however, approach the subject from this point of view. He regarded the whole question as one of political economy in its widest sense of the conduct and government of the State. The greatness of kings, he said, is measured by the number of

their subjects, and then follows this famous passage, "Tel
est le grand et très noble Royaume de France, le mieux
situé de l'univers en égard à tout ce que l'on voudra. Il
est rempli d'un peuple três nombreux sous un même Roi.
Il est naturellement belliqueux et capable de tous les arts
et disciplines, très obéissant et aimant ses Rois, jusqu'
à prodiguer libéralement leurs vies et leurs biens pour eux.
Il est d'ailleurs très fertile et abondant en tout ce qui peut
être nécessaire à la vie. C'est enfin le plus beau Royaume
du monde et rempli des meilleurs sujets. Il faut donc les
considérer, et en toutes manières rallier, et rappeler ceux
que les misères passées et les chagrins des conversions ont
fait sortir du Royaume, et ménager ceux qui y restent, au
lieu de les vexer et tourmenter." It was a noble appeal
on behalf of the persecuted and oppressed, and Vauban
was absolutely right in his forecast. Many of the best
craftsmen and tradesmen of France left the country for
ever and settled in England, Holland, Denmark, Sweden,
Germany and even in Ireland,[1] and the persecution in
France was so intolerable that within ten years of Vauban's
second mémoire, there broke out that tragic war of the
Camisards in the Cevennes, when for several years a
handful of mountaineers defied the troops of Louis
XIV, cost him losses that he could ill afford in men and
money, and intensified the hatred with which he was
regarded by all the Protestant powers. This was the war
in which Mme. de Maintenon and the Jesuits did in fact
hope to exterminate the Protestants, the alternative
which Vauban had condemned as "horrible", the war in
which the Bishop of Alais adjured all good Catholics
"par les entrailles de notre divin Sauveur" to withold
any help from Protestants, and "d'essayer de les extermin-
iner par le fer et le feu. Par ces moyens la majesté divine,
l'honneur de l'Eglise Catholique, et la dignité royale du
Prince, demeureront inviolables dans tous les siècles".
Alais is a small town at the foot of the Cevennes, and

---

[1] It was said that fully 300,000 Protestants fled from France between 1686
and 1705. For an account of the war in the Cevennes see *Byways*, Chapters VI
and VII, by Reginald Blomfield (Murray).

Vauban had built a citadel here overlooking the River Gardon. The Bishopric of Gardon was only established in 1694, so no doubt the new Bishop was anxious to show his zeal. It is a pity that Vauban could not have set him to work in one of his trenches.

Vauban's protest was in vain. He sent the mémoire of 1689 to Louvois, who replied from Versailles, "J'ai lu votre mémoire, où j'ai trouvé de fort bonnes choses; mais entre nous, elles sont un peu outrées, j'essaierai de les lire à sa Majesté", but it is doubtful whether Louvois ever attempted to do so. His health was not good, he had many enemies, and even he, formidable as he was, did not care to incur the enmity of Mme. de Maintenon. Louvois died in the next year, July 1691. The King wrote a personal letter to Vauban on July 22, 1691. "Je ne doute point que vous n'ayez été fâché de la mort du sieur Marquis de Louvois", but he expressed no opinion as to Louvois' merits. He died quite suddenly after dining with the King, not without a suspicion of his having been poisoned, according to Dangeau. Saint Simon as usual has one of his unpleasant stories that Louvois' independence had become so intolerable to the King, that if he had not died, he would have been taken off to the Bastille, "d'où il ne serait jamais sorti". Mme. de Sévigné wrote to M. de Coulanges, her cousin, "Voilà donc M. Louvois mort, ce grand ministre, cet homme si considérable, qui tenait une si grande place, dont le 'moi', comme dit M. Nicole, était si étendu, qui était le centre de tant de choses. Que d'affaires, que de desseins, que de projets, que de secrets, que d'intérêts à démêler, que de guerres commencées, que d'intrigues, que de beaux coups d'échecs à faire et à conduire!" An anonymous epitaph of the time said:

> Ici git que tout plait
> Et que de tout avait connaissance parfaite
> Louvois que personne n'aimait
> Et que tout le monde regrette.[1]

Louvois was a strange mixture of good and bad. Harsh,

[1] Quoted by Rochas d'Aiglun, *Vauban*, II, 328.

arrogant and overbearing, ruthless in trampling on all
who opposed him, he was always a loyal friend of Vauban,
and in spite of his brusqueness, and a rather heavy irony
which he sometimes brought into play in answer to Vauban's cheerful humour, he comes out well in his correspondence with Vauban. He had saved Vauban early in
his career from complete catastrophe in the affair of Brisach, and whatever he may have said or written, he always
backed him when he could. Of his ability there could be
no doubt: only a man of his strong personality could have
maintained his position as first minister of Louis XIV for
the ten troublesome years that followed the death of
Colbert. He was loyal to the King and to what he believed
to be the interests of France. The rumours reported by
Saint Simon may be discounted. Saint Simon suspected
every one and for some reason disliked Louvois, though
he could hardly have known him personally, for Saint
Simon was only sixteen when Louvois died. The disastrous years that followed his death, the growing
disorganization of the state, and the mistakes in the policy
of the King, show the extent of the loss that France suffered by his death. Probably the worst service that he did
to France was to pass on his son, the Marquis de Barbezieux as his successor. Barbezieux, though only twenty-
three, became minister of war and held that position
till his death in 1701 at the age of thirty-three. According to Saint Simon he was a brilliant young man, but "Il
aimait tous les plaisirs et s'y perdait". The nepotism of
these ministers seems incredible. Barbezieux was one
instance. Seignelay, the eldest son of Colbert was
another. His father got him appointed as his successor
at the Ministry of Marine when he was only twenty-five,
and here he stayed till his death fourteen years later in
1690. Colonel Lazard says justly, "Ce que nous repro-
chons le plus à Louvois, comme aux ministres ses contem-
porains, c'est leur népotisme. Ils étaient bons ministres,
mais aussi bons parents."

CHAPTER XI

Vauban and a breach of professional etiquette—The abrégé *for* 1692—
*The siege of Namur—Racine's description—Vauban and Cohorn—Dauphiné
—Barbezieux—Nice—Niquet—The mountain forts—Want of trained men
—The Order of Saint Louis.*

VAUBAN must have been a splendid chief. He said of
himself that he had no use for "fripons", but he spared
no effort to help subordinates who served him well. On
the other hand, he insisted that things should be done
decently and in order. In 1690, an engineer named
Cladech had suggested to Louvois alterations in a design
by Vauban, without any reference to the latter. Vauban,
in a letter to Cladech, reminded him that "l'usage est
parmi les honnêtes gens de notre métier, de s'adresser
à moi avant toutes choses, et de me proposer leurs diffi-
cultés, et ce qu'ils trouvent à redire." Having thus
rebuked Cladech for his breach of professional etiquette,
Vauban went on to say that he was not drunk when he
made the design, and that Cladech, owing to his having
ignored Vauban's design, had committed a "quantité
d'absurdités condamnables "at Sedan. "Vous avez en un
mot si méprisé mes projets, que vous n'avez daigné les
demander, en quoi vous avez très mal fait, car c'est faire
le procès aux gens, sans vouloir les entendre." A formidable man when roused, yet Vauban never bore malice
and was in fact the most placable of men. He ended his
letter: "Je suis malgré toutes vos négligences toujours à
vous", and a little later wrote again to say, "Je suis toujours comme vous savez, et comme vous n'en pouvez pas
douter, de tout mon cœur tout à vous."

In 1691, Vauban's daughter was married to the Marquis
d'Ussé, and in April, after the capture of Mons, the
King gave him 100,000 livres and paid him the compliment of inviting him to dinner. In August, the King
wrote him a personal letter, desiring him to stay on at
Mons, so long as the Prince of Orange was in the

neighbourhood, and saying that Vauban's presence at Mons was worth more than any supplies that the King could send him, and that so long as Vauban was there "Je n'aurai point inquiétude pour cette place." The *Abrégé* for 1692 gives more details than usual, and I quote it in full as it is an excellent example of Vauban's concise register of his services, and also because it is typical of Vauban's professional life year after year. "En 1692 il servit au siège de Namur où le Roi commandait en personne. Il en conduisit les attaques avec tant de précaution, que cette place, que l'on croyait très forte, ne dura que trente jours de tranchée ouverte, ville et château, et on n'y perdit que 800 hommes, quoiqu'il s'y fit quantité d'action de main. Ce siège fait, il resta à Namur le temps nécessaire pour rétablir le désordre des attaques, et faire ce projet des ouvrages qui manquaient à ses fortifications pour les mettre en état. Ensuite de quoi il en partit, par ordre, pour aller visiter les places du Dauphiné où Monsieur de Savoie avait fait irruption. Il passa de là à Pignerol, et retourna par là en Provence. Ce fut aussi l'année où il fit le projet du fameux Mont-Dauphin." This was a characteristic year of Vauban's life. First a siege, then the capture of the place, then the repair of the fortifications, then he is sent off to the other end of France to see what the Duke of Savoy was doing, passes on to Provence, and ends up the year with the design of an important new fortress.

The siege of Namur was famous. The King was present in person, and there were also at the siege Racine as official historian, and Cohorn, the famous Dutch engineer, inside Namur with the defence, and thus for once the two most famous engineers of the 17th century (Vauban and Cohorn) were face to face. Vauban had made a careful reconnaissance of Namur in 1691, and had drawn up a report pointing out the difficulties of a siege and explaining how he proposed to deal with it. Namur, about 45 miles east of Mons, and rather less south-west of Liège, is a strong place on the Meuse, and the citadel stands on high ground on a tongue of land where the

Sambre joins the Meuse. The citadel commanded the town from which it was separated by the Sambre.[1] Racine described it as being "en plus haut de la montagne, et par conséquent pouvant commander aux ouvrages à cornes, qui couvrent le château de ce côté-là". The plan which I reproduce from the *Atlas Portatif* shows Namur as it was in 1695, presumably after Vauban had re-established the fortifications. Either he or Cohorn had constructed a line of fortification round the town from the Sambre to the Meuse, so that Namur was protected by the Meuse on one side, and by a continuous line all round the place, beginning down stream below the town, and joining the Meuse again above it. The fortifications round the town have disappeared and the Sambre is now canalized. Vauban made his attack from the high ground above the citadel and to the west of it, and seems to have completely bewildered the garrison by attacking from many points at once. Racine wrote three letters to Boileau describing the siege, giving technical details. Vauban laid out his lines, and Racine says that at the final attack the King was present in person at the head of his regiment, and gave his orders within a musquet shot of the fort; indeed, that he narrowly escaped being killed by a musquet shot which hit the gabion behind which he was standing, and wounded one of his attendants. The King all through the siege kept in close touch with Vauban, and late in the siege he wrote to him personally and said, "La conversation que nous aurons est de très grande importance." But the capture of Namur was as usual due to Vauban, who took infinite pains in preparing for the assault. Racine describes how he nursed his men, and how in order to save them from unnecessary risks, kept five drums beside him to be beaten when the men were advancing too far, and he also had stakes set out to mark the position of companies for the attack, and prevent them from getting mixed. "La chose réussit à merveille" and Namur fell after a siege of thirty days. Racine also relates a meeting of Cohorn and Vauban. Cohorn had

[1] This river is now canalized. Namur has stood at least five sieges.

made his last stand in a detached fort, being part of the citadel on the high ground to the north-west marked number 3 on the plan, and called on the map "Fort Cohorne", probably so called as a compliment to Cohorn, for Racine calls it Fort Guillaume. This fort had only been built the year before, "C'est un grand ouvrage[1] à cornes, avec quelques redans dans le milieu de la courtine selon que le terrain a demandé". Cohorn had designed it, and he now shut himself up in the fort declaring that he would die there. After Cohorn had been wounded, the fort surrendered, and Namur was captured. Vauban went to see Cohorn, and after warmly praising Cohorn for his defence of the place, asked him what he thought of the attack. Cohorn's reply was characteristic. The stubborn Dutch engineer always held to the direct frontal assault, as opposed to Vauban's method of attack by carefully planned lines of trenches, and he replied to Vauban that if the attack had been made "dans les formes ordinaires" he could have held out for another fortnight, but with trenches surrounding the whole place, further defence was hopeless, almost implying that this method of attack was hardly playing the game. The King gave Vauban 40,000 écus for the capture of Namur.

After repairing the fortifications of Namur Vauban was sent to Provence and Dauphiné, and in a reply to a letter from Vauban, Barbezieux, who had succeeded his father, Louvois, in 1691, as minister of war, wrote in very cordial terms "demandant bien sérieusement votre amitié que je veux avoir tout de bon, vous assurant . . . que ce n'est pas un compliment que je vous fais ici, mais bien que je suis avec sincérité tout à vous". The young man seems to have been genuinely anxious to carry on the traditions of his father in regard to Vauban, the one man in France on whom the King and his ministers could always rely. The south-east frontier was always a source of anxiety to Louis XIV. Nice, which had belonged to the Duke of Savoy, had been taken in 1691 by a French army commanded by that very able soldier

---

[1] Racine to Boileau.

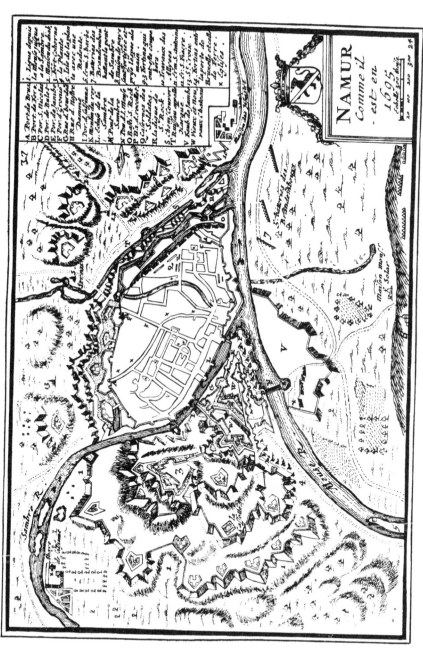

PLAN OF NAMUR
From "Atlas Portatif," 1702

Catinat, and a scheme for the fortification of Nice was got out by Niquet, and submitted to Vauban. The latter's criticism, courteously expressed, was that Niquet's scheme was too elaborate for execution in time of war, and not strong enough in time of peace, when expense need not be considered. Vauban took up Niquet's plan, and prepared a much more comprehensive scheme which would, he hoped, provide a frontier line of defence, "un pays fortifiée, que par ce moyen devient impénétrable à l'ennemie, par terre et par mer, et couvre merveilleusement la Provence par l'endroit le plus faible de la frontière". It was in this long distance view that Vauban was so far ahead of his contemporaries. He thought of defence as a whole, not as a matter of scattered and isolated details, and there was always in the back of his mind this idea of a ring fence, the strong barrier that would preserve the Pré Carré inviolate, and embrace the whole circuit of France. Starting eastward from Dunkerque, his line of defence moved along the Flemish frontier through Ypres, Menin, Ath and Mons to Namur, then south-east to Sedan and Luxembourg, Strasbourg and the frontier of the German states to Brisach, past the Swiss frontier through Belfort, to the frontier of Savoy, Mont Dauphin, Queyras and Briançon, then south to the Mediterranean and along the coast past Nice, Antibes, Hyères, Toulon, Cette and Port Vendres to the Spanish frontier. Some twenty-nine miles south-west of Perpignan he built the forts of Villefranche Conflent to command the valley of the Tet and Le Vernet, which runs north-west down to Perpignan, and fifteen miles south-west of Villefranche, high up in the Pyrenees he built the fort of Mont Louis at a height of 5,135 feet above the sea, to block the pass from Spain. Then to Bayonne, which he fortified. He had built the citadel in 1674 on the north side of the Adour, which bears over the entrance the proud inscription "Nunquam polluta". Then up the Atlantic coast—Brest, Belle Ile-en-Mer, La Rochelle, Oléron, and then up the Channel past S. Malo, Havre, Dieppe and Calais to Dunkerque. For the first time the defence of the kingdom of France was treated as a whole.

Vauban had now to prepare schemes for forts on the south-east frontier, more especially the new fort of Mont Dauphin, to be built on a mountain near Briançon at a height of 3,470 feet above the sea. The fortifications were built with the red marble of the district.[1] Vauban had to design these mountain forts on the Savoy frontier on very different lines from the forts of the plains. He had designed a fort at Castellana in the Alpes Maritimes at a height of 2,372 feet, the fort of "Mont Louis," the highest fort in France, at a height of 5,135 feet, the new town of Briançon at a height of 4,410 feet, and the re-modelling of the old fort of Château Queyras at 4,463 feet above the sea. All these places were in the mountainous country, overlooked by greater heights, and with no level sites on which the usual methods of fortification could be employed. In these forts he gave up the bastions, now almost sacrosanct by long tradition, and relied on strong walls with embrasures and crenellations, and his favourite device of the "Tours bastionnées". He wrote to Le Peletier in January 1693 that the fortification he proposed for Digne[2] was the only one possible on the site "où on est reserré et pressé de montagnes . . . car si d'un part on ne peut y faire de bastions, ni de demilunes, du moins on y pourra faire de bonnes et hautes tours, dont les flancs répétés, l'un sur l'autre, égaleront à peu de choses près ceux de bastions." Moreover the ground was so irregular, there were so many "plongées," that a rampart was scarcely possible and he had to rely on his towers. He even on occasion reverted to the use of the round tower of the medieval fortress. In 1693, writing to Catinat who was collaborating with him on the south-east frontier, he said "Toute cette frontière est si extraordinairement bossillée, qu'il m'a fallu inventer un nouveau système de fortification pour en tirer parti." In February 1693 he wrote again to Le Peletier[3] that as the places to be forti-fied were hilly (bossillées), and commanded by higher

---

[1] See Lazard, *Vauban*, Pl. XI, for an illustration of this fort which exists much as it was when built by Vauban.   [2] Basses Alpes.

[3] Le Peletier de Souzy had been appointed Director-General of Fortifica-tions on the death of Louvois in 1691.

ground, "il n'y a qu'une méthode de fortification à y observer qui est celle de tours bastionnées et des murailles couvertes, un peu fortes, percées d'embrasures et de crénaux." He added that for the last fifteen days he had been able to do nothing "parce que je suis accablé d'un rhume très opiniâtre, que me tourmente beaucoup". This was an old trouble from which Vauban constantly suffered. In January 1693 he had written to Le Peletier that the roads were all covered with ice and that he was "enrhumé à tousser tant que la nuit dure . . . je puis dire n'avoir point eu de repos depuis que je suis hors de ma grande maladie", but he wrote again in March, "le rhume s'est si fort relâché, que je ne m'en sens presque plus," and he thanked God that his daughter was, he heard, out of danger, one of his very rare references to his family.

In 1693 Vauban was employed on the fortifications of the Savoy frontier. He prepared schemes for Gap, Sisteron, Seyne, Saint Vincent, Colmars, Digne, Mont Dauphin, Château Queyras, Embrun and the new town of Briançon—citadel, church, fortifications and all. He was in constant communication with Le Peletier, to whom he sent graphic and very interesting reports on places visited. In describing Château Queyras, for instance, he pointed out the importance of its position as a fort on a high rock, commanding an entrance into Savoy, but the château was, he said, "extraordinairement petit" and "fort serré et environné de quatre grosses montagnes qui semblent le vouloir écraser." All he could do was to strengthen the walls so far as possible. He was not happy about the south-east frontier and wrote to Catinat from Nice: "Il est de la dernière conséquence de mettre au plus tôt, cette frontière en état en regard au présent et à l'avenir." Things too were not going well on the frontier further north. Rheinfels near Goar on the Rhine had been besieged by the French, but in consequence of a premature attack which failed, the siege had been raised. It seems that Tallard, who was in command, had been wounded the day after he arrived

9

at Rheinfels, and Choisy, an engineer who succeeded him, had been misinformed as to the strength of the place, and after an ineffectual attack had raised the siege—another instance of the incompetence which Vauban deplored. Vauban, who was at Nice, was very indignant and said "C'est une opération honteuse à la France, et très préjudiciable aux troupes . . . il n'est pas possible qu'on eût pu faire plus grande ânerie." Vauban was seriously concerned about the lack of trained officers in the French army. In a long letter to Le Peletier in February 1693, he said that in three sieges he could make any officers with a little sense "capable de la conduite d'une tranchée, d'un logement de contrescarpes, d'une descente de fossé, attachement de mineur, etc.," but that it took 15 to 20 years of hard work to make a man a good "bâtisseur". So many and such varied qualities were necessary that it was very seldom that they were possessed by any one man, and he said this of himself, "Le Génie [engineering] est un métier audessus de nos forces. Il embrasse trop de choses pour qu'un homme le puisse posséder dans un souverain degré de perfection. J'ai assez bonne opinion de moi pour me croire un des plus forts de la troupe, et capable de faire leçon aux plus habiles, et avec tout cela, quand je m'examine, je ne me trouve qu'un demi-ingénieur, après quarante ans de très forte application et de la plus grande expérience qui fut jamais." Rochas d'Aiglun says that when Vauban wrote this he had taken part in 45 sieges.

In 1693 Louis XIV established the Order of Saint Louis. The King and the Dauphin were to be Grand Masters, all the Maréchals de France were to be members. No patent of nobility was required, but all members must have served not less than 10 years. There were to be 8 Grand Croix, who were to wear a red sash with a gold cross on their coats, and were each to receive 2,000 écus.[1] Vauban, who was again disappointed at not

---

[1] The order was the forerunner of the Legion of Honour, but, like the patents of nobility, soon became a matter of price—Voltaire says that under Chamillart crosses of the order could be bought for 50 écus in cash.

CHÂTEAU QUEYRAS (HAUTES ALPES)

being made a Maréchal de France, was consoled by being made a member of the Order, and in June Louis XIV wrote him a personal letter, in which he said that though he did not always agree with him, Vauban was to continue to write to him whatever came into his head, and he assured Vauban "qu'on ne peut pas avoir plus de considération, d'estime, et d'amitié que je n'ai pour vous," a very handsome tribute from a King such as Louis XIV.

I think the promotion to the Order of Saint Louis marks the turning point in Vauban's career. He was yet to advance to further honours, but henceforward he was not to have the free hand which he had used so well in the service of France, when he had only the King and Louvois to deal with. The death of Louvois in 1691 was in fact a disaster for Vauban, for Louvois, whatever his faults of manner, had always been a loyal friend to Vauban, a strong defence against the intrigues of enemies and rivals. France was on the road downhill, the King was failing in health, judgment, and resolution, and power in the state had fallen into the hands of a weaker and inferior generation. The burdens borne by Colbert and Louvois were beyond the capacity of their sons Seignelay and Barbezieux. Seignelay died young, and when Barbezieux died in 1701, worn out by his excesses, he was succeeded by Chamillart, who was said to have commended himself to Louis XIV by his skill in billiards and by his astute administration of Saint Cyr for Mme. de Maintenon.[1] A generation had arisen that knew not Joseph, and were unable to appreciate the inestimable value to France of Vauban's ability and experience. There comes a time in the careers of distinguished men when Fortune seems to stay her hand. They may have reached the top of the tree, and the world may seem to lie at their feet, yet from this point they may move downwards not upwards. The Greeks

---

[1] Chamillart is described by Voltaire as "hommé modéré et doux", but quite unequal to the task of carrying on work which had taxed to the uttermost the energy and ability both of Colbert and Louvois. Through the influence of Mme. de Maintenon he was appointed Controller-General of Finance in 1699, and Minister of War in 1701. His efforts to raise money for the King made him so unpopular that he had to resign in 1709.

said well, "Call no man happy till the end." The wise man accepts the situation and retires from vain wrestling in the arena, but Vauban's immense vitality and burning patriotism would not admit of this. His choice was to go down fighting and to die in harness, and so one feels that in the last ten years of his life the tragedy was ever drawing nearer that was to end in his death, a broken-hearted man.

CHAPTER XII

Charleroi—The siege—Suggestions for surrender of useless places—The English raids—S. Malo—The defence and the Arrière-Ban—Namur re-taken by the allies—Strasbourg and Luxembourg—Capture of Ath—Peace of Ryswyk, 1697—Neuf-Brisach.

THE war of the League of Augsbourg dragged on—with few decisive battles but many sieges. The Maréchal de Luxembourg[1] had defeated the allies under William III at the battle of Neerwinden, in July 1693, and Louis XIV decided to attack Charleroi and wrote to Vauban "Votre présence y est absolument nécessaire." Charleroi[2] was a very strong place, about half-way between Mons and Namur. Vauban had long seen the dangers of leaving Charleroi in the enemy's hands. He wrote to Le Peletier in June, pointing out that Charleroi held "en échec Namur, Dinant, Charlemont, Mons, Maubeuge, Avesnes" and other places, "et nous oblige à tenir des gardes à 18 ou 20 châteaux et petites places." It was essential that this "place maudite" should be taken, and Vauban says that he had preached and repreached this, "mais il m'arrive ce qui arrivait à la pauvre Cassandre d'Homère . . . on ne me croit qu'après qu'ils (les malheurs) sont arrivés." Charleroi was the weak point on the frontier and must be taken. Vauban had fortified Charleroi some twenty years before. He knew the place well and the difficulty of taking it; so he proceeded with his usual

---

[1] François-Henri de Montmorency, Duc de Luxembourg, a brave and brilliant soldier, "mais si la sexe se trouvait près de là, il était inaccessible à tout" (Voltaire). After the capture of Namur in 1692 it was reported that William of Orange intended to besiege the place. Luxembourg was supposed to cover Namur, but it seems that he was in one of his "inaccessible" states, for he did not answer Vauban's letter, and Vauban wrote to him in July 1692, from Namur: "Si vous voulez sauver cette place au Roi, il est temps que vous preniez des mesures pour cela. . . . Nous sommes encore dans le désordre, où le dernier nous a laissés." Some of the French generals, such as Luxembourg and Vendôme, allowed themselves a licence which seems almost incredible.

[2] Charleroi is half-way between Namur and Mons, now a large, ugly and important centre of the Belgian coal and iron industry. The fortifications have long since been destroyed.

careful preparations. Some of the officers complained that Vauban was taking too long over it, and wanted a direct assault in the Cohorn manner. Vauban's reply was characteristic of his care for his men: "Brûlons de la poudre et versons moins de sang," and he was justified. Charleroi surrendered after a month's siege and a gallant defence, on which Vauban congratulated the commander of the fort. He reported that "ce siège a été beau par la conduite et l'industrie avec laquelle il a été mené, mais il y a de temps où je l'ai trouvé bien laid à cause des pluies fréquentes dans un terrain gras, où en moins d'une demi-heure on ne peut se tenir sur ses pieds, tant il fait glissant dans le fond des tranchées." Apparently the familiar duckboard had not yet been discovered. Vauban was also profoundly dissatisfied with his gunners, "J'ai beaucoup souffert par l'ignorance des canoniers et bombardiers," who he says were quite ignorant of the "règles précises" of artillery. He attributed this to the "routine et beaucoup d'interêt à la tête"—jobbery at headquarters. The Swiss officers, he said, knew their business much better than the French. He also complained again of the lack of any trained and organized company of engineers. In spite of all this, however, the fortifications of Charleroi had been knocked to pieces, and out of a garrison of 3,500 men, when the siege ended only 1,300 were "en état de combattre". The *Abrégé* says that though Charleroi was well defended "il (Vauban) ménagea si bien les attaques, que quoique cette place fût une des plus fortes des Pays Bas, il n'en couta pas au Roi 500 hommes". Writing to Le Peletier Vauban said, "La prise de cette place est une des plus nécessaires conquêtes que le Roi ait faites de son règne, et qui achève de lui faire la plus belle frontière que la France ait eue depuis mille ans." It completed the North Frontier. Fortresses might be taken, but unless they fell into place as essential parts of the line of frontier defence, Vauban regarded their capture as a waste of men and money.

After the surrender, the Spanish officers came and stood round Vauban "pour me voir à peu près avec la

BOMBARDMENT OF HAVRE

From "Atlas Portaiif," 1702

même curiosité qu'on voit l'ours à la foire Saint Germain". After this Vauban and the Spanish commander fell on each other's necks, and apart from their duties, swore eternal friendship, "et toujours bonne guerre". The officers of the French cavalry had complained that their horses had had nothing to do but move fascines, to which Vauban replied that these young heroes would sing a very different tune if they were exposed to the rain and tempest and all the dangers of the trenches, "en un mot, le courage d'un homme qui a les pieds chauds, et qui raisonne en chambre à son aise, quand il n'a pas tâté du peril, est fort différent de ce même homme-là, quand il s'y trouve." Vauban's attitude to war was peculiar to himself. It was not that of the bloodthirsty soldier anxious to kill anyhow and at any cost. He hated killing, and his attitude was that of the artist to his work. The siege of Charleroi he described as "beau, par la conduite et l'industrie avec laquelle il a été mené". Vauban felt no sort of animosity against his enemies; he was ready to fall on their necks "sauf nos devoirs" and all he asked for was "toujours bonne guerre". After the siege of Namur he discussed its conduct with Cohorn, much as two artists might discuss a work of art. When he sent Louvois his plans for the fortification of Maubeuge in 1683 he began his latter, "S'il y a quelque chose dans la fortification qui mérite l'admiration des hommes," it was to be found at Maubeuge, and he mentions "la belle symmétrie et solidité de son revêtement" and "la beauté de ses batteries". Vauban might have been a sculptor or an architect praising some notable work of art.

After the capture of Charleroi Vauban drew up a mémoire on possible savings in the conduct of the wars, and on places that the King could relinquish without injury to the State, and he took the curious course of sending this to the King through Mme. de Maintenon, possibly with some idea of conciliating that egregious lady after his bold appeal for the Huguenots.

In 1694 Vauban was appointed to the command of the Evêchés of Brittany. The successful piracies of Jean Bart,

Dugay-Trouin and others in the Channel had exasperated the English and the Dutch, and in the autumn of 1693 a small English fleet appeared off S. Malo to retaliate. A ship full of explosives was sent into the harbour of S. Malo to blow up the French ships. Unfortunately, it blew itself up instead, but the attack called the attention of Louis XIV to the weakness of the west coast of France, and in 1694 he sent Vauban to Brest to take command of the troops and see to the defence of the long broken coast line of the Channel, Brittany and the west. Vauban established fortified camps, his famous "camps retranchés", and left it to the local Militia and the "Arrière-Ban" to guard the coast. Of the latter force he had the poorest possible opinion. He had told Louvois in 1674, that the "Arrière-Ban" was drawn only from "noblesse fort gueuse et incommodée", was very badly armed and only fit for garrison duty. Twenty years later he found it worse than ever, and reported to the King that they could not march 200 yards without falling out of step. "Il n'y a pas d'escadron qui se puisse former en une heure de temps, ni qui puisse marcher 200 pas sans se rompre", and he implored Barbezieux not to send him any more of the Arrière-Ban. "Ils ne sont bons qu'embarasser par leurs désordres et piailleries[1] continuelles." However, a raid of the English was successfully repulsed in 1694. Louis XIV had heard of it beforehand from the Jacobites, and when a combined fleet of English and Dutch appeared off Brest and tried to land, they were defeated with a loss of one ship, 500 killed and nearly 1,200 prisoners. The French loss was reported to be only 40 to 50 killed and wounded. The *Atlas Portatif* has three plates showing the bombardment of Havre, Dieppe and Calais in 1694.

So far Louis XIV had been fairly successful, but he was now to suffer a severe reverse. Namur, captured by the French in the famous siege of 1692, was besieged by the forces of William III and the Electors of Brandenburg and Bavaria. Vauban in May had warned Le Peletier

---

[1] Squallings.

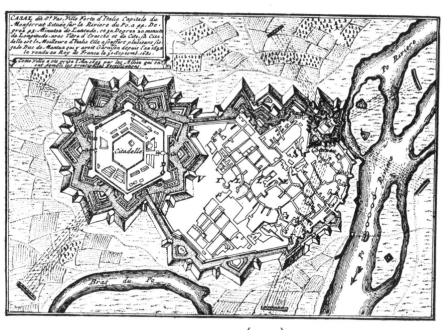

PLAN OF CASAL (ITALY)
From "Atlas Portatif," 1702

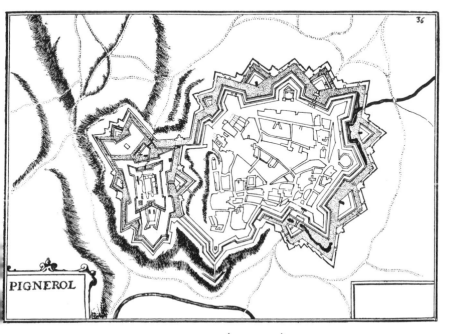

PLAN OF PIGNEROL (PINEROLO), ITALY
From "Atlas Portatif," 1702

that the only way to save Namur was to form an entrenched camp close by. His advice was not taken. The Maréchal de Luxembourg, as already noted, seems to have gone to sleep, or to have been occupied with his ladies, for he did nothing. In July 1696 the Maréchal de Boufflers threw himself into Namur, with 7 regiments of dragoons and the siege began on July 11. Cohorn who was in command of the attack, sent 6 columns of English grenadiers to attack the place, in accordance with his usual practice of direct assault. The Grenadiers advanced 600 metres, with colours flying and drums beating, and Vauban's comment was that he had never heard of such a gross error of judgment. Le Peletier, it seems, had regarded this as "un prodige de valeur". Vauban wrote to him in September, "Moi je le considère comme une des plus achevées sottises qu'on ait jamais faites en fait d'attaque de place"; he only hoped to God the enemy would attack like this again.

Boufflers capitulated in August after a gallant defence. The war was going badly for France and Vauban now prepared a mémoire giving a list of places that the King might surrender to secure a Treaty of Peace. This must have appeared a terrible list to a King who had been used to consider himself invincible. On the Italian frontier Vauban proposed to give up Casal, which Louis XIV had bought for 1,000,000 livres from the Duke of Savoy. Casal, on the upper part of the Po, was reckoned to be the strongest fort in Italy, with its hexagon citadel and very complete fortifications, but Vauban said that it cost the King 1,000,000 livres to maintain; and that it had taken 6,000,000 livres out of the country. He proposed simply to demolish other frontier forts on the Savoy border, Susa, Pignerol,[1] Montmelian, Nice and Chambéry. The attitude of Savoy was so uncertain that it was a waste of money to maintain these forts. Either the Duke would be friendly, in which case the forts would be unnecessary, or he would join the Allies, in which case Louis XIV would annex the whole of Savoy, and again there would

[1] Pignerol, now Pinerolo, had been bought in 1631 for 1,700,000 écus.

be no need for the forts. On the German frontier
Vauban advised the abandonment of Huningen on the
Rhine, Fribourg and Alt-Brisach. Fribourg cost the King
200,000 écus a year, but was of little use to France, and
Alt-Brisach on the right bank of the Rhine, cost him
850,000 livres a year, or Brisach might be exchanged for
Strasbourg, and a new Brisach built on the left bank—as
was actually done after the peace of Ryswyk in 1697,
when Louis XIV had to surrender Alt-Brisach. Vauban
seems to me to have been almost reckless in his proposals.
He was ready to abandon Kohl, Philisbourg and all
Fort St. Louis on the German side of the Rhine. As to
Philisbourg, this and Brisach, he said, cost the King as
much as a good province; the best thing to do would be
to demolish the fortifications, and hand the place over to
the Bishop of Spire, or exchange it for Strasbourg and
make the Rhine the boundary. He would demolish the
forts at Kaiserslautern[1], and even Mont-Royal, a fortress
built at great expense on a high hill above the Moselle in
1686. Dinant, he said, had never added a crown to the
King's revenue and was costly to maintain. This might
be exchanged for Luxembourg. Vauban was doubtful
about Namur,[2] and as to Charleroi (taken in 1693) if this
was handed back the fortifications should be destroyed.
Trèves was no use, and as the Elector was harmless this
might be handed back to him with permission to enclose
it with walls and round towers, but no bastions or hornworks. At Nancy he would destroy all the bastions, and
Longwy might be returned to the Duke of Lorraine. In
order to conciliate the Spaniards, Rosas and Belves might
be surrendered. Vauban estimated that this amazing
programme of surrender and demolition would save the
King in men, 82 battalions, and, in money, 10,400,000
livres a year. He added "on ne propose ceçi comme chose
à devoir absolument exécuter, mais comme un bon choix
à faire des places qui nous sont à charge et les moins utiles,
et dont on se peut relâcher pour conserver les autres, sans

---

[1] About 45 kilometres west of Mannheim.
[2] He wrote before its surrender in 1695.

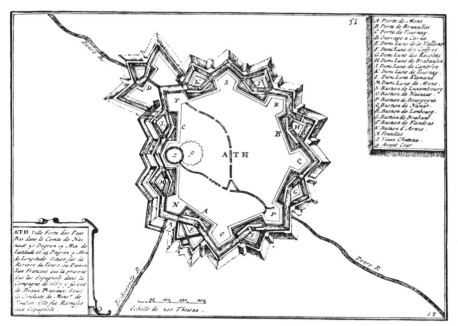

PLAN OF ATH
From "Atlas Portatif," 1702

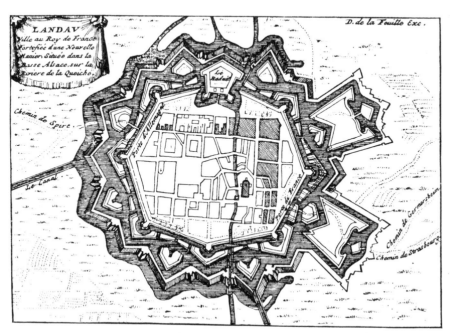

PLAN OF LANDAU (NOTE HORNWORKS ON THE RIGHT)
From "Atlas Portatif," 1702

préjudicier à la sûreté du Royaume". In 1694 Vauban thought so badly of the situation, that he was advising Louis XIV to cut his losses before it was too late, but a glance at the map will show how formidable Vauban's proposals were. The three places to which Vauban attached vital importance were Strasbourg, Mons, and Luxembourg, forming "une barrière impénétrable aux Allemands". Luxembourg in particular should only be abandoned after the complete destruction of the fortification, "démolition totale qui ne lassât pierre sur pierre dans toute l'étendue de la fortification vieille et nouvelle. Autrement il ne faut jamais le rendre," and this applied to Mons as well. This policy, Vauban argued, would keep the enemy quiet for the next twelve years, and during that time anything might happen.

It seems to me to have been a policy of despair. Yet Louis XIV followed it to the extent of coming to terms with the Duke of Savoy in 1696, by the surrender of Pignerol, Nice and other places in Savoy, after the destruction of their fortifications. Vauban was furious at the rumoured terms of peace, more particularly at the suggested surrender of Strasbourg and Luxembourg, which could only furnish the enemy "de quoi nous bien donner les étrivières".[1] Vauban seems to have forgotten the proposals of his own mémoire, and wrote a famous letter to Racine in September 1696 on "les conditions très déshonorantes", such as the suggested surrender of Strasbourg and Luxembourg. "Ces deux dernières places," he wrote, "sont les meilleurs de l'Europe. Il n'y avait qu'à les garder, il est certain qu'aucune puissance n'aurait pu nous les ôter. Nous perdons avec elles pour jamais l'occasion de nous borner par le Rhin. Nous n'y reviendrons plus." All that France had done in the last forty years would be wasted, and the loss of prestige would be irrecoverable. "Si nous la perdons une fois, nous allons devenir l'objet du mépris de nos voisins, comme nous sommes celui de leur aversion . . . on nous va marcher sur le ventre et nous n'oserons souffler."

---

[1] Stirrup leathers; as we should say, "a good leathering"!

Vauban fairly let himself go in this letter, and told Racine
to burn it. Racine did not do so, and it seems to have
reached the ears of jealous generals and the young men
at Court who were showing signs of impatience with the
practical knowledge and experience of Vauban. However, Louis XIV still supported him, and the peace was
not yet signed.

In 1696 Vauban did little except visit the forts on the
Flanders frontier. The last memorable events in the war
of the League of Augsbourg were the capture of Barcelona
with heavy losses on the French side, and the capture of
Ath from the allies in Flanders, "qui fut mené avec tant
d'art et de conduite, qu'il n'en coûta pas 100 hommes au
Roi"; but as Catinat had an army of 40,000 men in three
divisions, commanded by himself, Villeroi and Boufflers,
and the garrison consisted of only 3,600 men with 300
gunners and 200 miners, the capture of Ath was not a
very great exploit. Moreover, Vauban who had fortified
Ath thirty years before knew every inch of the place, and
Ath surrendered after a siege of 14 days. Vauban
attacked with two lines of trenches and used his "tir à
ricochet", but the defence was feeble, "aussi ne fut elle
prise, que par le canon, la pelle, et la pioche."[1]

Vauban, though now 65, spent ten hours a day in the
trenches, and though slightly wounded insisted on
carrying on. He was very proud of his work; never,
he wrote to Le Peletier, had a place been attacked and
taken with such art and such speed. Louis XIV was
greatly pleased and wrote to Vauban himself: "Vous
pouvez être persuadé que je suis très content de vous, et
que dans les occasions je serai bien aise de vous en donner
les marques", but Vauban had still to wait for his Field
Marshal's baton. The war was nearly ended, but
Louis XIV, emboldened by the capture of Ath, was
meditating further efforts, and in June 1697 wrote a long
personal letter to Vauban informing him that he was
resolved to besiege Oudenarde, and to flood the country
round by diverting the Scarpe into the Deulle, and that

[1] Pick and shovel.

the siege was to begin at once. Vauban agreed, though it was against his judgment, but nothing was done, and in August the King wrote Vauban another scarcely intelligible letter, from which it appeared that the King was casting about for honourable terms of peace. In September 1697 the Peace of Ryswyk was signed between France, and England, Holland and Spain. In spite of successes here and there France had steadily lost. By the terms of the Peace, Louis XIV had to surrender Barcelona, Charleroi, Ath, Courtrai and Luxembourg to Spain. He had to destroy Mont-Royal, Kirn and Ebenbourg. Philisbourg, Brisach and Fribourg were restored to the Emperor, and the Duchy of Lorraine to the Duke, though the fortifications of Nancy, Bitche and Hombourg were to be destroyed. The only important place saved from the wreck was Strasbourg. Perhaps Louis XIV would have done better had he followed the advice that Vauban had given three years before, and made peace with his enemy while he was in the way with him.

Louis XIV had to surrender Alt-Brisach in accordance with the terms of the Peace of Ryswyk, and it was made a condition of the peace that he should demolish a new town which had been built among the streams running into the Rhine below Alt-Brisach.[1] It was essential, however, that the bridge over the Rhine at this point should be defended, and it was accordingly decided to build an entirely new fort on the left bank of the Rhine, to be known as Neuf-Brisach. Vauban selected a site on flat ground at some little distance from the river in order to keep the fort out of range of guns on the higher ground of Alt-Brisach. He submitted three schemes to the King, who after close study approved of the third scheme, which provided an octagon fort with bastioned towers in the angles of the courtine, detached bastions, tenailles, demilunes, and moat filled from the Rhine.[2] The estimated cost was 4,048,875 livres, and the design was the last word in Vauban's method of fortification. Belidor who gives a model specification "pour une place neuve telle que le

[1] A plan of this is given in the *Atlas Portatif.*   [2] See Chapter VI.

Neuf-Brisac", to which I have already referred, says that he selected "Neuf-Brisac" as a "unique modèle" in preference to any other place "à cause de l'estime que l'on fait de la beauté de ses ouvrages. C'est effectivement à sujet le plus parfait que puisse être traité." His illustrations were from a second design made by Vauban which was altered in execution.

The specification deals with every part of the fortress: site, courtine, bastioned towers, gateways, posterns, subterranean passages, counterguards, tenailles, demilunes, redoubts, hornworks, moats, covered ways and places d'armes, glacis, bridges and guérites, and this specification is really a complete statement of the art of fortification at the point to which Vauban had carried it in his latest work. The place was immensely strong. Starting from the interior of the fort ("Corps de la Place" in the plan) there was first the rampart measuring some 66 ft. thick at the level of the ground inside the fort, then the moat between the rampart and the tenaille, 66 ft. wide, then the tenaille, another 66 ft., the moat again, 66 ft., the redoubt 72 ft., the moat of the redoubt 30 ft., the demilune 114 ft., then the moat of the demilune 72 ft., the chemin couvert 30 ft. and finally the glacis 120 ft. These measurements, though taken on the extreme line, show the great scale of Vauban's fortifications, and also the advance that he had made in military engineering beyond the point at which de Ville and Pagan left it. Neuf-Brisach was not completed till 1708, the date in the inscription over the main entrance.

CHAPTER XIII

THE *Abrégé* from 1698 to 1702 gives very scanty particu-lars of Vauban's work during the four years that preceded the war of the Spanish succession. As Chief Engineer he prepared plans for Neuf-Brisach, forts on the Savoy frontier and many other places, and Rochas d'Aiglun gives a list of 26 places for which Vauban prepared plans and reports. The *Abrégé* for 1699 says, "Le Roi lui ordonna de continuer la visite des places frontières", and this in fact described his work till war broke out again in 1702, but Vauban's active brain was never idle. All through his career he had been collecting notes and ob-servations, and he now began to put them together in that remarkable series of papers dealing with all sorts of subjects, which he called his *Oisivetés*. In the years 1694–1702 he wrote mémoires on the fortifications of Brest, on a uniform scheme of taxation at a rate of 7 per cent, to be levied impartially on all who could pay, a description of the district of Vezelay with statistics, showing how a census of the population and its resources could be taken, papers on "Caprerie" (privateering), on river navigation, on the re-establishment of the French colony in America, and on the reorganization of the Army. Vauban had intended that these and other papers were to be collected in twelve volumes, entitled "Oisivetés de M. de Vauban ou Ramas de plusieurs mémoires, de sa façon, sur différens sujets". These mémoires were not connected, and were, he says, written at odd times and in strange places, and when he had time to write. *Oisivetés* is a misleading title, for they are not casual papers, but serious studies based on some research and a first-hand acquaintance with facts. Vauban's own de-scription is best. In the essay on the reorganization of

the Army he says: "On ne sera pas surpris du peu d'arrange-
ment qu'on trouvera dans ces mémoires, si on veut bien
être informé que je n'y en travaillé que dans mes heures
de loisir, qui ont été rares, courtes et si entrecoupées et si
éloignées les unes des autres, qu'il y a de chapitres de 15
années d'ancienneté, d'autres de 10, d'autres de 6 et aussi
des autres, et qui plus est, ce n'était que des agendas fait
en vue de conserver le souvenir de mes remarques, et de
ce que me passait pour lors dans l'esprit, à dessein d'en
écrire un pour mon usage." Some repetition and even
contradiction was, therefore, he says, inevitable. "Ceci ne
doit donc être considéré que comme un ouvrage fait à la
hâte et à plusieurs reprises, dont quelqu'unes de si vieille
date que j'en avais perdu l'idée aussi bien que le souvenir."
This also accounts for the freshness of his writings.
Vauban never picked his words; he wrote probably much
as he talked, using the first word that occurred to him to
relieve the race of his volcanic brain.

Vauban was greatly concerned about the unfair incidence of taxation, and the iniquity of the "maltôtiers",
the tax collectors, and he wrote his mémoire on Vezelay
in order to show how taxation might be more fairly distributed, the revenues of the State increased, and an end put
to the "friponneries" of the tax farmers and collectors.
Vezelay was in his own country of the Morvan, and he
collected all the statistics he could of the numbers of the
population, their resources and even their morals, and
also of the agricultural and mineral possibilities of the
district. His idea was that the materials so collected
should form the basis of a simple system of taxation which
everybody could understand and nobody could evade.
In all that he wrote, Vauban aimed at clearness and above
all at facts, and the motives that inspired him were devo-
tion to the interests of the State and a keen anxiety to
help the poor and the oppressed. In his account of the
district of Vezelay there is this piece of vivid description:
"Le pays en général est mauvais, bien qu'il y ait de toutes
choses un peu. . . . Les hommes y viennent grands et
assez bien faits, et assez bons hommes de guerre quand ils

sont une fois dépaysés, mais les terres y sont très mal cultivées, les habitants laches et paresseux. Ils sont d'ailleurs sans industrie, art, ni manufacture aucune" which comes from their being starved, for the "bas peuple ne vit que de pain d'orge et d'avoine mêlées, dont ils n'ôtent même pas le son [bran]. Ils se nourissent encore de mauvais fruits la plupart sauvages, et de quelque peu d'herbes potagères de leur jardin, cuites à l'eau, avec un peu d'huile de noix ou de navette, le plus souvent sans ou avec très peu de sel." The "commun de peuple" did not eat meat three times a year, and it was not to be wondered that people so ill-fed and half-clothed were very feeble. Vauban knew the desperate poverty of the country people in the Morvan and he never forgot the "bas peuple, les pauvres gens", so poor that "s'ils ne ni sont pas encore réduits à la mendicité ils en sont fort près". Let the King redress the abuses of taxation, the revenues would be increased, and "cinquante mille fripons, sans compter les croupiers qui pillent impunément le Royaume, seraient reduits à gagner leur vie et à payer comme les autres."

It was with this aim of increasing the revenues of the State, and helping "le pauvre peuple", that Vauban wrote in 1701 his mémoire on Forestry, and the curious note on "La Cochonnerie", pig-breeding. The woods and forests of France had been cut recklessly, and had not been re-planted, and building timber was actually short in France. Vauban urged that forestry should be regulated by the State, and that there should be systematic planting, for which he gave detailed instructions. The ground was to be dug for at least 2 ft., left to lie for one or two winters, and then sown with acorns. The surface was to be kept clear of weeds and brambles and fenced in. At the end of 15 years the young trees were to be pruned, and again at the end of 32, 62 and 100 years. At the end of 120 to 140 years all dead wood and useless trees were to be removed, and at the end of 200 years, the trees were to be felled for timber. The forests, which should be planted by the State, should be planted with 250 trees to the acre set about 14 ft. centre to centre. Vauban concludes as usual with an estimate of the revenue that this planting would produce. He loved figures and statistics and he applied these in "La Cochonnerie", an elaborate calculation of the number of pigs that might be produced by one sow and its descendants in ten years, and he arrived at the amazing total of 6,000,000. Pigs are so easily fed, that every peasant could "élever un cochon de son cru par an: ce qui est capable de le mettre en état de ne point manger son pain sec les trois quarts de l'année."

The mémoire on "Caprerie" was suggested by what he had noted when in command of the defences of the coast, but twenty years before he had called the attention of Louvois to the injury done by the pirates of Gravelines to the Dutch fishing fleets, and had suggested that a hundred years of this properly supported would bring the Dutch to heel. He now urged that these raids should be organized and supported by the State. In 1675 he had written to Louvois: "Si les corsaires de cette ville[1] étaient un peu aidés et mieux soutenus qu'ils sont, il est constant qu'ils feraient beaucoup plus de mal aux Hollandais par leurs pirateries que toutes nos armées de terre," and at little cost to the King, would injure the Dutch where they would feel it most, namely in their trade. France, he said, was surrounded by enemies and had not a friend in the world. The English and the Dutch were the "principaux arcs boutants"[2] of the League of Augsbourg, and were able by their riches to buy the support of other powers. It was this wealth, the "nerf de la guerre", that must be attacked, and this could best be done by raiding their commerce. All the trade of England passed up and down the coast of France—Dunkerque, Dieppe, Havre, S. Malo, Brest, Honfleur, and La Rochelle. There was a grand opportunity for raids on English ships by bold buccaneers such as Jean Bart of Dunkerque,[3] but there

---

[1] Gravelines, now a derelict and untidy little town.   [2] Buttresses.

[3] Vauban had in 1685 commended Jean Bart to Seignelay: "C'est un très bon sujet à qui il est temps que vous fassiez faire un cran" (a step up). Jean Bart was then twenty years of age.

THE RAMPARTS, GRAVELINES (NORD)

must be systematic organization. So far privateering had only been carried out by individuals "peu intelligents et de peu de moyens". Moreover, they were harassed by legal chicanery in the award of prizes, checked by vexatious restrictions, and no help was given by the State. The consequence was that at S. Malo and Dunkerque, privateering had been given up. It should now be re-organized, and recognized by the State. Vauban had such belief in this policy that, like the gentlemen adventurers of Elizabeth's time, he invested money in it. He told Pontchartrain[1] in September 1695 that he had 1,000 écus invested in the ships of M. de Nesmond, another 1,000 écus in those of M. de Gennes, with two other smaller investments, and that it was only in the last winter that he had thought of making money by privateering. After the defeat of the French in the battle of La Hogue in 1692, organized privateering became an essential part of French maritime policy, and men such as Jean Bart, Forbin, Dugay-Trouin, Saint Pol, Pointis and others did much injury to Dutch and English trade, by their raids on convoys of merchantmen.

In 1699 Vauban drew up a long mémoire on the means of re-establishing the French Colonies in America. It seems that the French Colony was doing badly. It had from the first been one of the main aims of Colbert's policy to develop the trade and commerce of France. In 1664, he had established the "Compagnie des Indes Occidentales" with a monopoly of trade "dans les isles et terre firme d'Amérique". But the French Colonists in Canada protested against this monopoly, and Colbert had to withdraw it. In 1672 the Company's trade was limited to negroes and cattle, and in 1674 the Company was suppressed. After this fiasco, the King took control of the Colonies, the precedents of the Constitution of France were to be followed, with slight concessions to local

---

[1] Pontchartrain, much against his will, had succeeded Seignelay at the Ministry of Marine in 1691. He told the King that he knew nothing of naval matters, but the King insisted, on the ground that that he trusted Pontchartrain's zeal and honesty, but with the determination to keep the direction of the Marine in his own hands.

custom. The King assured the Colonists that he regarded them as "presque ses propres enfans", and Colbert urged that the only method of developing these waste lands was "La Peuplade". Every year girls, "saines et fortes", were sent out to Canada to increase the population, and Colbert informed the Governor[1] "nous préparons les cent cinquante filles, les cavales, chevaux entiers, et brebis, qu'il faut faire passer en Canada," and soldiers who did not marry one of the girls within fifteen days of their arrival were severely punished. Colbert had intended to exterminate the Iroquois, but he changed his mind, and decided that it was best to civilize them, "de façon de composer avec les habitants du Canada un même peuple"; but this did not suit the Jesuits in Canada at all. They had converted many of the natives, and wished to keep them apart, and to save them from the snares of the white man, and more particularly from his traffic in brandy. Louis XIV referred the matter to his Confessor, the Archbishop of Paris, who of course decided in favour of the Jesuits. Colbert also insisted on the necessity of keeping the Colonists together, but so far as possible he was ready to let them work out their own salvation, and he dreamt of building up a vast colonial Empire. The War with Holland put an end to his dreams, and in 1675 he had to inform the Governor of the French Colony that the King could no longer help him. The Colony was still in its infancy. In 1663 the number of settlers was 2,500; in 1680, with the help of the soldiers and the "filles saines et fortes" the population had increased to 9,400, and was still increasing, but very slowly, and the Colony was doing badly. Owing to his interminable wars, Louis could do nothing for Canada and the Isles; and it was this that induced Vauban in 1699 to write his "Mémoire: Moyen de rétablir nos Colonies de L'Amérique et de les accroître en peu de temps", and to place them "Sur un meilleur pied que celui de passé, qui a été fort languissant et incertain". Vauban's proposals were drastic, but except that he went into minute detail he, in

[1] Lavisse, *Hist. de France*, VII, I, p. 257.

fact, repeated the essential points of Colbert's policy. Colbert had been beaten by the Jesuits and the King's timidity, so Vauban's first proposal was to clear the air by expelling "les moines" (the Jesuits) from America. He would allow a few mendicant friars to remain, but he had no use for the Clergy of endowed establishments; they were, he said, "incommodes, intéressés, et suspects". He did not believe in the conversions of which they boasted, and said that all the clergy cared for was to enrich themselves. He would buy them out, and devote their property to establishing a seminary for the training of secular priests, who would make "bons Curés et Vicaires de paroisses", and would be paid and employed by the State. One or two Bishops should be appointed to look after the Clergy, "gens de bien, et d'un vertu Apostolique", also paid by the State "à fin de ne les point embarasser de temporel, et que toute leur application soit occupée au Spirituel, qui est justement ce qui doit remplir leur vocation".

Having thus disposed of the Clergy and got rid of the Jesuits, Vauban turned to the financiers and the monopolists. These he would simply suppress, and "laisser le commerce libre". At this point Vauban leaves the organization of the existing Colonies, and proceeds to sketch out a programme for the foundation of new ones, for Vauban's real interest was with new settlements. Here his proposals are very precise and read like some story of adventure in savage lands, with Red Indians with tomahawks and feathers lurking in the background to scalp the unwary settler. Every step was to be considered and provided for in advance. First of all, competent engineers should be sent to examine and report on the air, water, and the fertility of the soil, on possibilities of trade, on sites for forts, on rivers and how far they were navigable, on water power for mills, on forests for timber, ground suitable for grazing, vineyards and orchards and any other details that they noted. After the Engineers had reported, 5 or 6 battalions of soldiers were to be sent out, including as many "gens de métier" as possible, bricklayers, carpenters, joiners, smiths and so on, with extra pay. The battalions were to be relieved every five years, but those who wished to stay should be allowed to do so and given the land they had cleared. After a fortnight's rest each battalion was to go to its appointed place, and select the site for the camp which later on was to become the town, fortify it with a rampart, parapet and ditch, and build huts within the enclosure, ample space being left for future buildings.

This work would take three to four months, and after this the troops were to clear the ground round the camp. Vauban calculated that 200 to 250 men working 8 hours a day would clear 300 acres in a year, and at the end of five years the ground so cleared would be divided up among the troops according to ranks. Gardens were to be made, and within the enclosure a church, "Eglise provisionelle"; magazines, mills and a hospital were to be built, all machinery necessary, and all arms, munitions and tools of the trade were to be brought from France, and Vauban gives a statement of the provisions necessary for the first year, and a list of the artisans and tradesmen to accompany the troops:

Ironmongers .	10 to 12	Carpenters .	30
Smiths . .	6 or 7	Sawyers .	10–12
Armourers .	ditto	Joiners . .	8–10
Charcoal-		Gardeners .	3–4
burners .	20	Bakers . .	5–6
Stone-cutters .	15–20	Cutlers .	3–4
Masons .	20–30	Tailors and	
Bricklayers and		Drapers .	1–2
tilers .	5–6	Apothecaries .	1–2
		Doctors .	1

Having thus provided for the start of the colony, Vauban drew up regulations for its conduct.

(1) No one was to go more than 10–12 leagues from the Camp without leave.
(2) Theft was to be punished by death.
(3) Blasphemy or sacrilege and

(4) Drunkenness, assault, fighting, murdering and seduction were criminal offences.
(5) No slander.
(6) No cowardice, sedition or bad house-keeping.
(7) No cattle to be killed for meat during the first year except in cases of urgent necessity. The troops were to find provisions by hunting, shooting and fishing.
(8) The guard never to be relaxed, and no slackness allowed.
(9) No trade to be allowed except in the produce of the country.
(10) Young people to be married at the age of 18–20. No unmarried people to be allowed in the colony.

Regulation No. 1 seems odd. If it was necessary to start the settlement as a fortified camp one would have thought 10 to 14 leagues far too great a distance for settlers to be allowed to wander. Vauban, following Colbert's lead, seems to have been afraid of his colony breaking up and the settlers straying "en découvertes de nouveaux pays, ou par s'écarter dans les bois comme ils font présentement à la chasse de castors."[1] He considered it essential to the success of his colony that it should hold together as a unit, and if further settlements were made, they should be made not by individuals, but by bodies of settlers protected not merely by palisades, but by "remparts et fossés fraisés, et palissadés, et même plantés de haies vives sur les bermes." Without these precautions new colonies will be "toujours faibles et languissantes comme elles sont présentement, et en état d'être opprimées au premier jour par les Anglais, qui par le bon ordre qu'ils tiennent, accroissent fort en ce pays-là, où dans peu ils deviendront très puissants". Here, as in many other instances, Vauban's prescience was amazing.

Regulation No. 9 is characteristic. Vauban had a profound distrust of financiers and monopolists. They cared

---

[1] Beavers.

for nothing but their profit, and the only companies he
would allow would be co-operative associations of the
inhabitants, to which any could be admitted who could
put up 1,000 livres, but for the first thirty years all companies were to be run by Le Roi and nobody else. Vauban
had no use whatever for the capitalist who battened on
the labours of others, an admirable sentiment but quite
impracticable, as it is impossible to develop any under-
taking without capital, but Vauban was a strange mixture
of the idealist who dreamed dreams of the future, and the
realist ready to prescribe to the last detail the means of
realizing his dreams. He wished to banish "le luxe et
toute superfluité, de même que les moines rentés et la
chicane". The combination of the two is notable.
Vauban would expel the financiers, close the monasteries
and convert them into seminaries and colleges. I suspect
that whatever he might profess to be, Vauban was at
heart a Huguenot, at any rate he had a healthy dislike of
the intrigues and political influence of the Jesuits at the
Court. As to taxation, he would absolutely prohibit "la
taille" as a "peste publique" and the source of "mille
friponneries", a favourite word with Vauban.

Vauban proposed to deal with S. Domingo and "les
autres îles de l'Amérique" in the same way. France should
come to terms with the English on the island of St.
Christopher, and should establish a naval station at the
mouth of the Mississippi. He gives eight reasons to show
that these colonies would cost the King little and be of
immense value to France. Their establishment would be
a glorious action, even "une action pieuse et méritoire
devant Dieu", and what could be finer "que de peupler
un grand vaste et bon pays vide, qui n'est rempli que de
nations exécrables pour le plupart qui vivent en bêtes, ne
connaissent point de Dieu, et n'en veulent point con-
naître, qui n'ont ni foi ni loi, et qui n'occupent pas la
centième part de ce pays"? For once in a way Vauban's
large humanity was at fault. The native was not to be
considered; he was to be exterminated. Was Vauban
trying to conciliate Mme. de Maintenon, who at this time

was doing her best to exterminate the Huguenots of the Cevennes?

Whatever may be thought of the proposals of Vauban, "homme toujours occupé de projets les uns utiles, les autres peu practicables et tous singuliers",[1] it must be admitted that he had large and far-seeing ideas. Undaunted by Niagara, he wanted his colony to extend up the S. Lawrence to the Great Lakes; he hoped to find iron, and was very sanguine as to the growth of population. He calculated on four children to each couple and their descendants, and on this basis estimated that instead of the present population[2] of 14,000 in thirty years (1730) it would have increased to 100,000; and that by 1970 the population would be 25,600,000. Vauban loved these gigantic figures, as we have already seen in his "La Cochonnerie". People, he concluded, might say his scheme was chimerical; but one must look ahead. Unless colonies such as he proposed were founded, "cette grande et riche partie du monde que est l'Amérique", with all its possibilities of wealth, where "le soleil est beau et bon, et le climat le même que celui de la vieille France", this America will fall into other hands. Yet it was "incomparablement meilleur que le Pérou où on manque de pain au milieu de l'or et de l'argent." Nothing, Vauban said, could be more glorious, more right, less costly and more worthy "d'un grand Roi" than the establishment of such colonies as Vauban proposed. Vauban's forecast was curiously exact. America has fallen into other hands, and Canada and America are perhaps the richest lands on the face of the earth, but no notice seems to have been taken of Vauban's warning. France was sinking deeper and deeper into financial difficulties. Any attempt to balance the budget had long been abandoned, and Desmaretz, Controller-General of Finances in 1708, actually recommended the State to declare itself bankrupt. When Louis XIV died the State is said to have been in debt to the amount of over two milliards of livres.

---

[1] Voltaire, *Siècle de Louis XIV*.　　　　　[2] In 1699.

EARLY in his career, Vauban had noted the unsatisfactory
state of the French Army, and it seems that Louis XIV
himself was aware of its want of organization and serious
deficiencies. In 1670, Louvois told Vauban, "Le Roi n'a
rien dans la tête pour l'année que vient, que la perfection
de ses places et de son infanterie." Unfortunately, the
King's zeal was only a flash in the pan, for it took Vauban
another thirty years to obtain even such a rudimentary
Corps of Engineers as he had persistently asked for. As
for the Infantry, Vauban said at the end of the eighteenth
century: "Il y a plus de 35 ans que j'ai commencé à
m'apercevoir qu'il y avait de la défectuosité dans notre
infanterie", and he added that not only it was bad but
that it was steadily getting worse, and his criticism was
soon to be justified by the series of defeats that the French
suffered at the hands of Marlborough and Prince Eugene,
Blenheim (1704), Ramillies (1706), Oudenarde (1708) and
Malplaquet (1709). Vauban now drew up an elaborate
programme of reforms, with the title of "Moyen d'amé-
liorer nos troupes et de faire une infanterie perpetuelle et
très excellente."[1] War, he says, has for its father "interest", for its mother "ambition", and for its kinsmen all
the worst passions of man. War, Vauban continues, is
inevitable, and so has grown up "le grand art de la guerre
. . . et c'est de cet art terrible, que j'entreprendrai
d'écrire, non en termes élégants ni polis, car je n'ai point
d'étude et fort peu de lecture, mais en homme à qui

---

[1] Extracts are given in Rochas d'Aiglun, *Vauban*, II, pp. 265–345. The
original contained 530 folio pages. An edition published in 1707 contained
722 pages. In addition to this Vauban wrote separate papers on raising three
troops of artillery, and a corps of sappers (1691).

50 années d'expérience et d'application, joint à beaucoup de reflexions, ont appris quelque chose." The French, he says, love war when it can be sustained with honour, and their courage and intelligence make them well fitted for war; but the state of the Army is rotten. Service in it is disliked; there are constant desertions, and it is becoming ever more difficult to find a sufficient number of recruits for the multifarious campaigns of the King. Enlistment by force, and the press gang, caused serious discontent in the country because by taking able-bodied men, it deprived large numbers of women and "pauvres enfants" of the means of livelihood, so that a "grande quantité sont morts de famin et de misère, et plusieurs autres ont été réduits à la mendicité, pour avoir été privés de ceux qui pouvaient les faire subsister". Here, as always with Vauban, care for the weak and helpless is a dominant motive. Deserters were very severely punished, either sent to the galleys or hanged, and much as Vauban hated it, except for these punishments "tous déserteraient, et les armées seraient dépeuplées". Vauban himself had seen cases in the Nivernais, of young men burning their hands or pretending to be imbecile, in order to escape military service. There were, said Vauban, two ways of dealing with this state of things; one was to reform the methods of enlistment, the other to improve the pay and the conditions of service. It seems that when Vauban wrote there was no organized system of enlistment. Officers raised men for their regiments any way they could, there was no State supervision and the methods of recruiting were unjust and often brutal. In future, Vauban urged, recruiting should be the work of "le Roi", that is the State, carried out under proper control and on a definite system. The first step was to take a census of the population, house by house, in order to arrive at the number of men eligible for service, after the exemption of clergy, nobility on service, sailors, and lawyers, except an infinite number of "avocats" and "petits praticiens de village qui ne méritent pas exemption", and of widows and old men, "véritables mendiants"

and the halt, the maimed and the blind. The results of the census were to be divided into districts, and checked every five years, and an example is given from Vezelay how this should be done. The age for enlistment to be 18 to 45, newly married men to be exempt for the year following their marriage, and two brothers not to be drawn by lot at one and the same time. The enlistment should be for three years, after which the soldier should be given a free discharge, and provision for return to his home, and should be exempt from further drawings, till the whole canton had been drawn, but he should be allowed to enter for another term of service if he desired to do so. Vauban who loved details suggested that after the names of the recruits had been drawn, there should be a solemn ceremonial. The new recruits were to be placed in ranks by the sergeants under any flags available, and were to be presented to the Commissary, who would desire them to take the oath of service to the King, swearing by "la part que vous prétendez en Paradis" to serve him well and faithfully. After this the recruits were to be distributed to their several companies, given "une gratification sur la main" by their officers and introduced to the old soldiers of the companies. Vauban gives a model interview between the recruit and the Commissary at which the recruit was to swear (1) that he would serve the King faithfully; (2) would not desert; (3) would obey his officers; (4) inform them of any one hostile to the King's service; (5) would not steal; (6) or desert his officer in battle; (7) or suffer them to be despoiled if killed or wounded.

Next came the reforms of pay, service and equipment. In future the pay of the infantry soldier should be 6 sous a day,[1] with a "sol d'utensile", that is, the right of demanding fire and light, and a pot for their soup from the people on whom they were billeted. Regular barracks seem to have been very rare, though Vauban had constructed blocks of barracks round the central Place in the

[1] Voltaire says that in his time the pay of the soldier was still only 5 sous a day, a rate of pay dating from the time of Henri IV.

citadel at Lille, and in 1679 Colbert had instructed Vauban to prepare a standard design for barracks for cavalry and infantry, but Vauban says that the soldiers were herded together like pigs in a sty. Vauban hoped that if reasonably treated the soldier would learn to respect himself and his uniform. Accordingly he suggested a uniform, a coat of red cloth of Berry, with red buttons, breeches to match, a leather waistcoat, a hat with silk borders, and mark of rank sewn on the coat, but the really important matter was the soldier's arms. The troops of the time were armed with musquets, a very clumsy weapon fired by lighting the powder with a "mêche", tinder kept in a metal case. The objection to it was that the mêche did not always start the powder, and that in night attacks when it did, it gave away the position to the enemy. Vauban in a letter to Louvois written from Lille in 1687 called the musquet "la plus fautive" of all arms for these reasons, and also because it was difficult to aim with, the more so as the latest fad, "sottise très dangereuse", was to teach the soldier to place the butt "contre l'estomac pour avoir meilleure grace". Musquets were, Vauban said, no more use than slings. The men hated them, and they ought to be armed with "fusils", flint-locks on the model of those used by the buccaneers, with barrels 4 ft. 6 in. long, and bayonets, triangular in section, which could be taken off at will, and were fitted to the sockets, which Vauban had invented, so that they did not interfere with the fire. So armed one company of "fusiliers spontonniers"[1] would be worth two or three armed with pikes and musquets, and could defy cavalry far better with these, than with the "chevaux de frise" (calthrops) of the Germans. Each soldier should carry the charges of powder in special pockets, and all pikes and musquets should be withdrawn. He also proposed that officers as well as privates should be armed with fusils, it being absurd that those who were

---

[1] The bayonet when detached would be a "sponton", a half pike or dagger. Readers of Casanova will recollect the famous "sponton" made from an old bolt with which he made his escape from the Leads in Venice.

probably the best shots in the regiment should take no part in the fray.[1]

Vauban was greatly interested in armaments of all sorts, and was constantly making experiments with cannons and mortars. In 1672 he invented a light buckler made of some pliable stuff, not steel, which he calls "ouate" (wadding) which would be proof against bullets and weigh not more than 4½ pounds. He seems to have anticipated those stuffed linen waistcoats invented in the late war, which were said to be bullet proof. In the same year (1672) he reported to Louvois the results of his experiments with mortars 12 in. to 13 in. in diameter, which fired 30 stones, each the size of one's fist, a distance of 400 yards with such violence that the smallest of the stones buried themselves 6 in. in the ground. In 1686 he was making experiments with mines at Valenciennes, and at another time was trying the effect of hollow bullets. I have already referred to his "tir à ricochet".

Vauban offered no advice on cavalry, saying that he knew nothing about horses, though he must have spent much of his life on horseback. In his later years he travelled in a sort of sedan chair, slung on two mules, one in front and one behind, with a groom to lead them. He did, however, advise against the heavy horses used by the Germans. Unlike Frederic the Great, who would have no Grenadier less than 6 ft. tall, Vauban did not believe in size. "Rien n'est plus trompeur, et quand je vois toiser un homme, il me semble voir un nouveau marchand, ignorant son métier, qui achète à faux poids et à fausse mesure sans s'appercevoir." His experience was that big men had too much weight to carry, and he preferred men of average height and even small men. People, he said, should not be deceived by looks. "Le courage ne se mesure pas par la figure." Vauban gave no suggestion as to horses, but gives full particulars of arms, equipment, numbers and cost of light cavalry. The cost

---

[1] Vauban gives the complete number of a regiment as 1,842. This included a colonel, lieut.-colonel, a major and two aides, 32 captains, 32 lieutenants and sub-lieutenants, and 96 sergeants. The regiment was divided into 3 battalions, each costing 111,323 livres per annum.

of a regiment of cuirassiers he put at 297,756.6 livres per annum.

When it came to the artillery Vauban was on familiar ground. "L'Artillerie a tant de part dans les sièges, soit pour attaquer ou défendre, que j'ai un devoir ajouter le mémoire qui suit à ce traité." Writing soon after Louvois' death, he says the late M. Louvois in his early days knew nothing about artillery, and used to appoint as Grand Masters of Ordnance distinguished people who also knew nothing about it, but who were agreeable to the King, subservient to Louvois, and quite content to leave everything to him, so long as they enjoyed the emoluments and privileges "attachés à cette belle charge". The result was that the artillery of the French Army was inefficient. At Fleurus, for example, in 1690, after the first discharges, the cannons were silent, because there was nobody there who knew how to serve the guns. The artillery were treated as inferior to the infantry, whereas in Germany "où la discipline est très bien réglée" the practice was for Lieut.-Generals of the Artillery to issue their commands to the officers of the Infantry and Cavalry. The officers of Artillery in the French Army were badly paid, and the keepers of magazines were "gens de bas aloi", not to be trusted and easily bribed. There was a serious deficiency of skilled mechanics, and even of gunners, so that "on est obligé de se servir des soldats maladroits, qui ne savent par quel bout prendre un levier." There should be at least three regiments of artillery, the men specially trained as gunners with increased pay, the officers to have the same ranks and privileges as other officers of the Army. It is rather surprising to find that in the time of Louis XIV the artillery were treated as an inferior branch of the French Army.

The lack of any body of trained engineers to which I have already referred was another serious weakness in in the Army. Vauban had long pleaded for the establishment of an independent company of sappers and miners, with trained engineer officers. Louvois had promised this, but nothing had been done since his death, and in 1705

Vauban was still asking for his company. He wanted a company of 188 men with 12 sergeants, 12 corporals, 4 lieutenants, 4 sub-lieutenants and a captain to command the company. The men were to be chosen from among the bravest and most intelligent, and were to be specially trained. In view of their special knowledge, and the fact that they would run exceptional risks on service, Vauban asked for higher pay. The Captain, for example, should receive 10 livres a day; a lieutenant 5, and the total cost of the company he estimated at 50,000 livres per annum.

Vauban added a curious note on the Hôtel des Invalides erected from the designs of Liberal Bruant by Louis XIV in 1675 "pour les estropiez vieux et Caducs". The idea of the Invalides, Vauban says, was a good one, but badly carried out. The seven or eight hundred inmates were kept under severe discipline, and wandered about the building with nothing to do. Nobody in the provinces had ever heard of it, so that this establishment, though "juste, preux et très raisonnable de soi . . . ne fait pas tout l'effet qu'on en doit attendre". As for the "grand et beau dôme qui a tant coûté" it was no more use to the Invalides than a fifth wheel to a chariot.[1] Vauban suggested that the "Invalides" should be divided into three classes: (A) "parfaits", those who could do nothing at all, to receive 15 sous a day; (B) "imparfaits" who could do light work, wear the uniform, go to their homes and even marry, to receive 5 sous; (C) "Invalides de service" who might do garrison duty at 4 sous a day.

The mémoire on the reorganization of the Army concludes with some trenchant reflections on the appointment of officers. Vauban thought that officers might well be promoted from the ranks. "Dieu le Père et le Créateur de tous les hommes se moque de nos distinctions. . . . Tous les hommes sont les mêmes devant lui." Therefore where you find merit, take it to your heart, and pay

---

[1] In 1680 Bruant was superseded by J. H. Mansart, who tacked on the costly Church of the Dôme to the end of the Church of the Invalides already built from Bruant's designs. By the year 1695, a sum of nearly 3 million livres had been spent on the Church of the Dôme—another example of the insensate extravagance of "le Roi soleil" and his unscrupulous advisers.

no heed to wealth or social position. Vauban was not in the least impressed by the pretensions of the Court. Opportunities of promotion should be open to all ranks, and there should be graduated awards for merit open both to privates and officers. To a private, for example, for having killed two or three men in one action, saved the flag, saved an officer's life, captured the enemy's flag, been the first to scale the scarp or enter the city, or taken a boat by swimming when under fire. [Vauban recollected an exploit of his early days when serving under Condé.] The awards were to be made to officers, for such actions as the discovery of a spy or a plot, stopping a mutiny, surprising the enemy's miners and killing their leading man as he emerged from the mine. The awards were not to be given to officers above the rank of captain, in order not to tempt general officers to risk their lives. Officers should be the sons of gentlemen of small means, in order that having no private resources, they should take their careers seriously, and they should be "de bonnes mœurs, de bon corps, et de bon esprit". They should enter as cadets at the age of eighteen, and during their first year should carry a pack and arms and march on foot "comme les autres soldats". Vauban gives a list of the years for each rank in a service of thirty-two years, ending up with the rank of "Maréchal de France" if the officer ever got so far. His aim, Vauban says, was to make officers soldiers at all points. He should have some knowledge of "Belles lettres", for the soldier who knows nothing but his sword is a dull dog and no use. Therefore, instead of wasting their time on gambling, wine and women "qui leur font perdre un temps infini et en ruine la plus grande partie", they should study, have some knowledge of mathematics and of history, especially of the treaties of the last 300 years, and be able to draw. With some such reasonable knowledge when it comes to drafting treaties they will be able to dispense with lawyers, "gens de robe" for, Vauban says, there is a natural antipathy between soldiers and lawyers. The officer should not waste his money on eating and drinking and dressing up.

It was absurd that a lieutenant on a pay of 300 livres a year, should spend thirty louis on dress, simply in order to cut a figure and be like other people. "Il n'y a si petit officier que ne soit aujourdhui endentellé. . . . La Luxe s'empare des gens de guerre . . . comme des gens de cour, et Dieu veuille n'aille pas jusqu'à nous prétintailler[1] et mettre du rouge et des mouches" (patches). People, he continues, ate and drank far too much, they were fatter than they used to be and aged earlier, and the only way to suppress "ce vilain vice" was to condemn gluttony "comme un vice abominable", and to refuse to employ those who were guilty of it on any serious business.

Vauban saw no sufficient objection to soldiers marrying. He would rather they did not, but he admitted that married soldiers served well and deserted less. Besides, they helped to increase the population of the State, a point to which Vauban attached great importance. He would not tolerate blasphemy. There were young men devoted to wine and women, who suggested that they were atheists, hoping to pass as "esprits forts et des gens intrépides". Vauban would simply expel them from the regiment with ignominy, together with all "fripons et faussaires". St. Paul had said, "Have no fellowship with the unfruitful works of darkness, but rather reprove them." Vauban would simply have thrown them out of the camp. Yet he adds: "Il y aurait trop de monde à punir, il vaut mieux hasarder quelque chose et en demeurer là." Those who deny all religion seldom carry through to the end and repent too late. Besides this, not all officers have these vices. There are others, Vauban says, who by their virtues could give points to "les Capucins les plus réformés". Vauban's irony is refreshing.

---

[1] One of Vauban's own particular words. I take it to mean to prink oneself.

BY the end of the seventeenth century Vauban was recognized not only in France, but everywhere in Europe, as the first military engineer of his time. In 1689 a small book by M. Le Chevalier de Cambray, entitled *Manière de fortifier de M. de Vauban* was published at Amsterdam by Pierre Mortier, and dedicated to Frederic III, Elector of Brandenburg, the sworn enemy of France, who a few years later with the help of William of Orange and the Elector of Bavaria was to capture Namur (1695). Mortier the publisher said in an introduction: "Le nom de M. de Vauban fait tant de bruit, et tout le monde est si convaincu de son habilité dans l'architecture militaire", that he could assure his readers of the merits of this work by the Chevalier de Cambray who was, he says, one of Vauban's most brilliant pupils. The book would, he says, be of great service at the present moment, when all Europe was armed, and his Electoral Highness was on the eve "d'aller renverser les remparts de l'ennemi qui opprime si injustement l'Allemagne, et qui a porté le fer et feu" in the Palatinate. This little book seems to have been pirated in England, for in 1691 a book entitled *The New Method of Fortification as practised by M. de Vauban* was published by Abel Swall at the sign of the Unicorn in S. Paul's churchyard. A second edition appeared in 1693, but Vauban himself of deliberate purpose refused to publish anything; he had an intense dislike of dogmatic systems, and he himself would have been the first to repudiate the classification of his work into three distinct manners which ingenious French writers have attempted. Fontenelle who was his contemporary says definitely: "Il a toujours dit, et il a fait voir par sa pratique, qu'il n'avoit point de manière. Chaque place différente, lui en fournissoit une nouvelle, selon les différentes circonstances de grandeur, de sa situation, de son terrain." Vauban began with the ordinary methods of fortification and attack in use at the time, but his clear-headed practical sense and amazing eye for ground enabled him to develop these methods far beyond anything dreamt of by his predecessors. All through his career he had made notes on attack and defence, but it was only near the end of his life that he put these together in a mémoire, entitled "Traité des fortifications. Attaque et Défense des places", but he gave express directions that this was not to be published; it was to be treated as a State document, entrusted only to officers in command and returned by them to the Ministry of War.

Both in attack and defence, Vauban made a great advance on the methods of the first half of the seventeenth century. Hitherto the advance to a fort had been made by zigzag trenches, leading to temporary screens of gabions for the attack. Vauban introduced lines of trenches parallel to the place to be attacked. Instead of flimsy screens of gabions, he built up solid screens with steps for firing. He made the artillery much more effective by his "tir à ricochet". In defence, he improved the strength of fortified places by his skilful disposition of tenailles, ravelins, demilunes, hornworks, and other outworks varying them according to the nature of the ground, and also by his use of bastioned towers and cavaliers on the ramparts, and occasionally by means of a double enceinte such as that which he suggested for the defence of Paris; but no account can do justice to all that Vauban did in the service of France, to his inexhaustible resource, and his amazing instinct—genius, in fact—for doing the right thing in ever-varying conditions.

In his treatise on attack Vauban dwells on the necessity of having trained engineers constantly present in the trenches, and of personal reconnaissance. There was, he says, no difficulty in getting plans of most of the important fortified places in Europe. "La plupart même sont imprimés et se vendent dans les boutiques des graveurs et librairies de Paris," and he might have added Amsterdam, and these were the source of the admirable engravings in the *Atlas Portatif* and similar publications, but knowledge acquired from books was not enough; engineers must reconnoitre the ground, "afin de les (les places) pouvoir approcher et toucher, comme on dit, du bout du doigt". General officers should not be allowed to interfere with the engineers or override their plans of attack. If the King or royal Princes visit the trenches, special precautions must be taken for their safety. All the troops should stand to arms, and a handy little horse should be provided for the King, as it would be too far for him to walk round the trenches, but such visits should only be made on really important occasions. In the earlier years of his reign, Louis XIV was fond of appearing in person at sieges, no doubt at a respectful distance; and it is clear that he took an active interest in Vauban's plans, sometimes making suggestions for the attack. But the Royal visitors and their attendants were a great responsibility and they usually got in the way. Then follow 29 general maxims on the conduct of the attack. Nos. 3 and 4 say that there should always be three main lines of parallel tranches and that the trenches should not be opened till well advanced. Never attack a fort from a re-entering angle, as this exposes the attack to cross fire. No. 14 says, avoid direct attacks on account of the loss of life to which it would expose the troops. (This in Vauban's opinion was the mistake made by Cohorn who always wanted to rush things). No. 16 says, don't fire at the buildings inside the fortifications; it is a waste of ammunition to do so and involves the cost of rebuilding. No. 21 says, concentrate the attack on the citadel, because if the citadel is taken the town must be taken. Most of Vauban's maxims for the attack seem to a layman fairly obvious, but no doubt with the harum-scarum methods in use, Vauban thought it necessary to insist on the obvious.

Vauban opens his remarks on the "défense" with the comment that when he wrote his mémoire on the

"Attaque", he thought that nothing more would be necessary, "vu l'état florissant de nos affaires", but since then things had gone so badly that "je me suis résolu à faire ce traité, où j'ai mis, tout ce que l'expérience de plusieurs année d'application, la mémoire et l'imagination m'ont pu fournir de meilleur." The treatise on defence was in fact written in almost the last year of his life, on his return from Flanders in 1706. By way of introduction he says that defence depends not only on the strength of the fortification, but also on the skill and stout-heartedness of the garrison. Strong places were surrendered much too easily, "Car on ne manque jamais de prétexte pour excuser la médiocrité de leur résistance". He then gives his suggestions—"remarques importantes"—for the treatment of the garrison. Tobacco, for instance,—"cette manie"—is necessary for the soldiers. Nothing, he says, is better calculated "à désennuyer l'oisiveté, et à semousser[1] le grand besoin qu'ils ont de manger". Fasts, "jours maigres", should be observed, because men exposed to constant danger are likely to pay attention to their religion. But what is of vital importance is that there should be a standard calibre for guns, and that the guns should be of good quality. Cheap and bad guns were supplied by contractors, whose only object was "se mettre en état d'acheter tantôt une grosse terre, tantôt un charge considérable dans la robe (the law), et tantôt à faire bâtir de belles mansions, et enrichir ses croupiers, associés secrets, le tout au dépens du Roi et d'une infinité des braves soldats." In future all arms and munitions should be provided by State ordnance factories, and the guns should be of good metal from Conté, Dauphiné or Charleville, or from the Auvergne and the Ardennes. Sorties are undesirable. One man inside a fort is worth six outside[2] and in view of the heavy work of a siege, rations should be increased from $1\frac{1}{2}$ to 2 lb. of bread a day.

---

[1] Mitigate. One of Vauban's strange words, not to be found in ordinary French dictionaries.

[2] Vauban repeats this remark in his *Fortifications de la Campagne*, where he gives a "démonstration physique du mérite des retranchements, qui prouve qu'un homme bien retranché en vaut six qui ne sont pas."

Vauban is very severe on the governors of forts. These appointments are usually given or bought. The governors are usually senior officers who have never learnt their business, and spend all the time they can in Paris. When in residence they entertain freely, keep a table of cards, visit the neighbourhood and join parties for "la chasse". They seldom go the rounds, and at the end of ten years know no more about the fort than they did when first appointed, and when the fort is attacked, they do not know where they are. The general officers sent to the governor are no better. They know nothing about the fort, usually quarrel with the governor, and when the fort is captured each says it was the other fellow's fault— a slashing picture of incompetence in Vauban's best manner. There is no necessity, Vauban says, for the governor to keep open house, though he should be on good terms with his staff and treat them fairly. It would be well for him to keep a reserve of 2,000 to 3,000 pistoles, so that when on going the rounds he finds a soldier worn out with hunger, illness or fatigue he may give him something for himself. A few pence so given is worth a crown given them at their ease. These "petites libéralités" will endear him to the men. He might also help poor subalterns, who on their meagre pay have a very poor time, and Vauban thought this so important, that if the governor had not got the money, he advised him to borrow it for this purpose. The inhabitants of fortified towns should be told to store provisions for three months, and all wheat should be kept ground, as the mills might be put out of action during a siege. and if it was known that a place was to be besieged, all non-combatants should be sent away, "notamment les femmes, qui sont toujours criardes et jamais bonnes à rien"! Vauban had very old-fashioned views on women, and was not going to allow sentiment to interfere with the defence.

Vauban complained bitterly of non-resident governors and of the sale of these responsible posts to quite unworthy people, who had no experience and cared for nothing but their own advancement. As to bought appointments,

Vauban said, "On ne saurait trop condamner la conduite qui introduit la vénalité de ces charges." These posts should only be entrusted to veteran officers "choisis, expérimentés et reconnus capables de les défendre et de se donner toutes les applications nécessaires pour s'en bien instruire". Personal merit was the sole claim to be considered. In a service in which purchase was recognized, it was difficult to avoid "vénalité", but in the time of Louis XIV intrigue and bribery were rampant, and Vauban himself was one of the rare cases, of a man who started with no advantages, rising solely by merit to a great position.

However strong and however brave the defence, no place was impregnable. The attack must be defeated either by stronger force brought from a distance, or by Vauban's favourite device of an entrenched camp in the neighbourhood of the place attacked, from which diversions could be made and relief given to the garrison. Vauban gives a long list of historical precedents for the use of entrenched camps. They were used, he says, by Moses and the Israelites when they fled from Egypt, by the Greeks at the siege of Troy, by the Kings of Lydia and Assyria when attacked by Cyrus, by the Romans[1], by Attila, by the Huns, by "le faux prophète Mahomet", Tamerlane and others, and more particularly by Ziska, "Général de Hussites, qui de pauvre gentilhomme sans bien et sans appui, dans un âge déjà avancé et après avoir servi longtemps dans les plus bas emplois de la guerre, se fit un très grand capitaine". In this description of Ziska, Vauban might have been describing himself. He had a great admiration for Ziska, and devotes two pages to an account of his exploits and his fortified camp of Tabor in Silesia. He refers to the use of these camps by Alva in Flanders, by Henry IV at the battle of Arques, and in his own time, by Catinat at Suza, by Villars, who "l'an passé" stopped the advance of a strong Imperial force at Dillingen

---

[1] Curiously enough, Vauban does not mention Hyginus Gromaticus de Castrametatione. The sixteenth and seventeenth-century writers on fortification do not seem to have known of this treatise on the setting out of camps, though an edition was published at Antwerp in 1607.

on the Danube, and finally "en l'année 1705 qui est cette que j'écris ceci" by Prince Eugene at Salo on the Lago di Garda in Italy. Other instances follow, from the practice of the Turks and the "Mogols", and Vauban concludes with an apology which he had already made elsewhere: "Ce ne sont que des pensées ramassées pendant mes voyages et dans des temps fort éloignés les uns des autres." He had done his best to disentangle "débrouiller, ce chaos . . . Le style en est simple et grossier, mais il est d'un homme de guerre qui ne cherche qu'à se faire entendre." Then follow thirty-one maxims on the construction of entrenched camps. Maxim twenty-six advises that the only answer to cannon is cannon, "parce que l'un amuse l'autre, et que le cannon tire toujours à ce qui l'incommode". Elsewhere Vauban refers to the unanswerable argument of cannon. Fifteen obvious reasons are given why an army should entrench itself in a fortified camp. It was inevitable, Vauban says, that he should repeat himself, but the fact was that in the last few years of his life, Vauban was becoming just a little prolix, unable to resist the temptation to turn on his own work and pat himself on the back. There follows one of his curious calculations on the value of fire from behind a parapet. Taking as his unit half an hour, he says a soldier can fire thirty shots with a range of 400 yards in half an hour. Assume five men entrenched who will fire in the half-hour 150 shots, and assume an attack of thirty men advancing from a distance of 2,000 yards. The attack will take half an hour to cover this distance, during which the five men behind the parapet will have fired 150 shots from the steady rest of the parapet, as against the straggling fire of the advancing enemy. Assuming one shot in five fired from a rest to be fatal, all the thirty attacking will be wiped out. The argument seems to me inconclusive, for the thirty men advancing would have been out of range until they got within 400 yards of the defence, the thirty could hardly have missed everybody in their attack, and Vauban's five entrenched soldiers rather resemble Captain Boabdil's twenty gentlemen swordsmen, who were to kill everybody else without receiving a scratch.

Not content with his permanent entrenched camp, Vauban advocated a curious moving camp, known in Germany and Bohemia as a "Tabor, un mot allemand, bohémien, cosaque ou polonais. Peut-être un nom forgé à fantaisie qui signifie une clôture de chariots ou charrettes . . . une palissade roulante . . . un retranchement mobile, où l'infanterie trouve un bon couvert contre l'infanterie, et un obstacle invincible contre la cavalerie". The idea was that by ranging all the carriages and carts accompanying an army on the move on the flanks of the column, and fastening them by chains, the line would form a laager at night and would protect the flanks of columns by day. When stationary the carriages were to be filled with faggots and when on the march planks 12 in. wide and 2 in. thick were to be hung at the sides to protect the legs of the troops. This constituted the "Tabor". When on the march 200 to 300 men were to go in front to prepare the way, and cavalry were to reconnoitre the country. Vauban calculated that for a force of thirty-six battalions each 800 strong, 2,600 carriages and carts would be wanted. Vauban does not say whether these were to accompany the troops from the start, or be picked up on the way.[1] Altogether it seems rather a fantastic idea. Vauban says this device had not been adopted by France, though it was "la nation du monde qui se pique le plus de raffiner sur la guerre". One can hardly wonder that the French generals found it impracticable.

The brief summaries that I have given of the more important papers of the *Oisivetés* represent only part of Vauban's literary output, though "literary" is hardly the word, for Vauban expressly disclaims any sort of literary pretension. All that he wanted to do was to set down in writing some of the ideas with which his brain was teeming.

[1] The number of "chariots" (baggage wagons that accompanied troops on the march) seems incredible. Voltaire in his *Life of Charles XII of Sweden* says that Löwenhaupt, who was trying to join Charles XII before the battle of Pultowa in 1709, had with him some 15,000 men and 8,000 "chariots".

The wealth of detail with which he drove home his schemes, resulted in an immense mass of papers and pamphlets, and the *Oisivetés* represent only part of his multifarious activities. After Vauban's death his papers were scattered. Those on fortified places went to Paris and are now in the Musée de Génie. The rest of his papers were divided between his two daughters. His miscellaneous papers included subjects so remote as the immortality of the soul and the restoration of the Stuarts.[1]

---

[1] A full bibliography of Vauban's writings is given in Rochas d Aiglun's *Vauban*, I, pp. 81–100.

CHAPTER XVI

Vauban and the Académie des Sciences—Chamillart succeeds Barbezieux —Vauban a Maréchal de France—The siege of Brisach—Disappointment at not being given the sieges of Landau and Turin—La Feuillade's failure at Turin—The Order of Saint Esprit—Pensées.

IN 1699 the Académie des Sciences asked the King's permission to elect Vauban an honorary member of that body, and Fontenelle in his Eloge, says Vauban had brought down mathematics from the heavens to meet the needs of men. In the years 1699 to 1702 Vauban continued his reports on frontier places to Barbezieux and Le Peletier. These reports are not dry technical statements, but very vivid descriptions of the places visited. Here is one of Mont St. Michel. "Le Mont Saint Michel est une montagne ou plutôt un grand rocher qui s'élève en pain de sucre, sur le sommet duquel est une abbaye des Bénédictines très célèbre, qui a sa clôture particulière assez bonne, mais brouillée et confondue avec les autres bâtiments de l'abbaye et de la ville, qui est attachée au pied qui consiste en une grande rue en rampe et cinq ou six autres petites ruelles ou échappées, et quelque cinquante ou soixante maisons, tous cabarets merceries ou petits marchands faisant ou vendant collets, et écharpes de pèlerins garnis de coquillages. Les rampes de ce rocher sont occupées partie en jardinage partie en désert. Le bas est fermé par les escarpments du rocher, et partie par une ençeinte en maçonnerie flanquée de quelques tours et deux petits bastions." Here is the whole of Mont S. Michel, and it is a picture that only a man with an artist's eye for essentials could have drawn. I doubt if any official has ever written such readable letters as those that Vauban wrote to ministers of state. One would hardly find in an official letter addressed to the Admiralty or the War Office, such a passage as this, from his letter to Le Peletier, "Il faisait hier le plus beau de monde, et cette nuit voilà le sommet des montagnes tout blanc. C'est pourquoi il me faut hâter pour prévenir les mauvais chemins des montagnes de Provence qu'on dit être horribles." Barbezieux died in 1701; he was succeeded by Chamillart, whose chief qualifications were said to be his skill in billiards "et le zèle qu'il mit à gérer les affaires de Saint Cyr". Vauban, on hearing the news from Mme. de Grignan, the daughter of Mme. de Sévigné, saluted the rising sun and wrote to Chamillart, "Permettez-moi, s'il vous plaît, de m'en réjouir de tout mon cœur, en qualité d'homme de guerre et comme un homme pénétré et rempli d'estime pour toutes les excellentes qualités qui sont en vous." Chamillart turned out to be a complete failure.

Vauban was now seventy, but as indefatigable as ever. Boufflers proposed to attack Liefkenskoek, a fort on the left bank of the Scheldt about ten miles north of Antwerp. Vauban with three or four engineers made a reconnaissance of the place, and reported that he had got as near the place as was possible in the floods, but that Boufflers had better give up the idea of a siege. The fort was surrounded by water, and it was impossible to place any batteries for the attack, as "le paysage des environs de cet fort est terre de poldre, et par conséquent marécageux entrecoupé de fossés à watergang", and he reported that the Dutch were already opening their sluices. The report is interesting as showing the care with which Vauban laid out his schemes, and also his indomitable energy. In 1702 a rumour got about that the King was going to make a fresh batch of Maréchals de France. Vauban feared that he might be passed over again, so this time he wrote to the King himself, and reminded him that he was senior to most of the Lieutenant-Generals of France, and that his services were "mieux marqués que les leurs, dont je ne veux pour témoin que Votre Majesté". If on the other hand, the King decided not to promote him, he would accept the situation; indeed, it might be an embarrassing situation for a Field-Marshal to be constantly moving about among the workmen, but in the latter case he would ask His Majesty to state the reasons why he was not promoted, and to give him a house and garden in Paris. It was a bold letter to write to the King, but just a little wanting in dignity, and it might have been better if some one else had written this letter. The fact was that Vauban's nature was so frank and ingenuous that he could not keep silence; if an idea came into his head, it had to be set down then and there. Also Vauban unquestionably deserved promotion more than any man in France and he knew it, but he had to wait another year for his promotion to the rank of Maréchal de France. In January 1703 he was promoted with nine others, including Tallard who next year was to be defeated by Marlborough at Blenheim, taken prisoner, and for the next seven years confined very comfortably at Nottingham, where he amused himself with laying out a garden in 1706.[1] Saint Simon indulged in his usual caustic comments on the new Field-Marshals, always excepting Vauban, of whom he said: "Vauban, la valeur même, la bonté, la probité même, sous un extérieur rude grossier et brutal, était de bien loin le premier homme de son siècle dans l'art des fortifications et des sièges, et dans celui d'y ménager les hommes, et parmi cela la simplicité même." He adds that when the King informed Vauban that he intended to make him a "Maréchal de France", Vauban said that this honour was too great for him, and might lead to differences with other generals, but this characteristic modesty only increased the desire of the King "de la (vertu) couronner". This account hardly squares with Vauban's letter to the King of January 1702 reminding him of his merits. Yet Saint Simon's account may be true. Vauban for once may have played the courtier, and when he knew that he had won the prize, could afford to be modest. A few days after his promotion Vauban asked the King to let him take charge of the siege of Kehl (south-east of Trier), but the King said that this siege was not worthy of his rank, to which Vauban replied that he would willingly leave his Maréchal's baton behind the door, and help in any

---

[1] See *The Formal Garden in England*, Reginald Blomfield and F. Inigo Thomas, Appendix II, 240–41.

capacity, if the King would let him go, but the King would not hear of it, and said that he was reserving him to take charge of his grandson the Duc de Bourgogne,[1] who was now to take nominal command of the siege of Alt-Brisach on the upper Rhine. The reply of Louis XIV was disingenuous. He wrote privately to Chamillart that Vauban was not to be allowed to interfere with the Army, and that apart from the trenches, all orders were to be given by the "Maréchal de Tallard . . . sous le Duc de Bourgogne". The King was becoming suspicious and his judgment was failing, for Tallard was incompetent, and it was Vauban, as usual, to whom the capture of Brisach was due.

The trenches were opened on August 12. The garrison fought well, as Vauban admitted: "Les ennemis ont peu de canon, mais ils s'en servent fort bien et fort peu ou point de fautes." However, on September 6, after a three weeks' siege, Brisach was taken, thanks, Vauban says, to "la trahison du Rhin", which had made islands where they had no right to be, and so gave undue advantage to the attack. The siege of Alt-Brisach was brilliantly successful, but it was Vauban's last siege. He wrote to Chamillart asking to be appointed to "un siège considérable". Although he was advanced in years he was not, he said, going to acquiesce in retirement, and he would be grieved if he was not allowed "exercer mon petit ministère", as engineer. In September 1703 he assured Chamillart that he would not interfere in any way with the Generals, if appointed. "Au nom de Dieu, que le Roi ne se fasse aucune peine sur ma manière de servir. Je ne veux me mêler que de ce qui regardera la conduite des lignes et des attaques. Cela ne doit point donner de jalousie à son general auquel je serai aussi soumis que le pourrait être l'un de ses lieutenants-généraux pourvu qu'il me laisse exercer mon petit ministère, dont je l'estime assez le personnage pour ne le pas croire indigne d'application, je ne dis pas d'un Maréchal de France, je

---

[1] The grandson of Louis XIV, who died at Marly in 1712. There is a delightful little model of this prince on horseback in the Victoria and Albert Museum.

dis même d'un Prince des plus considérables . . .[If Vauban was not appointed] Le Roi me donnerait un chagrin, dont il ne me pourrait jamais guérir." But it was all in vain. Vauban's day was over; his colleagues of the higher command were jealous, and the King was no longer loyal to his devoted servant. Chamillart replied that the King appreciated his zeal, but that the entire command of the siege of Landau, which was now to be undertaken, would be given to Tallard, and that it was impossible to divide the command. Vauban, he said, would find nothing but "marques d'amitié et de satisfaction de la part du Roi"—the usual official formula; that the King desired his presence at Court, and was reserving him to add to the glory of the Duc de Bourgogne.

Vauban was not employed in 1704 and 1705, and the siege of Turin was entrusted to the Duc de la Feuillade, according to Saint Simon one of the most incompetent of men, and one of the worst scoundrels in France. Plausible and always on the make, he was, Saint Simon says, "un cœur corrompu à fond, une âme de boue". That a man such as this should be sent to command the French army at an important siege shows how far France had fallen since the days of Colbert and Louvois. Vauban was grievously disappointed. He had offered his services and said that he would stay two leagues away from the army in order to avoid any interference with La Feuillade. But it was no use. La Feuillade was Chamillart's son-in-law. In order to repair his shattered fortunes, La Feuillade had married Chamillart's elderly ugly daughter as his second wife, Chamillart having extracted from the King a dowry of 200,000 livres, and so by a scandalous abuse of patronage, La Feuillade was given the command of the siege of Turin. "Ce mariage a coûté cher à la France".[1] Vauban's plan was ignored, but in spite of this, at the personal request of Chamillart, he wrote a letter of advice to La Feuillade. Vauban, "le premier des ingénieurs, le meilleur des citoyens," as Voltaire[2] calls him, was ready to make any sacrifice in the King's service,

---

[1] Saint Simon.   [2] *Siècle de Louis XIV.*

and to place his vast experience at the disposal of this ridiculous man. He advised strongly against any direct attack "à la Cohorn". This was all very well in the case of "bicoques", little places such as Venlo, for instance, but unless a fort commanding Turin was taken, the place would never be captured. La Feuillade assured his father-in-law that he was one of those born to command, and wrote to the King that he took it on his head to capture Turin. The result was what was expected. La Feuillade failed and the siege was suspended. In 1706 it was decided to renew the attack and Vauban was consulted. Vauban who had once fortified Turin for the Duke of Savoy knew the strength of the place. He stated his requirements and expressed his readiness to undertake the siege, "pourvu qu'il fût le maître et de rien au delà", saying that he knew nothing of strategy or how to command an army in the field. The King and Chamillart said that Vauban's requirements were impossible. Vauban replied that he could not take Turin with less and declined. La Feuillade was again given the command and the assistance of an inferior engineer "aussi cette forte besogne roula tout entière sur deux novices fort ignorants et pour cela même fort entêtés."[1] Prince Eugene came to the rescue of the Duke of Savoy and the French were badly beaten on September 8, 1706.

The whole episode of the siege of Turin was characteristic both of Vauban and of Louis XIV and his ministers at the beginning of the eighteenth century. Vauban was ready to make any sacrifice to be allowed to serve the King. Neither his dignity, nor his health nor his personal interests, would be allowed to stand in the way of his duty, but the great days of Louis XIV were over, and the tragedy of his later years was closing in on him. His health was giving way, broken down by the excesses of his early days, and his judgment and will were failing. Frightened by Mme. de Maintenon and the Jesuits, he was becoming anxious about the future of his soul, and where once he had been resolute and direct, he was now faltering and

---

[1] Saint Simon.

uncertain. So though he had ready to hand the greatest military engineer of the time and perhaps of all time, and though he knew that he could trust Vauban absolutely to do what he said he would do, he allowed himself to be bamboozled by a self-seeking minister and a worthless braggart. Vauban must have sighed for the days when he could rely on the clear judgment of Colbert and the iron hand of Louvois.

In 1705 Vauban was made a chevalier of the Order of Saint Esprit, an honour which in Saint Simon's opinion should only be conferred on persons with at least fifteen quarterings, but Louis XIV when he wrote to Vauban now addressed him as "Mon Cousin". This, however, was not going to prevent Vauban from saying just what he thought. He was probably embittered by the persistent refusals to make use of his services, and finding himself with nothing to do, he fairly let himself go in his Thoughts of an Idle Man.[1] Here he said that he believed "les enfants naturels de nos rois"[2] were less dangerous to the State than Princes of the blood. If one looked back in history, "on verra que les Princes du sang des trois races qui ont régné dans ce royaume n'y ont guère moins cause de mal que les ennemis déclarés de l'état". He recommended that the royal princes should be given allowances paid quarterly, and should be kept under strict control "les reduisant simplement au nécessaire attendu que le surplus est inutile et à charge à l'état, et ne peut rien ajouter à leur grandeur qui réside tout entière dans leur naissance." There was no compromise here with royalties, and no beating about the bush. As for "les enfants naturels de nos rois," Vauban thought them less dangerous than Princes of the blood because they could never lay claim to the throne, but they were none the less mischievous owing to the high rank they assumed, their cost to the State, and because they rob those who have served

---

[1] "Pensées d'un homme qui n'avait pas grand' chose à faire."
[2] Louis XIV had 11 "enfants naturels": Louis, Conte de Vermandois, Marie Anne, Mdlle. de Blois; the Duc de Maine; Mdlle. de Nantes; Louise Françoise (Mdlle. de Blois), the Comte de Toulon, and four children who died young. For a genealogical list see Lavisse, *Hist. de France*, VIII, I, 442.

the State of the titles and preferments which they deserve. Also these "enfants naturels honorent trop des naissances naturellement condamnées par les lois divines et humaines . . . c'est à proprement parler couronner le vice et en faire parade, que de donner tant d'éclat à des naissances que la religion et la bienséance voudraient que l'on tint cachées." So much for the bastards of Louis XIV.

As for the King's Ministers, although they were slaves, they had far better opportunities of making their fortune than anyone else, and they abused their privileges without the least scruple. As for women, "Il n'y a rien de plus importun ni de plus dangereux que les femmes. Elles cabalent incessament ou elles demandent." Vauban would have nothing to do with priests, "moines" as he calls them—Kings who have them as their Confessors, entrust State secrets to "gens peu affectionnées" and "La France ne trouvera jamais son ancienne splendeur qu'en ruinant la moinerie" and "faisant divorce avec Rome, non en altérant la religion", or he might have added in persecuting dissent. He concludes his advice to Kings with "avis Chrétien de conséquence pour le salut." It should be the pious duty of the King, and of a Christian Prince who will have to render account to God for his administration of justice, to visit once a year all the prisons. He would find people long imprisoned for trifling and forgotten faults, or simply to gratify the animosity of some person in authority. "J'ai vu un Capucin à Saint Malo prisonnier depuis 25 ans et qui ne savait pas pour quoi il était là." He had seen women imprisoned in caves made in the piers of the Pont Saint Esprit,[1] only because they were Huguenots and refused to be converted, and other prisoners chained by a leg or an arm in narrow cells; three had died within the year and the others had gone mad. The Clergy accepted these things as a matter of course; only Vauban, the veteran soldier and engineer of fifty sieges, protested against this inhumanity.

---

[1] The famous thirteenth-century bridge over the Rhône some twenty miles north of Orange. See *Byways*, pp. 48–52.

CHAPTER XVII

MME. DE VAUBAN died at Bazoches on June 18, 1705, and was buried there the next day in the presence of "grande nombre de noblesse, officiers et plus de deux milles personnes de différents estats". So it would seem that this "haute et puissante dame", as the Register of Burials calls her, was a person of consideration in her own country, but the forty-five years since the day when Jeanne d'Osnay had married "le Capitaine Lieutenant Sebastien le Prestre, Sieur de Vauban," must have been rather a dreary time. She saw her husband only at very rare intervals, and through all these years she was buried in the country. Vauban was at Paris when she died, and was not present at her funeral, and there is no reference to her death in the correspondence of Vauban and Chamillart at the time. The inference I draw is that Vauban's attitude to his wife was conventional, and that his thoughts were elsewhere—on the frontier of France or his many projects of reform. He was now approaching the end of his life, and he decided that he must strike boldly for a policy that he believed to be absolutely necessary, if France was to escape disaster. The country was going from bad to worse. On August 4 1704, the English had taken Gibraltar, and nine days later the army of Louis XIV was defeated at Blenheim, with a loss of 27,000 killed and 13,000 prisoners. The siege of Turin had failed disastrously. Ramillies followed on May 23 1706, and Oudenarde and Malplaquet were to follow within two years of Vauban's death. In 1705 Saint Simon wrote "Hochstet (Blenheim), Gibraltar, Barcelone, la triste Campagne de Tessé, la révolte de Catalogne et des pays voisins, les misérables succès d'Italie, l'épuisement de France, celui de la France, que se faisait fort sentir, d'hommes, d'argent, l'incapacité de nos généraux, que l'art de la cour protègeait contre leur faute, toutes ces choses me fit faire des reflexions," and the result of his reflections was that peace should be made as soon as possible. Vauban had long come to the same conclusion, and in 1706 unlike Saint Simon who would not put his "reflexions" on paper, he drew up a "Projet de Paix assez raisonnable pour que tous les intéressez à la guerre présente en dussent être contents, s'il avait lieu, et qu'il plût à Dieu d'y donner sa bénédiction". France, he said, was in danger of utter failure from want of men and money, and also because "elle renferme dans soy un nombre infini de gens ruinées", who wished for any change anyhow, and a number of "Fanatiques ou plutôt enragés" who were only waiting for help from outside to start their revolt again.[1] The country was ruined. There was no discipline in the Army; enlistment was compulsory, and the soldiers deserted at the first opportunity; the officers were slack; there were too many general officers, and what there were, were no use. Robbery on the roads was common, and the only people who were doing well out of the war were the army contractors, their clerks and commis "qui se gorgent du sang de leurs concitoyens". Worst of all was the state of those who lived in the country, who like the "Bête de Somme" were laden with burdens too heavy to be borne, were reduced to skin and bones, and hoped for death before their natural terms. All this was the result of "le malheureux enchainement des guerres, qui n'ont fait depuis 40 à 50 ans que se succéder les unes aux autres". The French frontier was weak. France had been disarmed by the Treaty of Ryswyk and had not been able to make good since then. The country was in a very dangerous state, and those who held "le timon[1] de son gouvernement", ought to advise the King to recognize the position and make peace with his enemies, lest a worse thing befall him. Vauban gave a detailed list of the exchanges which might be made with the enemies of France. He would begin by surrendering all rights

[1] The Camisards in the Cevennes.   [2] The helm.

acquired by the will of the late King of Spain, and shows how his proposals would satisfy the Germans, the Dutch and others. As for the English "que nous ont fait la guerre de gayeté de cœur, très injustement et sans aucun prétexte raisonnable", they would be satisfied with the recognition of Queen Anne and the extension of their trade to India and America at the expense of Spain. He admitted that the King of Spain would not like it, but at any rate he himself would be safe. Vauban actually proposed that he should be sent to America to rule over the French colonies. "Le Maréchal de Vauban, le premier des ingénieurs, le meilleur des citoyens, homme toujours occupé de projets, les uns utiles, les autres peu praticables et tous singuliers proposa à la cour de France d'envoyer Philippe V régner en Amérique. Le Prince y consentit."[1] However, he never went, and finally succeeded in remaining on the throne of Spain. Vauban's mémoire was an able paper and bold even to audacity, but no notice seems to have been taken of it.

The war of the Spanish Succession continued and Vauban was given his last command on the north-west frontier with headquarters at Dunkerque, and a free hand was given by the King to "mon cousin" in a personal letter written from Marly, but in fact he was put on the shelf. Chamillart paid no attention to the letters that Vauban wrote him every few days, and the correspondence becomes colder and more formal. In October 1706 Vauban asked for leave, "car je ne fais plus rien ici, et le rhume commence à m'attaquer vivement", the beginning, in fact, of his final illness. He had not, he said, asked for the post that he held, "dont je me serais bien passé, vieux et incommodé comme je suis."[2] In November he seems to have taken the matter into his own hands and left for Paris.

---

[1] Voltaire, *Le Siècle de Louis XIV*, Ch. XXI, p. 296.

[2] Vauban had conducted 48 sieges and been wounded eight times. A list of sieges from 1653 to 1703 is given by Col. Lazard, *Vauban*, 344-5. Vauban had always suffered from a chronic cough, and once at least was very seriously ill, but the *Abrégé* says "Il a même eu le bonheur de n'être jamais malade quand il a été question de servir."

It was the end of a great career. In a few months he was to die, but he was yet to make one splendid effort on behalf of "le pauvre peuple", the distressed and toiling millions who from the first were dearer to him even than the King himself. Vauban had long meditated on the injustice and inequality of a taxation which ground the face of the poor, and the flagrant abuses of an administration by which the rich grew richer, and the poor poorer. The chaos and injustice of taxation in France in the time of Louis XIV was almost incredible. When Colbert died in 1683, the nett amount of revenue was 93 million livres, and the expenditure 109 millions—a deficit of 16 millions. In 1715 the receipts had dropped to 74 millions, and the expenditure had risen to 119 millions. The war budget, which in 1683 was 38 millions, was 100 millions in 1706, the year in which Vauban brought out his scheme of the "Dîme Royale". In 1697, after the end of the War of the League of Augsbourg, expenses were 219 millions, with receipts 81 millions. From the death of Colbert onwards, desperate efforts were made to meet the ever growing deficit—loans at high interest, conversions of interest, debasement of the coinage, the sale of offices and of patents of nobility[1]—but they were all in vain: the taxes were too heavy to be paid, their incidence was unequal, and there was a whole army of officials, tax farmers and collectors, whose sole concern from the Minister of Finance down to the lowest collector was to raise money somehow, part for the State, part for themselves. The officials were quite unscrupulous. Vauban says that the archers (police employed by the collectors) did not hesitate to remove the doors and beams of houses, after selling everything inside them, if the taxpayer did not pay. What made matters worse was that there were large exemptions. The Court, the clergy, officers of the law and finance, mayors and syndics were exempt from payment of the "Taille", and rich people

---

[1] In the year 1692 a sum of 1,788,000 livres was raised by the sale of "lettres de noblesse". No wonder that Vauban wrote a mémoire on "L'idée d'une excellente noblesse, et des moyens de la distinguer par les générations."

could buy exemptions by cash payments. The Gabelle, a tax on salt, was even more pernicious than the taille, which was a general tax on property. By the gabelle, everybody was bound by law to buy a certain quantity of salt, though some provinces were exempt. The tax was farmed out, and the tax farmers had the amount and disposition of the tax largely in their own hands. The inevitable attempt at smuggling salt was punished by the galleys, or death in case of armed resistance. In addition to the Taille and the Gabelle there were "aides", duties on merchandise of all sorts, octrois, tolls and customs which hampered trade, diverted money which should have gone to the State into the pockets of the tax farmers, and left the peasant and small owner in such abject poverty that some of them gave up their land altogether rather than pay these exorbitant taxes. Colbert and his successors were aware of the desperate state of the finances and of the deadly abuses of their administration, and had done their best to deal with them; but they had failed, and Vauban's "Dîme Royale" was a heroic if hopeless attempt to save the State from its impending ruin. He failed, and the French Revolution was inevitable.[1]

Nearly twenty years earlier Vauban had made a tentative draft of reform and sent it to Louvois, who treated it with contempt and ridicule and advised Vauban to destroy it, but that was not Vauban's way. An idea that had once formed itself in his mind was there to stay, and at length and in the last year of his life he drafted his famous proposal for "La Dîme Royale", a uniform method of taxation to be levied on all who could pay. This, while providing a revenue "suffisant pour tous les besoins de l'État, pourra donner lieu à la suppression de la Taille, des Aides, des douanes provinciales, des Dîmes du Clergé, et de toutes les autres impositions onéreuses et à charge du peuple de quelque nature qu'elles poussent être." Vauban says that his "vie errante" of the last forty years, had given him many opportunities of

---

[1] See Lavisse, *Histoire de France*, VII, I, 186–205 and VIII, I, 164–199 for an account of the finances of France in the time of Louis XIV.

acquainting himself with the state of France, and that it had been accurately described by de Bois-Guillebert in a work entitled *Détail de la France*.[1] He found that nearly one-tenth of the people was "réduite à la mendicité", and that in the whole population of France, there were not 10,000 households that could be said to be in easy circumstances, and that if the "gens d'affaires", the King's beneficiaries and a few merchants were excepted, there would hardly be any. Vauban proposed that a tax of one-tenth, never higher than one-tenth and never lower than one-twentieth, should be levied by the State on all property. Only in this way could justice be done to the "partie basse du peuple, que remplit encore à ses dépens les vides qui se font dans la haute par les gens qui s'élèvent et qui font fortune. C'est encore la partie basse du peuple que par son travail et son commerce et par ce qu'elle paye au Roi, l'enrichit et tout son royaume. C'est elle qui fournit tous les soldats et matelots de ses armées de terre et de mer, et grand nombre d'officiers, tous les marchands et les petits officiers de Judicature. C'est elle qui fait tout le commerce et les manufactures de ce royaume, qui fournit tous les laboureurs, vignerons et manœuvrieurs de la campagne, qui garde et nourrit les bestiaux, qui sème les blés et les recueille, qui façonne les vignes, et fait le vin, et pour achever de le dire en peu de mots, c'est elle qui fait tous les gros et menus ouvrages de la campagne et des villes." It was a gallant effort for those who could not speak for themselves, for "cette partie du peuple si utile et si méprisée, qui a tant souffert, et qui souffre tant de l'heure que j'écris ceci. . . . Quand le peuple ne serait pas si oppressé, ils se marieront plus hardiment, ils se vêteront et nourriront mieux, leurs enfants seront plus robustes et mieux élevés: ils prendront un plus grand soin de leurs affaires." Here again Vauban was ahead of his time, and went to the root of the matter. There was no hope for a half-starved people; the burden must be lightened, and the workman enjoy some of the results of his labours, if the State was to survive. Here

[1] Published in 1695.

was the true Vauban, racy of the soil, a countryman who
cared for the people more than for anything else in
France, and who saw clearly how things were drifting, as
in fact they did drift throughout the eighteenth century
till the cataclysm of the French Revolution.

It was a magnificent effort but it ended in tragedy.
The story is finely told by Saint Simon. We shall now,[1]
he says, "see how (Vauban) was driven to the grave by the
bitterness of his grief for that which did him the highest
honour, and which would have done so anywhere but in
France. . . . Patriot as he was, all his life he had been
touched by the misery and sufferings of the people. The
knowledge which his profession gave him of inevitable
expenditure, and the scanty hope that the King would
economize in his splendour and his armaments, made him
groan to see that there was no remedy to a burden which
increased every day. With this on his mind on all his
journeys—and he was constantly travelling up and down
the Kingdom—he took exact note of the value and produce of land, of trade and industry in towns and provinces,
and on the nature of taxes and methods of levying them.
He employed others to collect statistics for him at great
expense to himself, and devoted the last twenty years of
his life to these researches. Finally he convinced himself
that the land was the one solid asset of the State, and set
to work to draw up a new system of taxation. He was
well advanced with this, when there appeared several
small books written by M. de Bois-Guillebert, a Lieutenant-General and a man of much intelligence and industry, who had long held views similar to those of Vauban.
De Bois-Guillebert had already put his views before the
Chancellor, Pont-Chartrain, telling him that probably
he would take him for a fool at first, but that in the end
he would agree. Pont-Chartrain 'qu'était tout salpêtre',
laughed and said that he took the first alternative and
turned his back on de Bois-Guillebert. The latter returned to his command at Rouen, and produced a learned
and profound work which was favourably entertained by

---

[1] The passage is too long to quote in full and I translate it.

Chamillart who had succeeded Pont-Chartrain. De Bois-Guillebert's proposals were on the same lines as Vauban's, though the two men had not known each other and had arrived at their conclusions independently. Vauban met de Bois-Guillebert, discussed his proposals with him, and ardent for the relief of the people and the good of the State, put the finishing touches to his system of taxation, and proposed the abolition of all taxes then levied, and the substitution of a single tax of one-tenth, divided into two classes, one on the land, the other on trade. All who had any knowledge of the subject, admired the profoundness, the justice, the precision and the clarity of Vauban's 'Projet de la Dîme Royale'. But though it might save the people, it had one fatal defect. It ruined an army of financiers, clerks and employés of every kind . . . it sapped the foundations of those immense fortunes that one has seen born in so short a time; and this alone was enough to kill the scheme. It destroyed the authority, position and privileges of the Controller-General of Finances and all his department. As for the lawyers 'La robe entière en rugit pour son intérêt.' All vested interests conspired against it, and the King, warned beforehand, received Vauban very badly when he presented his book. And from that moment Vauban's services, his unique military capacity in his own line, his virtues, and the affection which the King himself had shown him, to the extent of believing that he was honouring himself with laurels in promoting him, all this disappeared in an instant. He (the King) no longer saw in Vauban anything but a man passionate for the love of the public and a criminal who attacked the authority of his ministers and, in consequence, of himself. Vauban died a few months later, seeing nobody, consumed with grief and a sorrow which nothing could soften." Saint Simon's account is vivid, though not quite accurate, for there is no evidence that Vauban ever presented his book to the King, and when the King heard of Vauban's last illness he at once sent him his second physician. Though the ministers of Louis XIV were ill-disposed to Vauban, the

King himself seems to have been distressed, and there seems to be no sufficient ground for accusing him of this base ingratitude.[1]

It was a tragic end to a great career. What actually happened was that Vauban had his mémoire printed "clandestinement" at Rouen, without having first obtained the royal "imprimatur" necessary for all books printed in France, and this technical illegality was the opportunity of his enemies. The mémoire had been printed on quarto leaves, which Vauban intended to have sumptuously bound for presentation to the King. He went in his carriage to the Port S. Denis, to receive the packet of printed pages, and took them to a widow Fétil, who saw to the bindings of his writings. The leaves were bound and a few copies distributed. On the afternoon of Thursday, March 24 1707, Vauban heard that by decree of the Council, his book was to be suppressed, and he at once sent his servant, named Colas, to the widow Fétil to withdraw all copies, but it was too late. His enemies had seen their chance and taken it. Colas was arrested and imprisoned in the Petit Châtelet in Paris for examination. On the evening of Friday, March 25, Vauban who was very ill with pneumonia took to his bed. On the Sunday he was slightly better, but greatly troubled by the thought that unintentionally he might have been disloyal to his King, and he sent a copy of the book to an Abbé in the Rue de Grenelle, asking him to examine the book and say if he thought there was anything wrong. Vauban had always been subject to colds and coughs. He was now dying of pneumonia, and was so tormented by his scruples that he sent copies to his doctor in the Rue S. Honoré and to his Confessor asking them to say whether he had done anything against his conscience, but it was too late. Vauban died on the Wednesday, the 30th of March 1707, in the arms of his son-in-law, Mesgrigny.

[1] Dangeau in his *Journal* quoted by Lazard, p. 94, says that when the King heard, on Tuesday, of Vauban's illness, he at once sent him the "premier Médecin de Monseigneur" and spoke of Vauban "avec beaucoup d'estime et d'amitié, il le loua sur plusieurs chapitres et dit: 'Je perds un homme fort affectionné à ma personne et à l'Etat.'"

So died the finest Frenchman of the long reign of Louis XIV. His death passed almost unnoticed. There was no grand State funeral with a military escort and the sad lament of a funeral march; a service was held in the Church of S. Roch, which was attended by Vauban's two sons-in-law, Mesgrigny and the Marquis d'Ussé; but there were no representatives of the King or the Army, and a few days later the body was taken to Bazoches and buried in the chapel of Saint Sebastien in the church of St. Léger-Foucherest. Fontenelle alone had the courage to give his Éloge before the Académie des Sciences a few weeks later, but he did not dare to refer to the Dîme Royale. A hundred years later by order of Napoleon, Vauban's heart was placed in the church of the Invalides in Paris in the presence of his descendants, the Ministers of War and Marine and other important persons. The ceremony was formal and dignified; a discours was given, "et une symphonie guérrière a été exécutée". The account does not say who composed it, but if ever any one deserved a funeral march on the death of a hero, Vauban did.[1]

[1] The Tercentenary of Vauban's birth was celebrated at the Invalides in 1933.

CHAPTER XVIII

*Vauban's will and the secret will—Mme. de Fériol—Fontenelle's tribute
and Saint Simon's—Vauban's generosity—His style and the man.*

WE have followed Vauban through his career, from the
days when he joined the army of Condé as a lad of sixteen down to his tragic end, but of his private life, of his
relations to his wife and family, we know practically
nothing, and the reason is that the owner of Vauban's
private papers refused to let them be published. Of Mme.
de Vauban we hear nothing. She spent her life far away
in the country at Bazoches, where she lived from 1675 till
her death in 1705. Vauban made her the executrix of his
will, drawn up in March 1702,[1] and left her all his
possessions "suivans la coutume". This will was an ex-
ceedingly proper document. Vauban left legacies to the
poor and the churches of five parishes, to certain poor
relations, to his secretary, his servants, and a legacy of
500 livres "pour une bague" for his secretary's wife, and a
legacy of 600 livres to "la petite Fanchon", the Secretary's daughter, little legacies characteristic of the
essential kindliness of Vauban's nature. But in addition
to this official will, Vauban drew up an additional secret
will, leaving a sum of 14,000 livres to be distributed by
Friand, his secretary, "suivant mes instructions dont je l'ay
informé", without his rendering any account of his dis-
bursements, "me remettant à sa bonne foy et à sa conscience pour cet employ". Vauban left secret directions
for the disposal of this money. "Il (Friand) exécutera ce
que dessus le plus secrètement qu'il sera possible, afin de
ni pas divulguer les uns ny les autres", but evidently
Friand did not carry out his instructions as to secrecy.
After the payment of certain debts at Forez near Toul in
Lorraine, in regard to which Vauban was uncertain ("Il
me reste un scrupul dont je me veux déchargé"), the will

[1] This will with its additional secret will was discovered by Rochas d'Aiglun
and is given at length in his *Vauban*, I, pp. 59-63.

gives instructions for the payment of legacies to five persons with whom Vauban had had relations at different times. One legacy of 2,000 livres was to a young widow at Bergues near Dunkerque, for the maintenance of a son of whom she asserted "avec de grandz serment" that Vauban was the father. The next legacy of 2,000 livres for a similar reason was to a Mdlle. Poussin at Paris "avec qui j'ay eu commerce il y a 16 ou 17 ans, bien que très rarement". Vauban said that he did not believe her, but "le scrupul que je m'en fait" obliged him to desire a settlement once for all. The third legacy of 2,000 livres was to a Mme. de la Motte, "Fame de Monsieur de la Motte, Capitaine d'Infanterie". The fourth legacy was to Mdlle. Baussant, who asserted that she was with child by Vauban (this was in the year 1702). Vauban in his will said that this might be so or not. In any case, Friand was to hand over to Mdlle. Baussant or her mother 1,000 écus, very secretly, "parce qu'elle et (est) fille de quelque callité". The fifth and most interesting legacy was to "une pauvre dame Irlandaise", who made the usual claim. Vauban was doubtful, but "je ne veux pas hasarder le salut de mon âme pour cela", so he left her 2,000 livres. Friand was to make enquiries after Vauban's death, and if any of the children were dead, he was not to pay their mothers, "que j'ay assez bien payées pour n'avoir pas de scrupul à leur égart", and the money so left was to be added to the legacy of "cette pauvre dame Irlandaise, qui étant fame de callité, hors de son pais, et comme abandonée de son mary, et (est) plus digne de compassion que les autres". The poor Irish gentlewoman seems to have been the only one of the five for whom Vauban cared. This secret will, written by Vauban with his own hand, with his characteristic idioms and spelling, such as "fame de callité", is of first-rate psychological interest. Vauban's admission of his relations was perfectly frank, and his only anxiety was to discharge what he took to be his duty. His standard of morality was simply that of the time in which he lived. He had before him the flagrant example of his royal master, and the

wandering life which his profession compelled him to live
no doubt placed the domestic virtues at a serious dis-
count. What is attractive in Vauban's secret will is the
total absence of any sort of cant, and his recognition of
personal obligation to those with whom he had had relations. He was not a mere sensualist, but he was hot-
blooded and of great vitality. Ever since 1697 he had
been carrying on a flirtation with a very charming lady,
Mme. de Fériol, sister of Cardinal Tencin, and wife of a
"complaisant" husband who was content to live at
Grenoble, while his wife lived in Paris. In 1701 he wrote
from Fontainebleau "je soupire . . . pour mon retour à
Paris, à portée de voir souvent la belle Angelique[1] que
j'aime assurément de tout mon cœur et que j'honore par
dessus toutes les femmes, bien que l'ingrate s'en soucie
fort peu . . . adieu, ma belle Reine, je vous aime et
honore de tout mon cœur et tout ce que peut s'imaginer
au delà." Vauban was still writing to her in 1703, but
the letters seem to have been quite harmless. In 1705
there was actually some sort of an affair with a Mdlle. de
Villefranche, a protégée of Mme. de Maintenon, who was
beloved by a young man of whom Mme. de Maintenon
did not approve. She thought that a more suitable
husband might be found in "quelque vieux seigneur"
who was known to admire the young lady. Vauban, a
widower of nine months, appears to have been the
"vieux seigneur" whom "le respect empêche de nommer". But the net was set in vain, and nothing came
of it. Vauban was not in the least above the infirmities
of human nature, and he never made any claim to
superhuman virtue.

When Vauban died, his enemies had prevailed against
him, the Court ignored him, and only Fontenelle paid a
gallant tribute to his memory, delivered on May 4 1707,
within five weeks of his death. "Jamais les traits de la
simple nature n'ont été mieux marquées qu'en lui, ni plus
exempts de tout mélange étranger . . . un sens droit et
étendu, qui s'attachait au vrai par une espèce de

[1] Mme. de Fériol.

sympathie, et sentoit le faux sans le discuter, lui épargnait des longs circuits par où les autres marchent, et d'ailleurs sa vertu étoit en quelque sorte un instinct heureux si prompt qu'il prévenoit la raison. Il méprisait cette politesse superficielle dont le monde se contente, et qui couvre souvent tant de barbarie, mais sa bonté, son humanité, sa libéralité, lui composait une autre politesse plus rare, qui étoit toute dans son cœur." This is finely said and every word of it was justified by Vauban's life. He was constantly helping the lame dog over the stile; if one of his subalterns was too poor, Vauban would supplement his pay, saying that he was only giving the surplus of what he had received from the King. Yet Vauban was not a rich man; he was always short of money himself, and left only a "fortune médiocre". Fontenelle continues that Vauban was devoted to the King, "sujet plein d'une fidélité ardente et zélée et nullement courtesan. Personne n'a été si souvent que lui ni avec autant de courage l'introducteur de la verité. Il avoit pour elle une passion presque impudente et incapable de ménagement." Vauban went for what he believed to be the truth at all costs; no regard for his own interests ever prevented him from saying what he thought to the King or Louvois or anybody else, if he was convinced that it was to the interest of the State that he should do so, and it is only fair to Louis XIV and Louvois to say that both of them recognized this.

Saint Simon's description of Vauban is famous. Saint Simon had three ways of dealing with the subjects of his portraits. If he disliked them, as he usually did, he simply wiped the floor with their characters. J. H. Mansart, for example, or Harcourt, or La Feuillade "cette âme de boue". In other cases, he so balanced their virtues and vices that the one cancelled the others. In very rare cases he dwelt only on their merits. Vauban shares this last distinction with a few others, indeed I can only find four others, Lenôtre, the designer of gardens, Boufflers, the brave but rather clumsy soldier, the Duchesse de Saint Simon, and Ninon de l'Enclos, in Saint Simon's view a

13

second Aspasia. Saint Simon begins his 35th chapter:[1] "Vauban s'appelait le Prestre, petit gentilhomme de Bourgogne tout au plus, mais peut-être le plus honnête homme et le plus vertueux de son siècle, et avec la réputation du plus savant homme dans l'art des sièges et de la fortification, le plus simple, le plus vrai et le plus modeste. C'était un homme de médiocre taille, assez trapu, qui avait fort l'air de guerre, mais en même temps un extérieur rustre et grossier, pour ne pas dire brutal et féroce. Il n'était rien moins. Jamais homme plus doux, plus compatissant, plus obligeant, mais respectueux sans mille politesses, et le plus avare ménager de la vie des hommes, avec une valeur qui prenait tout sur soi et donnait tout aux autres. Il est inconcevable qu'avec tant de droiture et franchise, incapable de se prêter à rien de faux ni de mauvais, il ait pu gagner qu'il fit l'amitié et la confiance de Louvois et du Roi." The "petit gentilhomme" is characteristic of Saint Simon, and his description of Vauban's appearance as "pour ne pas dire brutal et féroce" does not tally with his bust by Coysevox or the crayon study by Rigaud. Both of these show the face of a man who had thought and dared and suffered much, a man with a sense of humour more English than French as a French writer says, and above all compassionate; but no finer tribute than Saint Simon's has ever been paid to a soldier and no man has deserved it more. Vauban's care for his men was twice noted by Fontenelle. "L'étoit là son but principal la conservation des hommes, non seulement l'intérêt de la guerre, mais aussi son humanité naturel les lui rendoit chers." When ambitious generals tried to hurry him in order to win credit for some brilliant feat of arms, Vauban simply went on with his lines and parallels, so the soldiers loved him and "lui obéissoient avec un entier dévouement" not only because they trusted his ability, but because they knew that he cared for them personally and individually. Vauban never forgot "le pauvre peuple" whether they were serving in the army or toiling in the countryside.

[1] Vol. III, Ed. la Bédollière.

Another point which appears constantly in his official correspondence is his generous recommendation of any one who had served him well, or of deserving officers who were out of employment. "Quand on expose d'honnêtes gens à se faire tuer autant que je le fais, on doit du moins rendre témoignage de leur mérite et de leur bon cœur." In a letter to Louvois in 1674 he recommends three such officers. The first had served in Portugal as an engineer and been awarded the Order of Christ, then he had served with Condé and after that at Venice. He had been a prisoner in Spain for five or six years. He could draw well and speak four languages, yet now, with all these qualifications, "il est sur ses coudes" doing nothing at La Rochelle. The second had also served in Portugal. "C'est un génie tout à fait extraordinaire pour les mécaniques." He had invented a machine, based on the movements of fish, which enabled a ship to move in a dead calm, and other devices. The third was a young man who, owing to the misdeeds or misfortunes of his uncles, was now banished and had had his property confiscated. Yet he was a young man of excellent parts, anxious to serve his country. Vauban recommended all three for employment in the interests of the State. Then there were pleas for mercy, such as the case of Relief, who had been in charge of fodder and wood in the citadel of Arras, and had been accused of shooting hares. The Governor had sentenced him to two or three dozen "coups de bâton sur la tête et sur les bras". Relief complained to Louvois, and relying on this had returned to the citadel of Arras, when he had again been thrown into prison. Vauban assured Louvois that the man was quite innocent, that "cet homme n'a jamais pris lièvre qu'au plat," and that those who accused him had stolen the wood and fodder in his charge. Only ten days before Vauban had asked Louvois to spare a deserter, on the ground that he was a poor miserable men with 5 or 6 children. Twenty years later we find Vauban asking Le Peletier to show some consideration to a young engineer, who had been sent to survey a fort at Mont Dauphin, with only 100 livres in his pocket. "Comment croyez-vous que cela se puisse soutenir, dans un lieu où il fait deux fois plus cher vivre, que partout ailleurs", and where the survey was peculiarly difficult. The lad was, Vauban said, a little fool, but he could draw well, and in Vauban's hands he could become "doux comme un gant". It seems that in addition to having been starved on his pay, Villeneuve had been thrown into prison, and six weeks later Vauban wrote again in his defence, and said that Villeneuve was a hard worker, and that all he had done had been to stand up to the contractors, "ce que n'est pas un marque de volerie". Vauban told Le Peletier boldly that he had been much too summary in his judgment, and that for himself "je suis toujours pour le pardon des fautes d'esprit, parce qu'elles ne sont pas volontaires, que les hommes ne sont pas faits eux-mêmes, et qu'il suffit de l'être pour être sujet à faibler, mais je ne pardonne pas aux fripons avérés." People cannot help being fools, but there is no excuse for their being knaves. It is this large humanity which makes Vauban so lovable. He seems to me to have been incapable of ill-will to anyone; a candid soul giving to all their due, understanding their failures, and making the best of all who served him.

Throughout this book I have transcribed freely from Vauban's writings, and I have done so because, if ever the saying "Le style c'est l'homme" was true of any one, it was true of Vauban. He had the rare gift of writing as he spoke. He never struggled for his words; all he cared for was to make his meaning clear by the simplest possible means. If one compares him with Saint Simon the difference in style is exactly what one would expect from two radically different personalities. Saint Simon, acute and trenchant, but tortuous and rather laboured, so that sometimes one has to read him twice to get at his meaning; Vauban, sincere and admirably clear, with no thought of fine rhetoric, quite indifferent to what people might think of his free use of the vernacular. He thought in concrete terms, never in abstract, and he presented facts just as they struck him in any words that came into his head, and if the right word did not occur to him at once, he invented words of his own, or used such strange uncouth phrases as a "Corps de garde de croutes et de bousilles".[1] When he is describing hilly ground he calls it "bossillé". Elsewhere he speaks of the "gibbosité de la montagne". In 1668, writing from Ath, he complains to Louvois of the men sent from Paris to work in rocky ground, "je vous supplie de ne plus envoyer vos rocqueteurs de Paris parce qu'une partie sont enfants, les autres coureurs, et tous ensemble les animaux du monde les plus indociles." Speaking of the sieges of unimportant places such as the 22 places taken in Flanders before 1672, he writes contemptuously of "toutes ces bicoques de sièges".[2] When he applies to Louvois for travelling expenses he says that if these are not allowed he will be compelled "écorner" (blue) the 4,000 louis given him by the King, after the capture of Maestricht in 1673. Writing to Seignelay in 1685, to recommend Jean Bart, he says "C'est un très bon sujet à qui il est temps que vous fassiez faire un cran." "Cran" means a notch. Vauban uses it for promotion, one step up. When he has collected some 250 horses, he does not use such a term as "rassembler" but says "grapiller" (to glean). Vauban never troubled about his spelling. "Femme" is spelt "fame", qualité "callité", matériaux "matereaux", and he uses strange words such as "pretintailler", "gniole"[3] (check), "caprerie" (privateering), "goupillon" (draft of a mémoire), "minorité" (inferiority). "toutes et quantes fois" for "toutes les fois que", "tirer pays" (leaving the country), "se pétuler" (making petulant gestures). In nearly every letter some strange and novel word will startle the reader. He writes of the "infidélités", of the Rhine, and its "trahison". In a few words he can call up a whole picture; for instance, the description of the premature advance of the French at Offenburg on the Rhine in 1688, when the troops having marched all night, "et bien fait japper et

---

[1] A mud wall with mortar made of mud and straw.

[2] Twopenny-halfpenny sieges, as we might say.

[3] The dent made by the peg of a top. Boyer.

hurler tous les chiens des villages où l'on passe", found the gates closed against them and had to march back having done nothing but find "copy" for the gazettes. Describing winter in Flanders, he wrote: "Toute la terre n'était qu'une glace sur laquelle j'ai faillis vingt fois à me casser le cou . . . je serai fort heureux, si j'en quitte pour quelque bout de nez ou d'oreille gelés". In 1671 Vauban paid a visit to Nieuport to see what the Spaniards were doing on the other side of the frontier, and he gives a very dramatic account of his interview with the Governor, a punctilious old Spaniard, "de soixante-dix à quatre-vingt ans" . . . "il était orné d'une barbe à vieille façon méslangé de beaucoup de poils blancs, contre très peu de noirs, et d'une peruque noire à cheveux plats, surmonté d'un chapeau retroussé à petits bords." The interview was stormy; indeed, the parties threatened to shoot each other, and Vauban gives an admirable verbatim account of the meeting and of the conversation. Louvois replied very coldly, that the Governor seemed to be a decent sort of man and that it was a pity they had quarrelled. Louvois did not appreciate a quality rather rare in Frenchmen, a certain humour that underlay everything that Vauban wrote, or he may have thought that his young officer was getting a little beyond himself, and that it was time to head him off in his own interest. Vauban wrote a deplorable hand which sometimes exhausted Louvois' patience. Rochas d'Aiglun gives a facsimile of Vauban's writing, one to a M. de Caligny which is almost illegible, the other to Mme. de Fériol written in 1701 which is a little clearer. Vauban evidently wrote at a great pace; he said himself that he could never write a letter without blotting it, and one does not wonder that Louvois was annoyed at having to decipher his scrawls.

Vauban's letters are extraordinarily readable; they are those of an open-hearted generous man who said what he thought, never shirked an issue, and took his fences as they came; clear-seeing, fearless and indomitable, not Ajax "inexorabilis acer"; not Achilles swift of foot but

NIEUPORT

PLAN OF NIEUPORT
From "Atlas Portatif," 1702

detestable; with some touch of Ulysses πολύμητις but without the craft and cruelty of that rather unscrupulous adventurer. Human nature being what it is, one hesitates to call any one heroic, yet one might say it of Vauban, for his courage, his honesty, his loyalty, his burning patriotism, and his never-failing sympathy with the poor and the oppressed.

> Non possidentem multa vocaveris
> recte beatum: rectius occupat
> nomen beati, qui deorum
> muneribus sapienter uti
>
> duramque callet pauperiem pati
> peiusque leto flagitium timet,
> non ille pro caris amicis
> aut patria timidus perire.[1]

Vauban himself gives the description of true glory: "La véritable gloire ne se vole comme le papillon. Elle ne s'acquiert que par des actions réelles et solides. Elle veut toujours remplir ses devoirs à la lettre, son premier et véritable principe est la vérité, à laquelle elle est très particulièrement dévouée. Elle est tout généreuse, prudente, hardie, dans ses entreprises, ferme dans ses résolutions, intrépide dans les actions périlleux, charitable, désintéressée et toujours prête à pardonner, et à prendre la part de la justice. Toujours sensée en ce qu'elle fait, la raison seule la gouverne. Contente dans l'adversité, humble et affable dans la prospérité, comme elle est toujours judicieux, elle prend bien son part, et le soutient quand elle l'a pris, au prix de tout ce que peut arriver."[2] This was the ideal which Vauban set out to realize, and the only injustice to himself lay in the words, "la raison seule gouverne", for Vauban was governed by his heart. Fontenelle ends his Eloge with these words: "En un mot, c'étoit un Romain qu'il sembloit que nôtre siècle eut dérobé aux plus heureux temps de la République." There can be no nobler epitaph than the inscription in the little church of St. Léger Foucherest:

"Patriam dilexit, veritatem coluit."

[1] Hor. *Car. IV*, ix. [2] *Pensées diverses*—"La vraie et la fausse gloire".

A GLOSSARY OF TERMS USED IN FRENCH FORTI-FICATIONS IN THE SEVENTEENTH CENTURY

BASCULE: a gate at the entrance of a fort moved up and down by counterweights.

BASTION: the fortified work built at the salient angles of polygonal ramparts. "Tours bastionnées"—bastions of two or more storeys introduced by Vauban.

BANQUETTE: steps behind the parapets to enable soldiers to shoot over the parapets.

BERME: a level strip 3 ft. to 4 ft. wide left at the foot of the rampart next the moat. Also applied to a space left between the earth parapet and outer face of a redoubt, to take the "haie vive" (quickset hedge).

BOYAU: a communication trench.

CASCANE: hole sunk by the defence in the platform of the rampart to provide an escape for mines, or made by the attack as a way up from mines made below the moat.

CASEMATES: vaulted chambers for guns.

CAPONNIERES: protected passage ways communicating with works outside the rampart.

CAVALIERS: a raised work on the rampart for purposes of look-out and a longer range of fire. Also used by Vauban for purposes of attack on the glacis.

CHANDELLES: posts for screens to conceal the defence.

CHEMIN COUVERT: a level walk on the further side of the moat, protected by the parapet formed by the higher part of the glacis, with "places d'armes" at intervals.

CHEMIN DE RONDES: the rounds, a walk between the earth parapet of the rampart and the brick or masonry parapet of the revetment of the rampart, going all round the fort.

CITADEL: a fort with four to six bastions. These were usually at one corner of the fortified town, but connected with it. The citadels at Lille and Arras are pentagons with five bastions.

CORDON: the rounded stone moulding or band below the parapet of the revetment of the rampart going all round the fort.

CORNES (ouvrage à cornes): hornwork—a work outside the fort and detached from it, with two half bastions ending in acute angles on the front to the attack. (See plan of Sedan.)

CONTREGARDES: protective works in front of bastions.

CONTRESCARPE: the sloping outer side of the moat next the covered way, usually revetted.

OUVRAGES DE COURONNEMENT: crown works, fortifications supplementary to the hornwork.

COURTINE: curtain, the long straight front of the rampart from the re-entering angles of the junction of the bastions with the front of the rampart.

CUVETTE: a narrow secondary trench sunk in the centre of the moat.

DEMILUNE: a detached triangular work, built in the moat.

EMBRASURES: openings in parapets for guns.

EPAULE: a rectangular recess at the junction of the flanks of bastions with the courtine.

FAUSSE-BRAYE: a space left at the foot of the rampart next the moat for defence, protected by a parapet. This was given up after the middle of the seventeenth century.

FACE: the sides of bastions facing the attack and meeting at an angle at the salient point of the bastion.

FLANKS: the sides of the bastion returning to the courtine from the face.

FLANC FICHANT: fire from a flank to the bastion opposite.

FLANC RASANT: fire that passes the "face" of the bastion opposite.

FOSSÉ: moat, dry or wet.

FRAISES: stakes 5 in. square, 7 ft. to 8 ft. long, fixed horizontally on the outer slopes of grass parapets.

GABION: vertical baskets filled with earth to form temporary defences.

GORGE: the entrance to the bastion from the platform of the ramparts.

GLACIS: the ground, sloping from the top of the parapet of the covered way till it reaches the level of the open country.

GUERITE: a sentry-box corbelled out from the angles of ramparts, also called "Échauguette".

LIGNE DE DEFENSE: line of fire from the angle of junction of bastion and courtine to the salient point of the opposite bastion.

MADRIER: long plank.

MANTLET: a movable shield or screen of 3 in. planks, 5 ft. high, sometimes covered with tin on wheels.

MERLON: the solid part of masonry or brick parapets between the embrasures.

MOULINET: a turnstile.

ORGUES: a defence for the entrance to forts; long, heavy pieces of wood shod with iron, hung singly and dropped separately to block entrance.

ORILLON (*see* EPAULE): rounded recess at junction of flanks of bastion, with the courtine.

PATÉ or PATÉE: a small outwork of earth well rammed, usually horse-shoe in plan.

PARAPET:(1) the main parapet of earth covered with turf on the top of the rampart; (2) parapet of masonry or brickwork protecting bastions, chemins des rondes and other works; (3) the parapet to the covered way formed by the upper part of the glacis.

PALISADES: defences made with posts 9 ft. long, 6 in. or 7 in. square, fixed 3 ft. in the ground in rows with 3 in. spaces between the posts. Set in the covered way at a distance of 3 ft. from the inner face of the glacis.

PLACES D'ARMES: spaces left at intervals in the covered way and other outworks for soldiers to assemble.

QUEUE D'ARONDE: an outwork in plan like a swallow's tail.

RAVELIN: a small detached triangular work with two "faces" placed in the fossé opposite the courtine or in the rear part of demilunes.

REDANS: works set out in a serrated line, like the teeth of a saw.

REDUIT: a small fort to which the garrison can retreat, or larger forts to enable the garrison "contenir et reduire les Bourgeois" (Fournier). Also applied to the ravelin in the rear of the demilune.

SCARP: the revetted face of the rampart.

TALUS: the slope of banks.

TERRE-PLEIN: the platform on the top of the rampart behind the parapet.

TENAILLE: a detached oblong work with ends projecting outwards at an obtuse angle—in the moat and usually in front of and parallel to the courtine.

TIR-À-RICOCHET: plunging fire.

APPENDIX II

A List of Places Fortified by Vauban

Antibes (Alpes Maritimes)
Arras (Pas de Calais)
Ath (Nord)
Bapaume (Pas de Calais)
Bayonne (Basses Pyrenees)
Belfort (Aude)
Belle-Ile (Ile de)
Bergues (Nord)
Besançon (Doubs)
Béthune (Pas de Calais)
Blaye (Gironde)
Bordeaux (Gironde)
Boulogne (Pas de Calais)
Brest (Finistere)
Briançon (Hautes Alpes)
Brouage (Charente Inf.)
Calais (Pas de Calais)
Cambrai (Nord)
Casal (Italy)
Cette (Herault)
Fort Chandane (Doubs)
Charlemont (Ardennes)
Charleroi (Belgium)
Charleville (Ardennes)
Château-Queyras (Hautes Alpes)
Cherbourg (Manche)
Collioure (Pyrenees-Or.)
Colmars (Basses Alpes)
Condé-sur-Escaut (Nord)
Courtrai (Belgium)
Dieppe (Seine Inf.)
Digne (Basses Alpes)
Dinant (Belgium)
Dôle (Jura)
Doullens (Somme)

Dunkerque (Nord)
Embrun (Hautes Alpes)
Gap (Hautes Alpes)
Granville (Franche)
Gravelines (Nord)
Huningue (Alsace)
La Fère (Aisne)
La Kenoque (Belgium)
La Rochelle (Char.)
Landau (Alsace)
Le Havre (Seine Inf.)
Le Quesnoy (Nord)
Lille (Nord)
Longwy (Meurthe-et-Moselle)
Luxembourg
Maubeuge (Nord)
Menin (Belgium)
Mons (Belgium)
Mont Dauphin (Hautes Alpes)
Mont-Louis (Pyrenees)
Mont-Royal (Moselle)
Namur (Belgium)
Nancy (Meurthe-et-Moselle)
Neuf-Brisach (Alsace-Lorraine)
Nice (Col de)
Nieuport (Belgium)
Oléron (Ile de)
Oudenarde (Belgium).
Peronne (Somme)
Perpignan (Pyrenees-Or.)
Phalsbourg (Alsace-Lorraine)
Philippeville (Belgium)
Philisbourg (Alsace-Lorraine)
Pignerol (Italy)
Port-Vendres (Pyrenees-Or.)

Rochfort (Char.-Inf.)

Château Belin ⎫ Forts out-
Saint André ⎭ side Salins

Saint Louis (Alsace)

Saint Malo (Ille-et-Vilaine)

Sainte Ménehould (Marne)

Saint Quentin (Isère)

Saint Venant (Pas de Calais)

Saint Vincent (Isère)

Salins (Jura)

Sarre-Louis (Germany)

Sedan (Ardennes)

Seigne (Basses Alpes)

Sisteron (Basses Alpes)

Strasbourg (Alsace-Lorraine)

Toul (Nord)

Tournai (Belgium)

Valenciennes (Nord)

Verdun (Meuse)

Villefranche (Alpes Maritimes)

Villefranche le Conflent
(Pyrenees)

Ypres (Belgium)

ninety-two places

This list is not exhaustive. The *Abrégé* for 1692 says: "Il [Vauban] fit des projets de fortification pour les vingt-deux places que nous avons occupées dans ces pays-là" (Flanders): the names are not given. Rochas d'Aiglun says that the *Archives de la Section technique* for 1698 contains mémoires prepared by Vauban for the fortification of twenty-five places—Belfort, Charlemont, Montmédy, Colmars, Condé, Schelestadt, Einsisheim, Fort Louis, Huningue, Landau, Landskron, Longwy, Marsal, Metz, Neuf-Brisach, Phalsbourg, Toul, Sarre-Louis, Stenay, Mouzon, Villefranche-sur-Meuse, Strasbourg, Thionville, Valenciennes and Verdun. Voltaire says that Vauban constructed or repaired the fortifications of 150 "places de guerre", but Voltaire's figures are usually liberal. Vauban's energy was inexhaustible. He not only designed all these works, but he had to see that they were properly carried out, and in addition to this, wherever there was a siege, Vauban, the "preneur des villes", was indispensable, not only at his drawing-board, but in the trenches. He is said to have directed fifty sieges.

LIST OF AUTHORITIES

ON VAUBAN

AUGOYAT, Lieut.-Col. du Génie: *Abrégé des Services du Maréchal de Vauban*, Publié par M. Augoyat 1839. *Mémoires inédits du Maréchal de Vauban* 1841.

LAZARD, P., Colonel du Génie: *Vauban, 1633-1707.* 1934.

ROCHAS D'AIGLUN, Colonel: *Vauban—Sa famille et ses écrits, ses Oisivetés et sa Correspondence.* 1910.

FONTENELLE, Le Bovier de: *Éloge des Académiciens de l'Académie Royale des Sciences.* 1731.

SAINT SIMON: *Mémoires.* Ed. É. de la Bédollière. Paris 1856. A complete bibliography of works relating to Vauban is given in Col Lazard's *Vauban*, pp. 635-643.

VOLTAIRE: *Le Siècle de Louis XIV.* (Garnier. Paris 1929).

ON MILITARY FORTIFICATIONS IN THE SIXTEENTH AND SEVENTEENTH CENTURIES

BUSCA, GABRIELLO: Milanese. *Architettura Militare*, Milan 1619. Busca also wrote a work on the taking and defence of forts 1585 and 1598.

BELIDOR: *La Science des Ingénieurs dans la Conduite des travaux de fortification.* 1729.

CASTRIOTTO, Il Capitan Giacomo: Three books on the fortification of cities in conjunction with Girolamo Maggi. Venice 1563.

CATANEO, GIROLAMO: *Dell' arte Militare.* Libre tre 1559, Third Ed. 1571. French version *Le Capitaine de Hierosme Cataneo.* Lyons 1573.

DE CAMBRAY, M. le Chevalier: *Manière de fortifier de M. de Vauban.* Amsterdam 1689. Eng. trans, by A. Swall. London, 1693.

ERRARD J., de Bar-le-Duc: *La fortification demonstrée et reduite en art.* 1594-1604-1620.

FOURNIER, S. J., Le R. P. Georges: *Traité des fortifications ou Architecture Militaire.* 1647. Third Ed. 1661.

MAGGI, GIROLAMO: *See* Castriotto.

MAROLOIS, SAMUEL: *Architecture Militaire et fortification.* 1628. English trans. 1638 by Henry Hexam.

207

MARTINI, FRANCESCO DE GEORGIO: *Trattato di Architettura civile e militare.* Promis 1841. *Life of*, by G. Selwyn Brinton 1934–5.

PAGAN: *Les fortifications du Comte de Pagan.* Paris 1645.

PERRET, JACQUES: *Des fortifications et artifices*, 1594, Third Ed. 1620.

SCAMOZZI, VINCENZO: *Idea dell' Architettura Universale*, Book II, Chapters XX–XXIX. Venice 1615.

DE VILLE, Le Chevalier: *Les fortifications.* 1628 and 1656.

DA VINCI, LEONARDO: *Les Monuments de Léonard de Vinci*; reproductions by Ravaisson Mollier. Vols. 1881–1891.

VILLE-NOISY, Cosseron de, General: *Essai historique sur la fortification.* 1869.

ZANCHI, GIOVANNI BATTISTA. *Di Modo di fortifier le cita.* Venice 1560.

ATLAS PORTATIF: "Ou Théâtre de la Guerre en Europe—Contenant les cartes géographiques, avec le plan des villes et forteresses les plus exposées aux Révolutions présentes". Amsterdam 1702.

INDEX